THE TORAH OF LEADERSHIP

ESSAYS ON THE WEEKLY PARASHA

Yeshiva University
THE RABBI LORD JONATHAN SACKS-HERENSTEIN
CENTER FOR VALUES AND LEADERSHIP

מגיד
MAGGID

Erica Brown

The Torah of Leadership

Essays on the Weekly Parasha

Maggid Books
Yeshiva University – The Rabbi Lord Jonathan Sacks-Herenstein
Center for Values and Leadership

The Torah of Leadership
Essays on the Weekly Parasha

First Edition, 2024

Maggid Books
An imprint of Koren Publishers Jerusalem Ltd.

POB 8531, New Milford, CT 06776-8531, USA

& POB 4044, Jerusalem 9104001, Israel
www.korenpub.com

The publication of this book was made possible through the generous support of *The Jewish Book Trust.*

ISBN 978-1-59264-681-4, *hardcover*

Printed in the United States

With our deepest love and appreciation,
we dedicate this book to our dear wife and mother,

Audrey Wagner עמו"ש,

who has taught us all the importance of leadership. Throughout her life she has provided the sound advice, mentorship, and leadership that are so inherent in her nature, character, and world outlook. Whether through her years of teaching and influencing thousands of students at HILI, Hillel, and HAFTR, or her active involvement in benefiting children in Eretz Yisrael through AMIT, ALYN hospital, and other communal organizations, she has instilled in us the importance of reaching out to help and inspire others. This is something she witnessed in the home of her parents, Tessie and Julius Bienenfeld *z"l*, and has passed on this beautiful *mesora* to her children, grandchildren, and great-grandchildren.

It is fortuitous that Dr. Erica Brown decided to present to her devoted readers a book on Jewish leadership, because Audrey Wagner is just that, the quintessential Jewish leader, in both family and community matters. She truly understands and taught us that the "We" is more important than the "I," the primary requirement of any leader.

It is our hope and prayer that the *Ribbono shel Olam* grant our dear wife and mother many more years of health and happiness, so that she can continue to provide our family and community with her unique abilities to mentor, advise, and lead.

Max Wagner
Susan Wagner and Alan Klinger
Stephen and Tamara Wagner
Shmuel and Terri Wagner
Barbara and Gavy Simon

Author's Dedication

In memory of

Captain Daniel Shimon Perez

who died serving the State of Israel on October 7, 2023.
You taught us that heroes do not wait
to answer the call to leadership.

And in honor of Daniel's parents,

Shelley and Doron Perez

You taught and continue to teach us
hope in the darkness
and that everyday kindness is a form of redemption.
The redemption will come.

Contents

Preface: What's New About Jewish Leadership Today? xiii

Introduction: Reading Leadership into and Out of the Torah xxiii

LEADERSHIP IN THE BOOK OF GENESIS

Bereshit: A Garden of Possibility 3

Noaḥ: The What and Why of the Ark 7

Lekh Lekha: The Reputation Nation 11

Vayera: Still He Delayed 15

Ḥayei Sara: "I Will" 19

Toledot: The Lies of Leadership 23

Vayetzeh: Leadership Dreaming 27

Vayishlaḥ: The Gift 31

Vayeshev: Wait For It 35

Miketz: Attracted to Problems 39

Vayigash: The Anxiety of Approach 43

Vayeḥi: Leading Through Darkness 47

LEADERSHIP IN THE BOOK OF EXODUS

Shemot: Making It Good 53

Va'era: When You Discover You're Like No Other 57

Bo: Leadership and the Prayer Community 61

Beshallaḥ: Confusion and Control 65
Yitro: Celebrating Success 69
Mishpatim: Cursing the Leader/Blessing the Leader 73
Teruma: Sacred Work 78
Tetzaveh: Dress for Leadership Success 82
Ki Tisa: The Stiff-Necked People 85
Vayak'hel: Work and Rest 89
Pekudei: Leadership Gems 93

LEADERSHIP IN THE BOOK OF LEVITICUS

Vayikra: The Power of Invitation 99
Tzav: The Perpetual Flame 103
Shemini: When Leaders Atone 106
Tazria: Taking the Lead 110
Metzora: Where Leadership Lives 114
Aḥarei Mot: Leadership and the Scapegoat 118
Kedoshim: Thanks for the Feedback 122
Emor: Scrupulous Leadership 126
Behar: The Eternal Stranger 129
Beḥukotai: What is Life Worth? 133

LEADERSHIP IN THE BOOK OF NUMBERS

Bemidbar: Navigating Uncertainty 139
Naso: To Be a Blessing 142
Behaalotekha: Leadership Through Separation 146
Shelaḥ: Leadership and Diversity 149
Koraḥ: When What You Have Is Not Enough 153
Ḥukat: Have a Little Faith 156
Balak: What the Eye Can't See 160
Pinḥas: The Zealous Leader 164

Matot: Adjusting Sights 168
Masei: Leadership of the Land 172

LEADERSHIP IN THE BOOK OF DEUTERONOMY

Devarim: Leadership Stars 179
Va'etḥanan: Words on Fire 183
Ekev: Leadership and the Destination Postcard 186
Re'eh: The False Prophet 190
Shofetim: Leadership and Bias: Blinding Wise Eyes 194
Ki Tetzeh: Leadership and Favoritism 197
Ki Tavo: Climb Every Mountain 201
Nitzavim: Stand Strong 205
Vayelekh: After Leadership 209
Haazinu: Healing Leadership 213
Vezot Haberakha: The Greatest Leadership Legacy 216
Hadran: Finishing and Beginning Again 220

Acknowledgments 225
Notes 227

Preface

What's New About Jewish Leadership Today?

My first book, *Inspired Jewish Leadership,*[1] was published in 2008, over fifteen years ago. My publisher at the time encouraged me to explain its contents with a subtitle: *Practical Approaches to Building Strong Communities.* He advised putting most of the table of contents on the front cover in case a reader was unsure of the relationship between the words "Jewish" and "leadership." Despite the thousands of books on Christianity and leadership, there were almost no books utilizing Jewish sacred texts that seriously integrated leadership concepts through an organic Torah lens. There were even fewer that applied these ideas to the unique, often idiosyncratic realities of Jewish leadership structures and challenges today with vignettes from professionals and lay leaders serving in Jewish nonprofit organizations.

Several years later, in 2015, Rabbi Lord Jonathan Sacks published *Lessons in Leadership: A Weekly Reading of the Jewish Bible,*[2] his collected essays on the subject that followed the Torah reading of the week. That book put the subject of leadership more squarely on the map as an integrated discipline worthy of study and application. His essays on the

Torah portion of the week, *Covenant & Conversation,* often contained leadership observations that emerged from a close reading of Jewish texts. His death was a profound loss to world Jewry and to those of other faiths who were inspired to learn and to lead. Every essay in this book contains a pearl of his wisdom as a tribute to his influence in cultivating leadership.

In the intervening years since I wrote that first book on leadership, I've been blessed to work closely with hundreds of lay and professional leaders in nonprofit organizations: rabbis, board members, volunteers, philanthropists, and donors. Much has stayed the same in terms of the governance issues and challenges they deal with on a daily basis, and there is still, thank God, an enduring desire to leave the world a little bit better than we found it. On every level, people are leading purpose-driven lives and devoting time and energy to doing "what's right and good in the eyes of the Lord" (Deut. 6:18). Leaders are still moved by compassion and social justice, even if the expression *tikkun olam* has too often become denuded of its Jewish significance. We believe in the power and mandate of collective, community organizing. We can produce positive, transformative change together and do so as Jews committed to both our community and our humanity. We still want to serve. We need to serve.

So, what has changed in the past two decades? Much has evolved that leaders must leverage, pay attention to, and address:

Jewish wisdom is more accessible than ever. Access to the rich storehouse of Jewish texts and tradition is now, due to technology, just one click away. Technological advances have also created online participation in study sessions and synagogue services, a special boon to the sick and elderly and to those in isolation, enabling them to connect to community in meaningful ways.

Judaism's low-barrier approach, however, has often resulted in low commitment. Reduced membership fees, free trips to Israel, and discounted Jewish services can create the impression that Jewish life requires little material sacrifice or genuine time commitment. People value what they work for and put effort into creating and sustaining The strategy of getting people through the door by lowering the bar to entry has not necessarily resulted in people coming through the door and staying a while. Low barriers to entry can also translate into low substance. Despite having more access to Jewish texts and traditions than ever before, Jewish literacy has been eclipsed by Jewish celebrities, Jewish culture, and Jewish cuisine. Jewish clichés are no substitute for Jewish learning.

Jewish continuity is at greater risk than in any other time in history. Rates of intermarriage have been consistently climbing every decade in North America. The immense push for inclusion has, over time, resulted in fewer and fewer genuine Jewish links across multiple generations. So many Jewish grandparents today do not and cannot share the language of Jewish life and commitment with their grandchildren. Not in terms of ritual. Not in terms of social networks. Not in terms of Jewish giving. The chain has been broken in too many places.

Support for Israel wavers. During the decades since its founding, Israel was consistently regarded as the great unifier of Diaspora Jewry and the joint project of our people. But, just before October 7, 2023, Israel was at a point of fragmentation over its complex politics, the Middle East conflict, and the thorny issues around judicial reform. It was a polarizing place for many Diaspora Jews. People took sides. Rabbis, our spiritual leaders, confessed their fears of speaking in public about Israel lest they be vilified for their views. Over a decade ago, in 2013, the Jewish Council for Public Affairs surveyed 552 rabbis, mostly Reform and Conservative, and "found that a third of them hesitate to speak honestly to their congregations regarding their feelings about Israel." This trend grew as issues of perceived threats to democracy and religious pluralism heightened. A senior rabbi from a large East Coast city told me that he never expected, after over thirty years in his current pulpit, to think twice before mentioning Israel in a sermon. "What has our world come to?"

The events of October 7, however, changed the conversation about Israel dramatically. Most Diaspora Jews were, more or less, unified in their support for Israel and their desire to combat antisemitism, particularly on college campuses. The strong sense of *aḥdut,* unity, enhanced morale and reminded us of what it means to be a family in pain who show up for each other. The solidarity the war inspired was a source of solace, strength, and comfort. But many of the fissures that existed before the war were not inherently resolved, making their reappearance inevitable.

Antisemitism is on a precipitous climb upward. Anti-Israel rhetoric often has antisemitism at its core. At least this challenge unites us to combat injustice at the same time it reminds us that hate is here to stay. This plague of irrational animosity was responsible for the single largest antisemitic attack on American soil in 2018 and the war against Hamas in 2023, collapsing the Jewish sensibility that the world learned its lesson after the Holocaust and that, as a society, we are becoming ever more enlightened with each coming year. Leaders are expected to have answers and strategies to situations that are punishingly cruel and unpredictable at a time when local Jewish communities are often more fragmented, more afraid, and less aligned.

Politics has become more coarse, more tribal, and more venomous. Reaching across the aisle as a leader is regarded as a sign of weakness rather than an emblem of courage. Identity politics have become chokingly particularistic and can take inadvertently increasingly pronounced and self-absorbed notions of the individual's importance above the directive to build diverse communities. We lead in an increasingly parochial way, less on behalf of joint values across diverse populations and more for those who confirm or can magnify our own values in opposition to those of others. We play the victim rather than the resilience card when those values are challenged. We cancel those whose views do not accord with our own. Some date the expression "cancel culture" to as early as 2014. Others put that date in 2017. In 2008, we didn't have words to describe an ironically radical and casual nullification of others – usually but not always strangers – who do not conform to our notions of correctness.

Technology has moved apace with the speed of the Tower of Babel's construction but with little governmental regulation. Whenever we master one form of technology, we seem to be thrown another. People can find us at all hours and anywhere across the world. Leaders are expected to respond instantly if not sooner to everyone's texts, tweets, or email missives. Imagine receiving two hundred pieces of mail a day in your mailbox at home, carefully formulating responses to every last one of them, sealing and stamping the envelopes, and then checking the mailbox the next day to find two hundred more. We've become edgy about getting back to people because every response gets a response. Adam Grant advised us to stop apologizing for not writing back: "Apologizing for slow replies is a symptom of unrealistic demands in an always-on culture."[3] Over-responsiveness can communicate that our own work/life balance is way out of alignment.

Technology has also encumbered a progressively younger generation with the burden of a Wild West of adult content to navigate with few tools. Search engines blessedly give us access now to mountains of information, but without filters to help us understand the authority or veracity of what we are reading. It's hard for leaders to keep up, given the wealth of information and news. It's hard, in Wayne Gretsky's words, to "skate to where the puck is going," when the rink has no boundaries. No child should have to manage the poison of cyber-bullying, but every child with a smartphone must today. Leaders in schools and youth groups are struggling with how to guide the next generation to responsible use when technology changes faster than regulations do.

While we are ever connected, we are also more lonely. America's Centers for Disease Control publicized a study conducted in 2020 by the National Academies of Sciences, Engineering, and Medicine that reported a spike in social isolation and loneliness, especially in older adults. Over a third of adults aged forty-five and older are experiencing loneliness. That percentage jumps up to a quarter for adults aged over sixty-five. Better preventative care and advances in medicine are keeping us alive longer, while loneliness has come with the unanticipated health risks of depression, anxiety, suicide, increased heart disease, and risk of strokes. We have not figured out how to lead older, more vulnerable populations and ensure they are integrated and cared for within our communities.

Our greater affluence presents immense opportunity and its own surfeit of challenges. As a Jewish community, our affluence is a reassurance to many nonprofits, but tuition and membership rates are much higher than the rate of inflation. The costs of being Jewish and living in Jewish neighborhoods have risen. The space between the Jewish haves and have-nots is increasing. Board members tend to be more uniformly wealthy today – a worrying trend, because boards are meant to be as diverse as our communities are to be truly representative of our major constituencies. In this climate, leadership can become more about status than about skills. Rabbi Jonathan Sacks writes that we must "make it clear to all that leadership is service, not a form of status."[4]

In a related issue, the constant push to raise money can undermine energetic and inspired lay and professional leadership if it becomes their sole and exclusive responsibility and the criterion by which we judge a leader's success. Institutions need to be well-funded. We cannot be pollyannish about or dismissive of the important and necessary role that philanthropy plays in the long-term success of leaders and their organizations. Sometimes, we even tolerate bad leadership because the person in the most senior role is a great fundraiser or generous contributor. But the never-ending task of raising money for Jewish nonprofits too often prioritized over the higher goal of building meaningful relationships. Just consider the endless call for water when the Israelites traveled in the wilderness. Receiving "quality gifts" involves investing in quality relationships. Anything more shallow leads to transactional treatment. Sometimes community-wide agendas are dwarfed by the singular idiosyncratic voices of local and national philanthropic organizations and family foundations that pursue individual interests and fund their preferences. That is their right. But, as a result, professionals on the frontlines of the work can feel increasingly powerless to determine collective directions, especially when their expertise is marginalized, sidelined, or belittled. Genuine communal needs can inadvertently become ignored.

The talent pipeline risks drying up. In many cases, the hierarchy of wealth and power has damaged an already fragile lay-professional relationship, with many senior executives, from JCCs to synagogues to day schools, in position for fewer than five years. We don't need a succession pipeline as much as a talent intervention; our talent pipeline has been drying up for years. Good people do not want to face a steady stream of criticism or move their families from one place to another because they got on the wrong side of a powerful board chair.

To illustrate, I'd like to introduce you to Rabbi Josh. He told me that a while back, someone in his congregation died on a Friday night. Relatives came to his home and knocked on the door. He was in his bathrobe but welcomed them into his living room with the kindness one needs in such moment of loss. New to death and confused, these family members didn't know what to do. Rabbi Josh handed them a phone book and advised them to start making calls to organize the logistics as he took care of other details. Sometime later, one of the synagogue officers at a board meeting yelled at him in front of other trustees about this specific interaction: "You didn't let them in. You didn't help them. You cracked the door open and threw the phone book in their faces." What hurt Rabbi Josh the most was that the family knew this wasn't true, but they didn't deny it. The board member's accusation poisoned the rabbi's dignity: "He was the kind of guy – the clergy killer – who spent the whole time finding fault with me. I know what I did, and I would do the same thing again. You want to say something, but you can't always." Looking back with hindsight and more experience, he now realizes that the people who held so much power over his job at the time were mean and unforgiving. It was the beginning of what Rabbi Josh now describes as his own depression. Even though he knew what they said wasn't true, he struggled to make sense of his career choice, to lead others spiritually while facing constant criticism. When reflecting on the board, he shrugs: "To this day, they are just as dysfunctional, and I feel so lucky I'm not there. Water takes the shape of its container." He admitted how nervous his senior colleagues are about being let go – at any time and for anything. "In the rabbinate, there is always the overriding fear of losing your job." Can anyone lead successfully in this kind of tense environment?

Navigating uncertainty is now a certainty in leadership. A major change in the past twenty years is that we lived through a global pandemic, which was followed a few years later by a catastrophic war in Israel and a sharp and intense rise in global antisemitism, especially on college campuses.

Rabbis, Hillel directors, educational leaders, nonprofit CEOs, and senior board members confessed to me that they questioned themselves or broke down in different ways – lots of times. When Covid hit, there was no leadership manual to prepare them for this new, horrifying reality. Initially, they did not know how they could keep their organizations alive and functioning for an unclear duration of time. How would anyone get paid? Should they just shut down? Should they adjust their mission, downsize their staff, bring people back with conditions, or change the rules altogether? Some people could not stay in this zone of proximal tolerance. The burnout rate depleted our already shrinking pool of educators. One crisis after another left us all unsure, exhausted, and crestfallen. I heard what many of us heard and even said: "I didn't sign up for this." And either during the pandemic or not long after it, many left leadership roles altogether. They are blameless. The war in Israel prompted another wave of uncertainty that came with its own leadership difficulties.

The irony is that if you are a leader, you actually *did* sign up for this. You signed on to leadership in a world that is constantly changing and one that can produce surprises you never anticipated. A rare breed of leaders even leaned in during the pandemic and thrived. After finding imperfect solutions to imperfect situations, these leaders got creative. Because the entire world felt like an experiment, they had freedom they never would have had otherwise to consider radical possibilities. They worked collaboratively to restructure and to rethink, to reconsider their human resources on a board and professional level, to make serious decisions about strategic directions, and to reorganize their budgets to adopt more cost-saving efficiencies.

So much has changed in these last decades. How do we address these many new challenges? We need to promote more effective leadership dispositions that are less rigid and more durable, ones that reflect what Robert Jay Lifton describes as a protean self: "We are becoming fluid and many-sided. Without quite realizing it, we have been evolving a sense of self appropriate to the restlessness and flux of our time. This mode of being differs radically from that of the past and enables us to engage in continuous exploration and personal experiment."[5]

A new leadership framing is necessary to face these enormous challenges, one that emerges from a posture of humility about the world and greater realism about the human condition. In his bestselling book, *Thinking, Fast and Slow*, Nobel Prize winner Daniel Kahneman studied, among other issues, the way we diagnose situations and make decisions. "The idea that the future is unpredictable," he writes, "is undermined every day by the ease with which the past is explained."[6] We make mistakes when we lead in a way that is based on too-easy assumptions about the past to inform the organizational leadership of the future. "When faced with a difficult question," Kahneman contends, "we often answer an easier one instead, usually without noticing the substitution."[7] This can create a lack of realism about how we chart a course for change: "We are prone to overestimate how much we understand about the world and to underestimate the role of chance in events."[8] Kahneman identifies the problem starkly when he writes that we have "an almost unlimited ability to ignore our ignorance." To combat this and acquire the skills necessary to lead in the world requires "rapid and unequivocal feedback about the correctness of thoughts and actions."[9] We need more constructive feedback to lead well. We need to create feedback loops in real time because organizations undergo more rapid transitions today.

We also need to move from the ubiquitous language of journeys to the more compelling language of commitments. Several years ago, I had the good fortune to meet and interview Pete Davis. Pete is a young man who works on projects to strengthen democracy and solidarity in these times of increasing division. Upon graduating Harvard, he gave a commencement address on commitment that has been viewed by millions of people. There he cites the French philosopher Jacques Maritain, who said that the meaning of life is "self-mastery for the purpose of self-giving."[10] Pete then describes the great task his generation now faces: We say we love commitments, but we keep acting like browsers in the way we shop, date, watch TV. This culture of browsing seeps into a way of thinking and being in the world that comes down to three fears:

> First, we have a fear of regret: We worry that if we commit to something, we will later regret having not committed to something else. Second, we have a fear of association: We think that if we commit to something, we will be vulnerable to the chaos that that commitment brings to our identity, our reputation, and our sense of control. Third, we have a fear of missing out: We feel that if we commit to something, the responsibilities that come with it will prevent us from being everything, everywhere, to everyone.

The only way to combat these fears and cultural trends is to interrogate them and discover our core convictions. "This is the challenge of growing up – to turn the corner from self-mastery to self-giving. What is the moment at that corner – between inwardness, growth, and concerted self-development and outwardness, public interestedness, and other-centeredness? Commitment." Pete coined a phrase, explaining that what we need right now, in an age of browsing and too much choice, are "long-haul heroes." *Our community needs more long-haul heroes.*

Leadership suffers from a lack of commitment. I once described this shift in attitude with the help of a restaurant menu. Many decades ago, when people in the United States moved, they sought out and joined a myriad of Jewish organizations to feel belonging. They joined a synagogue, sent their children to Jewish day schools or Hebrew schools, and their teenagers to Jewish youth groups. They gave money to their local Federation, exercised in a JCC, and became members of multiple Jewish social clubs. We'll call this the fixed-price menu to community building. Then we moved to the *à la carte* menu of communal options, which slowly eroded the accepted communal norms. People joined Jewish organizations that serviced their needs at the time. They came in and out of synagogue membership depending on the stage of their families. They gave to charities episodically. According to demographic studies of various communities, people might, for example, send their children to Jewish day schools but not be members of a synagogue. Costs were often a deterrent. But today, "doing Jewish" for most Jews in North America most closely resembles a tapas menu. People come in and out of Jewish synagogue services, if they go at all. They go to events rather than commit to organizations. And, as a result, organizations suffer, especially when it comes to attracting younger members and supporters.

Leading now requires a cultural sea change. We cannot turn back the hands of time, but we can educate for commitment. We can move away from the language of journeys and engagement – those ever-amorphous terms of loose involvement – to asking people about their convictions and commitments and providing meaningful spaces to discover them. There is a lot of work to do. A lot.

Much of that work is discussed in the pages ahead. These essays are designed to amplify some of the leadership messages that are organic to each Torah portion and support them with the insights of contemporary leadership experts. With each weekly *sedra*, I found that heroes come in all forms, that some leaders are born into greatness and others are shaped by circumstances. Each leadership lesson jumps off the page and into life, provoking us to think bigger and to do more. For this reason, I conclude each essay with a personal leadership question.

Thank you for reading, and thank you for leading.

Introduction

Reading Leadership into and Out of the Torah

Leadership appears everywhere in the Torah in black words on white parchment. We need not read leadership *into* the Torah as a forced theme or a modern imposition on a sacred text. We read it *out* of the Torah on almost every page. Whenever there is a problem, we look to our leaders – in life and in Tanakh, the Hebrew Bible. Something goes right, spectacularly right, and we turn to leaders to give them thanks, credit, and praise. Something goes wrong, terribly wrong, and we turn to leaders to provide direction, inspiration, strength, moral guidance, military wisdom, if necessary, and hope. We also apportion blame. That was true then, and it is still true today.

A new leader in Tanakh is the key to actualize a vision, to carry out an assignment, and to respond to a crisis. The new leader is the builder of an ark, the founder of a faith, and the ancestor who put a stake in a land. The new leader confronts enemies, calls for a social justice revolution, brings down the law in tablets of stone, and inspires the building of a sanctuary where God can dwell among the people. The new leader escorts millions across the Jordan River and conquers a land full of enemies. The new leader sits under a tree and teaches the law until she goes out to war or faces down the head of an empire to beg for the life of her people. The new leader assures continuity by assigning or grooming a successor. The ancient talent pipeline was constantly flowing because a new leader was always necessary and available.

God alone, with omnipresent power, can save human beings from any form of distress, but in Tanakh, God almost never acts alone. God always chooses a human partner to act as a broker, an emissary, a teacher, an ambassador, an agent, a guide, an enforcer, a motivator, a challenger, a critic, and a parent. In virtually every one of the Bible's revolutionary stories, be they small family dramas or large battlefield scenes, God works with a leader to advance a mission. From the first chapter of Genesis onward, humans were created to take leadership roles – to work and to watch a garden, to have governance over the natural world and to steward it responsibly. Adam and Eve were tasked with co-creating the next generation and filling the world. All of this was to be done in God's likeness: Observe the way God creates with care, intention, separation, and evaluation, and then rest. We are to lead the way God leads as an expression of being created in God's image.

Our job is to be careful and impassioned Torah readers so that we can become careful and impassioned Jewish leaders. And this is a problem, because many have lost touch with this elemental, educational aspect of the Torah's challenge to us. For some, the Tanakh is a foreign book with outdated assumptions written in an unfamiliar or vaguely nostalgic language. It cannot be our teacher if the book is closed. For others, it is a deeply familiar guide to living a life of Jewish law and practice, informed by stories that have become their master narratives of ethics. But even then, it has not necessarily translated itself into the mandate to lead others, only to live a meaningful spiritual life of mitzvot in relation to God and in community. This approach, too, misses much of the Torah's messaging. It is ultimately a call text to inspire us to see the plight of the needy – to those who live in Isaiah's darkness or Ruth's poverty or Malachi's mediocrity – to feel compassion, to take action, and to change the conditions around us so that we can live in a world that is just, moral, and fair. The Torah asks us to be valiant, to be brave, and to be different. If we reduce the Torah to stories or to laws alone, it will not give us its fullness. By presenting so many leaders in so many different situations, it stimulates us to consider our own surroundings, our crises, our institutions, our boundaries, and our options and then to do something to make things better. We are *not* here to live passively. The Bible's pages remind every one of us in subtle and vivid ways to take initiative, to act with integrity, and to lead passionately.

To illustrate, we will travel way back in time to a biblical leadership story that resonates with contemporary sensibilities. This example is one of dozens that present what we'll call the cycle of leadership redemption. It is stamped all over Tanakh. The problem: a foreign enemy. The solution: a leader.

A long time ago, under a blazing Near Eastern sun, a young warrior named Gideon was charged with saving the Israelites from their tormentors, the Midianites, who were "swarming as thick as locusts" (Judges 6:5). Odds were stacked against the underdog. The same biblical verse tells us that the Midianites "and their camels were innumerable." With soldiers and strong animals, the "Midianites would invade the land and ravage it." We know variations of this story all too well. Oppressed Israelites cry out to God begging for salvation. God sends them a prophet who offers them words of solace and reassures them that just as God had freed them from Egypt's house of bondage, God would once again relieve them of their suffering. The solution is always the same: a new leader.

Back to our young new leader Gideon. In the midst of Israelite misery, God sent an angel to sit under a terebinth tree while Gideon, a farmer, was beating out his wheat, which was hidden in a winepress so the Midianites would not steal his harvest. "The angel of God appeared to him and said to him, 'God is with you, valiant warrior!'" (6:12). The angel essentially named Gideon the leader of his generation. But Gideon was not honored by this visit, nor did he feel privileged to lead his people in battle. Instead, he used the meeting as an opportunity to berate God: "Please, my lord, if God is with us, why has all this befallen us? Where are all those wondrous deeds about which our ancestors told us, saying, 'Truly God brought us up from Egypt'? Now God has abandoned us and delivered us into the hands of Midian!" (6:13). Gideon's accusation reflected a faithless generation. The God who freed the Jews from slavery once upon a time is now blamed for neglecting their descendants.

God directly responded by ignoring the insult and entrusting Gideon to be His human partner, replicating our familiar pattern: "God turned to him and said, 'Go in this strength of yours and deliver Israel from the Midianites. I now make you My messenger'" (6:14). But Gideon rejected the call. He, like Moses before him and Jeremiah after him, questioned his capabilities: "Please, my Sovereign, how can I deliver Israel?" (6:15). He also claimed he was from the smallest tribe and was the youngest in his family; surely there were people more adept, mature, and experienced? God responded the way God replied to Moses and Jeremiah in their times of insecurity and hesitation: "I will be with you, and you shall defeat Midian all at once" (6:16). At this point in the leadership cycle, we expect Gideon to change his mind, say, "*Hineni*" – I am here and ready – and outfit himself for war. That did not happen.

Gideon, at the very moment of this invitation to lead, questioned God's very existence: "If I have gained Your favor, give me a sign that it is You who are speaking to me" (6:17). But God did not show anger. God acquiesced and told Gideon to prepare an offering and place it on a rock, and it was immediately consumed by fire. This should have been sufficient proof. But not for Gideon. Even after he began the task of leading, Gideon tested God again, then a final time as a guarantee that he could beat the Midianites were he to lead them to war:

> And Gideon said to God, "If You really intend to deliver Israel through me as You have said – here I place a fleece of wool on the threshing floor. If dew falls only on the fleece and all the ground remains dry, I shall know that You will deliver Israel through me, as You have said." (6:36–37)

The next morning, the fleece was soaked through with water, a whole bowlful of it. Gideon needed a sign, and God responded with a surplus. Yet Gideon was still unsatisfied. With signature chutzpah, he prodded God again:

> "Do not be angry with me if I speak just once more. Let me make just one more test with the fleece: Let the fleece alone be dry, while there is dew all over the ground." God did so that

> night: Only the fleece was dry, while there was dew all over the ground. (6:39)

When Gideon needed another sign, God gave him another. God saturated the fleece, then dried it. This was an odd request given the miracles God was capable of performing, a test more suited to a shepherd than a farmer. But this time, Gideon had no more excuses. Finally, finally, as our chapter closes and the next opens, Gideon led his troops into battle.

Gideon eventually assumed the very leadership role he initially rejected, so what was the function of testing and retesting God?

I believe the story communicates with the starkest reality the anxiety of leadership that must be overcome to fight any battle: military, spiritual, or emotional. Gideon first did not believe in himself and then did not believe in the authority of the One giving him the assignment. His, like ours, was an age of disbelief and cynicism.

A biblical book earlier, the Israelites transitioned from Moses to Joshua. They finally reached the Promised Land and were motivated to fight for it. For the most part, Joshua was successful. The Israelites conquered the land, and the tribes settled. But Joshua never appointed a successor, the way that Moses did. As soon as Moses's death warrant was issued, Moses understood that his people required the stability of new leadership: "Let the Lord, Source of the breath of all flesh, appoint someone over the community who shall go out before them and come in before them, and who shall take them out and bring them in, so that the Lord's community may not be like sheep that have no shepherd" (Num. 27:16–17). Thus, Joshua was named as Moses's successor. In contrast, the closing chapter of the book of Joshua ends with the death of both the military leader, Joshua, and the spiritual leader, the high priest Eleazer. No replacements are mentioned in the book. Not surprisingly, in the early chapters of Judges, the people began to worship idols, lost military ground, and suffered, for the most part, the incompetency of multiple ill-equipped leaders. Failure to put a leadership pipeline in place spelled political and spiritual disaster.

The book of Judges is strikingly modern in its depiction of a generation bereft of godliness and good leadership, and Gideon was its chief representative. Gideon didn't believe in himself, but he also didn't believe in anyone else or in the God of old. He and his generation lacked inspiration and ambition. Pummeled by an enemy nation and unable to live and work freely (remember, he hid his work in a wine vat), he did not experience God's presence in his life – only God's absence. It is hard to lead when you lack conviction and drive, when you need constant proof that God exists and that leadership is a worthwhile use of your time. Even with proofs, Gideon continued to hesitate and had to test. He had internalized the pessimism of the defeated and lost the impulse to resist and to fight. He felt God had betrayed His people, and he regarded leadership as a second-rate endeavor. He deigned to lead only when badgered enough.

The leadership messages embedded in this story are sharp and powerful. I've distilled five:

1. **Offer leaders meaningful encouragement and support.** Taking the lead when it is very necessary and when no one else is stepping up to the plate often requires a double dose of reassurance. When people test others repeatedly – in this case, God – it is usually a sign of their own insecurity that masks itself as a false display of intransigence and arrogance. Unwittingly, Gideon was testing himself. Did God really think Gideon was up to the task? He did. He let Gideon know it. God had more faith in Gideon than Gideon had faith in God.
2. **Don't take "No" for an answer.** Ask again. And again. When leadership is the only answer, "Will you lead?" becomes the only worthwhile question. God could easily have lost patience with Gideon's offensive refusal and sought out another leader. Yet God did not dismiss the tests Gideon requested. He honored them and did not judge Gideon.
3. **Create a leadership pipeline early.** When good people do not step up to lead, those less noble and competent will occupy the vacuum. This happens a few chapters later. Gideon, in the end, was a highly successful military leader, who, like Joshua, failed to appoint a successor, despite having seventy sons (Judges 9:2). When the succession pipeline is broken, danger ensues. An unprincipled son of his, Avimelekh, consequently took control and

"hired some worthless and reckless fellows, and they followed him" (9:4). Avimelekh was such a troubled leader that he had to pay his followers. He then killed sixty-eight of his brothers to make sure there was no competition for the top seat. The youngest brother, Yotam, however, ran and hid. He came out of hiding on the day of Avimelekh's inauguration, stood on top of a mountain, and delivered a parable about bad leadership, asking the people to think carefully before formally appointing Avimelekh. Yotam thought he might shake the people out of their cognitive dissonance. They all knew what trouble Avimelekh was.

Yotam's words fell flat. Avimelekh reigned for three years, until the relationship between him and the people soured. The people sought a replacement, but Avimelekh resisted and went to war against them, eventually destroying the inhabitants of the city of Shechem, where this story takes place. He hired followers and killed followers. The pattern of no leadership, then good leadership, then bad leadership repeated itself because Gideon created the possibility of change without instituting continuity to enhance leadership stability. The result was mutiny, chaos, and death.

4. **People need to be led with greatness.** Leadership greatness is a combination of aspiration, inspiration, strategic thinking, competence, and character. Few leaders start out with all of these dispositions and behaviors. Gideon's hesitation transformed, over time, into real leadership drive, and he was successful at conquering the demons within and the enemies without.
5. **It takes only one person to reverse the cycle of defeat.** God did not call upon the community at large to change the political landscape. He called upon one person, and that one person was able during his lifetime to shift the winds of defeat into the courage of triumph.

Today, we are the inheritors of Gideon's leadership. We stand with Gideon in his moments of doubt, not sure if we can lead, not sure if this is what we want or God wants, and not sure of the people we are leading. We work hard, we fail, and we try again.

But, whatever Gideon's failings, he *did* provide a leadership solution for a limited period of time. And that's all we have: a limited period of time. No one leader can solve every problem for all time. This makes the need for selecting, training, and retaining good leaders all the more pressing. Every trend, challenge, and problem requires its own unique diagnosis and treatment. Every leader needs to marshal his or her own resources to achieve a modicum of victory. There will always be losses and disappointments. That is real and undeniable.

People will treat the leader unfairly. There will be gossip and ingratitude and complaints. Moses managed forty years of it when ushering the Israelites through the wilderness. Maybe that time period offers us a guide. Not only must we put up with the difficulties and everyday challenges of leadership, we must also sustain our work for the long game. Moses freed the Jews from slavery, gave them the law, built the *Mishkan* – the portable Sanctuary – and took the people to the edge of the Promised Land. These are achievements of service across a lifetime. With faith, enthusiasm, and luck, we can make the world a little bit better in our own time, not for all time.

We are lucky to wake up in a state of blessing and thank God that we are here to do something meaningful and useful for others, in the spirit of Mary Oliver: "It is a serious thing / just to be alive / on this fresh morning / in this broken world." And because that is all we can do with our one "wild and precious life," that has to be enough.

Leadership in the Book of Genesis

פרשת בראשית • *Parashat Bereshit*

A Garden of Possibility

The joy of starting the Torah cycle again is twinned with the sense of new interpretive possibilities that once again unfold. We may have read the first chapter of Genesis dozens, if not hundreds of times, but we bring a new self to it this week, a self that is a year older and made wiser through new experiences and insights.

We'll begin where our most foundational story began: in a garden. Why a garden? Everything about a garden thrums with new growth and possibility. Remember those little seeds in cups we planted as young schoolchildren? Remember the excitement of watching the first green sprout appear from the soil? In a garden, we cultivate that delight again and again.

Richard Powers, in his Pulitzer Prize-winning novel, *The Overstory*, writes, "This is not our world with trees in it. It's a world of trees, where humans have just arrived."[1] The book of Genesis opens with the verdancy of a tree-filled world. We humans only arrive later. On the third day, God said, "'Let the earth sprout vegetation: seed-bearing plants, fruit trees of every kind on earth that bear fruit with the seed in it.' And it was so." The text continues, as speech brings forth action followed by evaluation: "The earth brought forth vegetation: seed-bearing plants of every kind, and trees of every kind bearing fruit with the seed in it. And God saw that this was good" (Gen. 1:11–12). Seeds speak to the generational continuity of creation; every living thing in this special garden can replicate itself.

Humans, new scientific research tells us, are similar to the trees that preceded them in creation. Humans were not only in the Garden, we were *of* the Garden. Formed from the dust, our namesake – Adam – signifies the loamy earth – the *adama* – that produced us. In Genesis 2, the Garden is described as a bare landscape in desperate need of a human-divine partnership: "When no shrub (*siaḥ*) of the field was yet on earth and no grasses of the field had yet sprouted, because the Lord God had not sent rain upon the earth, and there was no man to till the soil" (Gen. 2:5). Later, in Deuteronomy 20:19, humans are compared to trees, prompting the midrashic comment: "This teaches that human life comes only from the tree" (*Sifrei* 203).

The Spanish medieval exegete Nahmanides observes that although vegetation was created in Genesis 1, its continued growth relies upon God's rain and the human gardener described in Genesis 2. God created a water supply and a person to tend and steward nature: "But a flow would well up from the ground and water the whole surface of the earth. The Lord God formed man from the dust of the earth. He blew into his nostrils the breath of life, and man became a living being" (Gen. 2:6–7). This image is both primal and poetic.

Rabbi Abraham ibn Ezra, the twelfth-century Spanish poet and commentator, defines the *siaḥ* of Genesis 2:5 – typically translated as "shrub" – as a fruit-bearing tree. He then offers another definition for *siaḥ*: "conversation." This meaning is borne out by a quick study of the word's appearance throughout Tanakh. *Siaḥ* can also mean to sing (Judges 5:10), to speak (Job 12:8), to pray (Ps. 55:17), to meditate (Ps. 77:6), to praise (I Chr. 16:9), and to complain (Job 7:11).

Is it possible that a word for many types of trees also signifies the varieties of speech? Yes. Speech, Ibn Ezra conjectures, is the fruit of our mouths. The similarity between humans and trees is not only in form, he writes, but in what we produce. Trees produce fruit. We produce words. Ibn Ezra then offers us a panoply of tree images we use to describe humans: limbs, trunks, roots, fruit, branches. Powers in *The*

Overstory makes the comparison genetic: "You and the tree in your backyard come from a common ancestor. A billion and a half years ago, the two of you parted ways. But even now, after an immense journey in separate directions, that tree and you still share a quarter of your genes."[2]

Ibn Ezra may have been onto something by alerting us to the linguistic "root" shared by trees and language. In 2015, Peter Wohlleben, a German forester who has devoted his life to the study of trees, published the bestselling book *The Hidden Life of Trees: What They Feel, How They Communicate.*[3] He challenges our common misconception of trees as loners that compete with other vegetation for water, sunlight, and nutrients. Mounting scientific evidence suggests that trees form alliances with other trees, even those not within the same species. They not only live cooperatively, they also communicate at the root level. Above ground, they use scent signals and pheromones to speak to each other. Through these complex, interconnected networks, trees send distress signals about drought, disease, and insect attacks. Wohlleben calls it the "wood-wide web."

Powers, through one of his characters, described this majestic undergrowth in this way: "A forest knows things.... There are brains down there, ones our own brains aren't shaped to see. Root plasticity, solving problems and making decisions. Fungal synapses. What else do you want to call it? Link enough trees together, and a forest grows aware."[4]

God's decision to create humans in this Garden may have been a way to communicate to Adam and Eve that they entered an interconnected natural world that predated them and required their leadership and tender care to bloom. The Garden was their classroom, where they were to learn from trees how to nurture an interdependent universe that communicated under and above ground. By creating through the process of separation, God was showing Adam and Eve that on a cosmic level, we are all profoundly connected. Trees were the best living example of this for the new couple. In *Studies in Spirituality*, Rabbi Jonathan Sacks writes, "If I were asked how to find God, I would say: Learn to listen. Listen to the song of the universe in the call of the birds, the rustle of trees..."[5]

It's not hard to understand the implications of the tree/human comparison for leadership. "Root cause analysis" in leadership is the study of all that is unspoken underground that may shed light on organizational problems, prompting us to search for creative and lasting solutions. Examining underlying, causal issues can prevent problems from reemerging. Moreover, taking the tree metaphor seriously in leadership implies alerting others to our inherent connectedness, especially when it is not obvious, especially in times of divisiveness. We lead when we select our words with intention and use them to create new possibilities. As the saying goes, what we pay attention to grows.

We are born "to work and to watch" this remarkable garden. The blessing of the very first psalm is also the blessing of what a great leader can do to protect and inspire us, "...like a tree planted beside streams of water, which yields its fruit in season, whose foliage never fades, and whatever it produces thrives" (Ps. 1:3). Leaders help others flourish. John Gardner, in his book *On Leadership*, compares mentors to farmers.[6] Every word we utter can be a seed to help someone else thrive. As we begin the Torah anew, we are challenged to think about how to tend to the world around us and within us.

Personal Leadership Reflection

As we begin this sacred Torah cycle anew, who and what will you be growing this year?

פרשת נח • *Parashat Noaḥ*

The What and Why of the Ark

My grandchildren love to play with my collection of wooden Noah's ark figures. Some have movable animals and a small Noah holding a staff. When I clean up after the children, I make sure to keep the animals in pairs. The children adore the Noah story. The image of the ark appears on kids' wallpaper and in their books; it's the stuff of toys.

The only problem is that the Noah story is not for children. It's an unhappy story of immorality, loss, and despair. The land takes its revenge on society and destroys all within its path. Even the closing covenant God made with Noah contained a note of the tragic: "Never again will I doom the earth because of man, since the devisings of the human mind are evil from youth; nor will I ever again destroy every living being, as I have done" (Gen. 8:21). God's promise never to destroy the world again is predicated on a lowering of expectations. Humans will forever be flawed. I'm not going to tell my young grandchildren the whole story just yet.

Maybe the only way we can understand this story is by standing with Noah before he built the ark:

> God said to Noah, "*I have decided to put an end to all flesh, for the earth is filled with lawlessness because of them: I am about to destroy them with the earth.* Make yourself an ark of gopher wood; make it an ark with compartments and cover it inside and out with pitch. This is how you shall make it: The length of the ark shall be three hundred cubits, its width fifty cubits, and its height thirty cubits. Make an opening for daylight in the ark, and finish it within a cubit of the top. Put the entrance to the ark in its side; make it with bottom, second, and third decks. *For My part, I am about to bring the Flood – waters upon the earth – to destroy all flesh under the sky in which there is breath of life; everything on earth shall perish.*" (Gen. 6:13–17)

Imagine, for a moment, a divine voice calling out to you with an important task that you, and only you, can actualize. Aside from a few family members, there will be no one to assist you. You are on your own. Your world will narrow into this one responsibility for the foreseeable future, but surprisingly, it is to create something rather prosaic. You are told to build a ship and to populate that ship with a pair of animals from every species. You try to prepare yourself mentally for the assignment, but you still cannot understand its significance. Unsure of how large this boat should be, you pay careful attention to the dimensions God commands.

You read the instructions a dozen times and make a list of what you'll need. You don't want to get it wrong. The job is too important. You create an architectural rendering of the ark. You wake up with the sun. Hammer in hand, you spend all day in the hot Near East nailing boards together. Everyone around you laughs. They jokingly look for the body of water where you are going to place your ship. They act as if you've lost your mind. But the word of God is a constant whisper in your ear that keeps you focused.

It's only when the rain first beats on the roof and you rush your family and the animals inside that you realize you've missed something critically important. You just closed the door on all of humanity. Holed up in the ark's dark and cavernous inside, you review the directions repeatedly to see where you went wrong. Suddenly, you see what you failed to see before. With your singular focus on following directions, you missed that in the opening and closing of the instructions, God presented an apocalyptic vision of the world. And now it is too late to do anything to help all those you left behind. All you can do is monitor the sea and pray.

This is the fate of Noah.

God told Noah exactly what to do. But God also told Noah why. Noah focused on the what and bypassed the why. The directions he was given form a unique and unusual passage, because the Tanakh rarely offers concrete recommendations. Abraham was told to go to another country and start a nation with no GPS. Moses was commanded to free the Jews from slavery and take them out of Egypt with no map and no guidance other than a staff. Esther was told by Mordecai to save her people but was given no script. Ruth made a covenantal commitment to Judaism without any explicit instructions. Why is it that Noah, of all people, was given such clear guidelines?

There is a powerful framing to God's technical instructions. Every few lines, God explicitly told Noah about the moral state of the world. Noah responded by taking out his tools and concentrating on the skylights. Noah missed the larger driving factor behind the situation. Rashi notes this and cites a passage of Talmud (Sanhedrin 108b) to support his reading. There are numerous ways, Rashi notes, that God could have saved Noah. Why select an ark? "So that the men of the generation of the flood might see him constructing it for 120 years and might ask him, 'What do you need this for?' and so that he might answer them, 'The Holy One, blessed be He, is about to bring a flood upon the world' – perhaps they might repent."

According to the Talmud, the ark's significance was not in its use during the flood, but its very presence long before the water hit. Noah's neighbors would be curious about this building project – how could they not be? – and badger him with questions. Noah could use this conversational opportunity to discuss the larger forces in society that prompted this task and perhaps convince others to repent.

They could have all built arks, every last one. The ancient seas could have, without much imagination, been filled with many other arks captained by all of Noah's friends and neighbors. But if any such conversations existed, they are not recorded in our *sedra*.

Noah was righteous, one midrash states, in *his* generation. Rashi offers two readings of the word "his": Noah was either truly righteous or relatively righteous in comparison to others who lived at the same time. This is both compliment and criticism. Rabbi Jonathan Sacks, in *Lessons in Leadership,* concludes that "Noah was a good man who was not a leader."[7] Noah was, in the words of leadership experts Ron Heifetz and Marty Linsky, a master of technical leadership. He focused on what he had to do logistically, but that ironically blinded him from seeing what he had to do adaptively. Adaptive leaders do more than solve problems. They examine causes, assess risks, and anticipate challenges and resistance. They learn the skills that will help them manage contingencies and crises.

When Noah left the ark, he offered a sacrifice – an act of giving to repair a world once flooded with theft and lawlessness. But Noah also planted a vineyard, produced wine, and got drunk in his tent. The enormity of the trauma he experienced was overwhelming. We understand his desire to lose himself in obliviousness. Drinking might have temporarily numbed Noah to all he ignored when building the ark, but at some point, the sobering reality set in. Noah had to construct a new world immune to the moral challenges of the one he left. His technical skills would be of little use. Everything about the new world required adaptive leadership.

One day, when my grandchildren are ready, I will tell them the whole story and remind them to listen to directions and always ask why and what they can do to help. Because that's what leaders do. Simon Sinek, in *Start with Why: How Great Leaders Inspire Everyone to Take Action,* writes that "regardless of WHAT we do in our lives, our WHY – our driving purpose, cause, or belief – never changes."[8] Leaders who only ask "what" questions are liable to forget the "why." But it's always the "why" that catalyzes true and meaningful change, one raindrop at a time.

Personal Leadership Reflection

What's your leadership "why"?

פרשת לך לך • *Parashat Lekh Lekha*

The Reputation Nation

Warren Buffet famously said, "It takes twenty years to build a reputation and five minutes to ruin it." Digitally, we can ruin someone's reputation even faster than that. One negative tweet, Uber rating, restaurant posting, rate my professor rant, or newspaper comment can damage someone's reputation irrevocably. There are websites today that try to manage or defend reputations to "help professionals develop and promote a truthful and positive online image through proactive reputation management strategies."

If it were only that easy. Gossip, cancellations, and trash talk don't just disappear, especially in this polarizing climate. Buffet, in his quote above, puts the onus on the person rather than his or her critics. "If you think," he says, about how quickly your reputation can change, "you'll do things differently."

Understanding the importance of a sterling reputation is as old as the first Jew, Abraham. One of the most astonishing and understudied encounters between Abram, as he was then called, and his neighbors appears in *Parashat Lekh Lekha*. In chapter 14, Abraham found himself amidst a battle between four kings and five kings when he tried to rescue his nephew Lot. The verses are not easy to follow, given the number of leaders involved and the complex geography.

All war brings confusion and collateral damage. As the battle ends, "King Melchizedek of Salem brought out bread and wine" and blessed Abram. The Jewish ritual of blessing wine and breaking bread originates with a foreign king. Abram gave a tenth of what he owned to King Melchizedek, likely as a form of tax or tribute. Then the king of Sodom, another of the warring kings, said to Abram, "Give me the persons, and take the possessions for yourself" (Gen. 14:21).

When wars are over, it's time to tally up losses and split rewards. Abram, however, was not willing to take a thing. "Abram said to the king of Sodom, 'I swear to the Lord, God Most High, Creator of heaven and earth: I will not take so much as a thread or a sandal strap of what is yours; you shall not say, 'It is I who made Abram rich'" (14:22). Rashi observes that Abram was confident that God would provide him with wealth, implied in Genesis 12:2. He did not, therefore, want a human being to take the credit.

Abram wanted nothing from these skirmishes. He gave a portion of what he had without taking as much as a shoelace. He did not even take a small and insignificant item. The Talmud (Ḥullin 89a) concludes that Abram's descendants would therefore merit two commandments that involve a string or strap: the thread of sky-blue wool worn on ritual fringes and the strap of the phylacteries. Abram, it seems, wanted to make a statement to those around him about his personal integrity as a leader and about the kind of God he served. Abram attributed his success to God alone. War to him was not about bounty, captives, or exploitation of the vulnerable. It was about mediating unfortunate obstructions to the divine promise he received.

According to the king of Sodom, Abram was within his right to take what he wanted, but he gave away his money instead. By not taking the loot of war, Abram was making a positive character deposit in the minds of the leaders who surrounded him. Abram was forgoing short-term gains for the long-term investment that was his reputation. When it comes to our reputations, there are no shortcuts.

Later, in Genesis 34:30, after Dinah was taken and violated by Shechem, Jacob chastises his sons Simeon and Levi for creating and implementing a devious plan to punish Shechem's community: "You have brought trouble on me, making me odious among the inhabitants of the land." The Hebrew expression *akhartem oti* literally means "you have made me odious" in the eyes of others.

A smell is invisible but can leave a highly potent signature of one's presence. The medieval Spanish commentator Abraham ibn Ezra explains Jacob's fears: "They will hate me as one loathes something that gives off a horrible odor." While there are many interpretations of Jacob's behavior here, one message Jacob tried to teach his sons is that our reputations matter. Even when others hurt us profoundly, we must always seek higher ground.

Abram's defense of his personal integrity as a leader brings to mind another dramatic biblical moment. As the prophet Samuel aged and effectively retired from service, he publicly pledged his honesty.

> Then Samuel said to all Israel, "I have yielded to you in all you have asked of me and have set a king over you. Henceforth the king will be your leader. As for me, I have grown old and gray – but my sons are still with you – and I have been your leader from my youth to this day. Here I am! Testify against me, in the presence of the Lord and in the presence of His anointed one: Whose ox have I taken, or whose ass have I taken? Whom have I defrauded or whom have I robbed? From whom have I taken a bribe to look the other way? I will return it to you." They responded, "You have not defrauded us, and you have not robbed us, and you have taken nothing from anyone." (I Sam. 12:1–4)

One view in the Talmud (Nedarim 38a) is that Samuel, like Abraham, was wealthy; he did not need to rely upon the bribes and handouts of his flock. But there is something deeper going on in this odd summative speech.

Samuel was a steward of the Israelites from his youngest years. His mother Hannah pledged him to the Temple under the high priest Eli when he was a child. As he aged, he recounted a lifetime of devotion to his people, culminating with a testament about the many storms they weathered together: "Here I am!" Despite it all. Because of it all.

I am still here with you. Samuel needed his flock to affirm that after he was gone, his noble reputation would stay intact. If there had been any misunderstanding or misuse of his authority, let it be known now. The people let it be known. Samuel, they responded in unison, took nothing. He was outstanding in character and in trustworthiness.

Reputations are fragile. Rabbi Jonathan Sacks affirms this in *Essays on Ethics*: "When people associate religiosity with integrity, decency, humility, and compassion, God's name is sanctified. When they come to associate it with contempt for others and for the law, the result is a desecration of God's name."[9]

Leaders can control many things. But they cannot control what is said about them. What they can do, as Abraham, Jacob, and Samuel teach us, is protect the reputations they already have. The same is true of us all. We must work hard. Serve. Apologize often. Compensate for error. And, most importantly, assume others have good intent. The fact that someone may not judge us favorably does not mean we should do the same. And, in the worst-case scenario, we must remember that we are not the sum total of the worst mistakes we have ever made. Reputations, our reputations, are built on justice and a thousand small acts of kindness.

Personal Leadership Reflection

Describe something you've done to protect or rehabilitate your leadership reputation.

פרשת וירא • Parashat Vayera

Still He Delayed

"He who hesitates is lost," goes the well-known proverb. I heard this as a teenager for the first time and wondered what it meant. I get lost when I don't know directions. I don't get lost when I take too long to make a decision. Or do I?

There's an incredible moment in *Parashat Vayera* that happens just as the sun is about to rise. It's the time of day when possibility opens, when another morning is about to unfold and with it, a sense of limitlessness. It's the moment that explains why he who hesitates is lost. Tentativeness can make us unsure of who we are. Our indecision can make us feel untethered. It is was at this liminal hour when Lot was approached by an angel with an important message, telling Lot to save himself and his family from the catastrophe about to plague Sodom and Gomorrah: "As dawn broke, the angels urged Lot on, saying, 'Arise, take your wife and your two remaining daughters, lest you be swept away because of the iniquity of the city.' Still he delayed" (Gen. 19:15–16).

Lot ignored the metaphor of the dawn. With doom on the horizon but the glimmer of light that this day could be different for him and those he loved, "still he delayed." Rashi writes that Lot delayed to save his property, putting money above his life and that of his family. Radak, a medieval French commentator, expands on this reading. In Genesis 19:12, at an earlier stage, the angel permitted Lot to take what he could with him. As time passed, every hour became increasingly consequential. Lot was forced to forgo his possessions and leave at dawn with only the clothing on his back. Hesitation has its costs. Still Lot wasn't ready.

The Hebrew word used for delay in the verse is "*vayitmahema.*" The root of this word is "*mah*" – which sounds like the Hebrew for "what." It is as if in delaying, we are asking "What, what, what shall I do?" The word itself sounds like the hesitation that it represents. It only appears in Tanakh nine times. *Strong's Exhaustive Concordance* also defines this word as to question, to be reluctant, to linger, to stay, or to tarry. The Torah reader unnaturally extends the musicality of the word when chanted in the Torah cycle, as a rare cantillation note, a *shalshelet,* appears above it, making the word itself tarry.

The second appearance of this word in Genesis also comes at a life-threatening time. Judah petitioned Jacob to allow him to bring Benjamin down to Egypt at Joseph's command. Every delay brought the family closer to starvation: "For we could have been there and back twice if we had not *delayed*" (Gen. 43:10). The word's association with food appears again in Exodus as we were leaving Egypt: "And they baked unleavened cakes of the dough that they had taken out of Egypt, for it was not leavened, since they had been driven out of Egypt and could not *delay*..." (Ex. 12:39). The prophet Habakkuk awaited the fulfillment of a prophecy, no matter how long it took to come to fruition: "Even if it *tarries,* wait for it still; for it will surely come, without delay" (Hab. 2:3). A psalm tells us never to put off a mitzva: "I have hurried and not *delayed* to keep Your commandments" (Ps. 119:60).

Lot characteristically miscalculated and misjudged the long-term implications of his actions, always missing opportunities. He consistently, until his very end, made poor decisions. This time was no different. He could have been heir to Abraham and the next leader of a new nation. Instead, he fathered two sons through incest who grew into two nations that were archenemies of the Jews. There are long-term implications of inaction.

Several years ago, management consultant and bestselling writer Ron Carucci wrote that "too many leaders avoid making tough calls"[10] He conducted a ten-year longitudinal study of more than 2,700 leaders and found that fifty-seven percent of new executives confronted decisions that were "more complicated and difficult than they expected." As a result, many leaders make excuses for not making hard decisions because they don't want to lose status with followers. Carucci boils down these excuses into three common phrases:

> *"I'm being considerate of others."*
> *"I'm committed to quality and accuracy."*
> *"I want to be seen as fair."*

Let's consider each of these expressions.

"I'm being considerate of others" is a catch-all statement of avoidance. Leaders put off decisions because morale is low, yet it usually gets lower when those in charge evade honest conversations; this only leads to greater dysfunction. Ignoring problems to avoid disappointing people also means putting off creative solutions and leaving those very people "demoralized and confused by their leader's deceit." Decision that should have been made weeks, months, or years ago have been intentionally avoided.

"I'm committed to quality and accuracy." Some leaders have difficulty making decisions that have a long-term impact because not knowing outcomes generates high levels of anxiety. They fear looking stupid, Carucci observes, so they ask for more data or seek prolonged consultations. They often ask too many people. "Taking action in the face of incomplete data," Carucci writes, "is an executive's job. You sometimes won't know if the decision was 'right' until long after it's made." When leaders avoid hard decisions because of these factors, they communicate that looking right is more important than doing what's right.

"I want to be seen as fair." It's not hard to understand why leaders want to be seen as caring and just. To avoid playing favorites, however, they risk creating environments in which everyone is praised equally or no one is. This, Carucci argues, is also unfair and disrespectful. High performers need acknowledgment if you want great organizations. People

who underperform also need to know it, even if some difficult decisions and conversations follow.

When leaders repeatedly make excuses for inaction, they are, in effect, telling others that self-interest and self-protection are more important than the organization, the family, or others in their orbit.

When Lot and his family were forcibly brought outside Sodom, the angels were not subtle in their demand: "'Flee for your life! Do not look behind you, nor stop anywhere in the plain; flee to the hills, lest you be swept away.' But Lot said to them, 'Oh no, my lord! You have been so gracious to your servant and have already shown me so much kindness in order to save my life; but I cannot flee to the hills, lest the disaster overtake me, and I die'" (Gen. 19:17–19).

Once again, Lot made excuses. Even when given another chance, he could not commit, and he thus brought doom to his family. On some level, Lot never truly left Sodom. In *Morality*, Rabbi Jonathan Sacks writes, "Moral hazard occurs when one party is involved in risk-taking, but knows that, should the decision turn out to be a bad one, someone else will pay the price. When this happens, there is a distortion in the decision-making process."[11] Lot's distortion had immense moral implications for his family and eventually for our history.

Abraham picked up his life, changed it for the good, and changed the known world as a result. Lot, however, ended his life in ignominy. Ambivalence is rarely neutral. Indecision is also a decision. It's a decision to abdicate responsibility. Uncertainty makes us feel lost. Yet every day, we wake up to a new dawn and the new decisions dawn brings. With each rising sun, we have another chance to rise, to shine, and to make better choices.

Personal Leadership Reflection

When has indecision been a decision for you?

פרשת חיי שרה • *Parashat Ḥayei Sara*

"I Will"

I once tasked a group of leaders to come up with a six-word mission statement in the spirit of Ernest Hemingway's famous six-word short story. A person in the back of the room shared, in six words, a life lesson he carried with him from his father: "Always do the right thing. Period." These six simple words continue to give him moral clarity. Rebecca has her own two words of clarity: "I will."

Rebecca had a moment when a complex decision suddenly became abundantly clear. Eliezer, Abraham's servant, was tasked with finding Isaac a wife. He traveled to relatives of the family and devised a test of kindness. This, above all other qualities, was essential for a member of Abraham and Sarah's household. Rebecca's kindness, we are told, took the form of watering Eliezer's many camels. Camels consume great amounts of water; the offer to provide them with water was a sure sign that Eliezer had identified Isaac's future soulmate. Later, Rebecca rode one of those camels to meet Isaac. She was kind to the camels, and one of those camels, it seems, reciprocated. Rebecca was so taken with Isaac upon first sight that she actually fell off her camel!

But enough about camels. Focusing on Eliezer's camels minimizes other important and overlooked details in this romantic story. Rebecca's kindness was evident before this famous gesture. When Eliezer encountered her at the well, he asked for a little water for himself. *Then* she gave him water. *Then* she watered his camels. *Then* Eliezer checked if Rebecca was a relative of Abraham's. *Then* he asked if there was room in her father's house for guests. With each request, Eliezer asked more of Rebecca. This, too, may have been part of Eliezer's test.

Rebecca's reply was full of self-assurance: "'I am (*anokhi*) the daughter of Bethuel the son of Milcah, whom she bore to Nahor.' And she went on, 'There is plenty of straw and feed at home, and also room to spend the night'" (Gen. 24:24–25). Rebecca invited Eliezer to join her family of her own accord. She did not wait for her father's permission. It is this that Eliezer noticed immediately. He suddenly bowed and thanked God for making his job so easy: "Blessed be the Lord, the God of my master Abraham, who has not withheld His steadfast faithfulness from my master. For I have been guided on my errand by the Lord to the house of my master's kinsmen" (24:28).

Later, after negotiating with the family, Eliezer wanted to take Rebecca back to his people. The group sought out Rebecca's opinion, and with that same confidence and clarity she displayed earlier, Rebecca responded. "'Will you go with this man?' and she said, 'I will'" (24:58).

Rashi explains Rebecca's assertion: She would go of her own accord, even if her family did not consent. Rebecca knew her own mind. Rashi's grandson, Rabbi Samuel ben Meir, adds that it was common courtesy to ask the bride if she wanted to spend her engagement period with her family or go to her new family. In saying, "I will," Rebecca was confirming her desire to make her future happen rather than waiting for it. Rebecca looked forward. Rabbi Jonathan Sacks advises us to always do the right thing. Period. "Don't wait for the world to get better. Take the initiative yourself. The world is waiting for you.[12] When you have lucidity on the course of action before you, don't wait another minute. And Rebecca didn't.

In these two scenes, Rebecca took charge of her destiny. It is only in Genesis 25, when her pregnancy proved painful and mysterious, that she questioned her existence. When twins struggled in her womb, she said, "If so, why do I (*anokhi*) exist? (Gen. 25:22). So she marched up to God with her characteristic curiosity and directness, and God answered her. There is an authenticity to Rebecca because of her I-awareness that is both profound and disarming.

Rebecca's strong sense of self was suddenly altered by her pregnancy. The first biblical character who acknowledged a personal identity had to negotiate, with twins in her belly, the transformation within from one to three. Children shifted her from an "I" to a "we"; this is a joyful transition but one that can also be untethering. Dr. Avivah Gottlieb Zornberg, in her book *The Murmuring Deep: Reflections on the Biblical Unconscious*, contends that Rebecca "was the first biblical character to speak the word *anokhi* as a term of identity.... With total assurance she had initiated the construction of the human subject as *anokhi*.... What has eroded her confident subjectivity?"[13]

In their article "Managing Yourself: Stop Holding Yourself Back," Anne Morriss, Robin J. Ely, and Frances X. Frei speak to the personal identity of leaders. Those who construct a false identity for the public may find themselves tottering: A "common impediment to leadership is being overly distracted by your image – that ideal self you've created in your mind. Sticking to the script that goes along with that image takes a lot of energy, leaving little left over for the real work of leadership."[14]

Maintaining an inauthentic identity has genuine psychic costs: "Once you've crafted your persona and determined not to veer from it, your effectiveness often suffers. The need to be seen as intelligent can inhibit learning and risk taking, for instance. The need to be seen as likable can keep you from asking tough questions or challenging existing norms. The need to be seen as decisive can cause you to shut down critical feedback loops." These authors argue that the difference between image and impact, between looking powerful and empowering others, forces a terrible choice "between impersonating a leader and being one."

Rebecca offers us a model of authenticity. She impersonated no one. She was determined to help, determined to chart her future, and determined to understand why she suffered. All of this came out of her I-awareness. God honored this in her by responding to her directness. God made her the mother of not one nation but two. Reading about Rebecca's fierce courage prompts us to ask our own identity questions.

Personal Leadership Reflection

In leadership and in life, when has betraying who you are led to loss and shame? When has honoring and articulating who you are helped you have greater impact?

פרשת תולדות • *Parashat Toledot*

The Lies of Leadership

In the painting "Rebecca Presents Jacob to Isaac" (1768), the artist Nicolas-Guy Brenet shows Isaac sitting up straight in his bed with one arm held high and his legs tangled in sheets. Isaac's other arm is wrapped around Jacob's shoulder, whose red tunic matches the ruddiness of his face. Rebecca stands in the background, holding up a tent curtain so she can quietly watch the scene from a distance. Isaac is old and blind but, the artist suggests, his body knows the truth and protests. Isaac's silent movement registers deception. The son with the pelt collar designed to imitate the manliness of his older twin was not Esau.

Toledot paints dishonesty with words rather than images. "'Father,' and he [Isaac] said, 'Yes, which of my sons are you?' Jacob said to his father, 'I am Esau, your first-born; I have done as you told me. Pray sit up and eat of my game, that you may give me your innermost blessing'" (Gen. 27:18–19). Jacob requested an innermost blessing while wearing an outer layer of betrayal. Jacob said, "I am Esau." The verse, by using names simply and lucidly, calls out the lie that would haunt Jacob for the rest of his life.

Later, Laban, his father-in-law, tricked Jacob by switching brides; Jacob married Leah instead of the love of his life, Rachel. Jacob's sons tricked him by giving him Joseph's striped coat dipped in goat's blood; Jacob naturally concluded that his favorite son had been killed by a wild animal. While Joseph did not trick his father outright, Joseph's long disappearance in Egypt without contact overwhelmed Jacob with grief. We are told many times that Jacob's hair greyed and he was ready for death. Joseph rose to meteoric heights of leadership in Egypt while Jacob mourned him and languished in Canaan. All of this was the consequence of one lie.

In *Morality,* Rabbi Jonathan Sacks writes that "without moral commitment, the still small voice of truth is inaudible beneath the cacophony of lies, half-truths, obfuscations, and evasions. Without truth, no trust; without trust, no society. Truth and trust create a world we can share."[15] Jacob was terribly aware of this break in trust and told his mother so directly: "But my brother Esau is a hairy man, and I am smooth-skinned. If my father touches me, I shall appear to him as a trickster and bring upon myself a curse, not a blessing" (Gen. 27:11–12). Jacob and Esau were different in every way. Jacob couldn't imagine getting away with this lie, nor did he want to. He didn't want to be labeled a trickster forevermore.

Although Jacob was a necessary actor in the story, it was Rebecca who hatched this deception and carried it out in detail. She demanded that Jacob hunt for meat to make Isaac his favorite dish from his favorite son. "Rebecca then took the best clothes of her older son Esau, which were there in the house, and had her younger son Jacob put them on; and she covered his hands and the hairless part of his neck with the skins of the kids. Then she put in the hands of her son Jacob the dish and the bread that she had prepared" (27:15–17). Rebecca took the meat. She brought the coat. She put gloves on Jacob's hands and placed the food in his arms. Jacob was an adult who could have dressed himself, but in his stiff, unyielding gestures, it is as if Jacob communicated that he wanted no part in his mother's plan. Why else would the Torah have gone into this level of detail to inform us what was happening backstage?

Behavioral economist Dan Ariely believes that the will to lie touches us all: "...our sense of our own morality is connected to the amount of cheating we feel comfortable with. Essentially, we cheat up to the level that allows us to retain our self-image as reasonably honest individuals."[16]

Jacob did not willingly participate in his mother's plan, because his own self-image was not as a deceiver. Rebecca, however, was comfortable with this lie because God told her while she was pregnant that her younger twin would be the rightful heir: "Two nations are in your womb. Two separate peoples shall issue from your body; one people shall be mightier than the other, *and the older shall serve the younger*" (Gen. 25:23).

A few verses later, we read that "Isaac favored Esau because he had a taste for game, but Rebecca favored Jacob" (25:28). Commentators fill in the gaps, trying to explain these loves. In *Haamek Davar,* Rabbi Naftali Zvi Yehuda Berlin suggests that Rebecca's love was based on the higher vision she had for Jacob that God placed in her mind during her pregnancy.

We lie most often for personal benefit, what Ariely calls "rational economic motivation." Sometimes we lie "to view ourselves as wonderful human beings" (this is the psychological motivation). This explains many of the lies that leaders tell. They lie or fudge the truth to protect themselves or others, to maintain morale when it's low, or to facilitate a better bottom-line. Lies make life easier in the short term but dissipate trust in the long term. Jacob understood this all too well.

Rebecca's motivation, of course, was never for personal gain. After all, Esau was her son also. No matter how different children are, mothers want every child to thrive. Rebecca had a different agenda; she needed to make good on God's prediction. Yet every time I read this story, I wonder why Rebecca never reported to Isaac what God said about the fate of their twins. Perhaps the two could have found a way as parents to grow Jacob into his leadership role without having to snatch a birthright from Esau. It could have spared heartache for all four of them.

Trust could not be more critical now in leadership or more absent in our everyday discourse. "A world of truth is a world of trust," writes Rabbi Sacks in *Morality*. "In it, there is something larger than individuals seeking their own interest. Truth becomes the intellectual equivalent of a public space that we can all inhabit, whatever our desires and predilections."[17] It's our responsibility to instill and restore trust so that it fills a public space we can all inhabit.

Our *sedra* reminds us that honesty is not only a characteristic. It's also a choice.

Personal Leadership Reflection

Think of a lie you could have told that would have made your life easier, but you didn't tell it. Think of a lie that had long-term consequences. Consider a truth that hurt but was necessary. Each of us can erode trust through lies or build trust through truth.

פרשת ויצא • *Parashat Vayetzeh*

Leadership Dreaming

Avimelekh, king of Gerar, had the very first dream recorded in the Torah (Gen. 20:3). The second occurs in our Torah reading of *Vayetzeh*. Jacob had a powerfully symbolic dream: "A ladder was set on the ground and its top reached to the sky, and messengers of God were going up and down on it" (28:12). The dream established a connection between heaven and earth at a time of immense vulnerability for Jacob. He tricked his father for Esau's blessing and had to leave his family home under the threat of death. It was a time for nightmares, not majestic dreams. We can only truly understand this dream if we travel with Jacob *after* the dream.

As the narrative progressed and the dream unfolded, it is God's voice that Jacob heard beckoning to him: "Your descendants shall be as the dust of the earth; you shall spread out to the west and to the east, to the north and to the south. All the families of the earth shall bless themselves by you and your descendants. Remember, I am with you: I will protect you wherever you go and will bring you back to this land. I will not leave you until I have done what I have promised you" (28:14–15). The gift of protection was exactly what Jacob needed. In his despair and his loneliness, he needed an intimate connection with God and assurance of his very survival. When he woke from his sleep, Jacob realized that something remarkable had happened, even if he did not understand all its contours: "Surely God is present in this place, and I did not know!" (28:16).

Israeli novelist Meir Shalev writes in *Beginnings,* his book of biblical firsts, that Jacob was bestowed with a guarantee of protection that even Abraham had not received. Jacob responded with wonder but also with conditions: "Jacob then made a vow, saying, 'If God remains with me, protecting me on this journey that I am making, and giving me bread to eat and clothing to wear, and I return safe to my father's house – God shall be my God'"(28:20–21).[18] Jacob's reaction is puzzling and a seeming insult to God's magnanimity. God will only be Jacob's God if God provides food, clothing, and safe passage for him? We have a word for this: chutzpah!

The classic commentators all feel a need to explain Jacob's bold vow. Rashi, citing a midrash, relates Jacob's speech to a verse in Psalms: "For I will not forsake you" (Ps. 37:25). One who has to beg for bread is called forsaken. Jacob was asking for external signs of love, nourishment, and care. Nahmanides focuses on the word "if" that begins Jacob's vow. It does not indicate doubt, he writes, but future fulfillment: "When the condition is satisfied, then the deed will be fulfilled." The sixteenth-century Italian exegete Rabbi Ovadia Sforno offers a brilliant reading. Jacob asked God to provide these basic needs to relieve Jacob from prosaic pressures. Then, and only then, could he focus attention on the greater purpose God laid out for him.

With these conditions, Jacob makes, in Shalev's words, emendations to his own dream.[19] It was not enough to be protected. Jacob wanted his material needs met. It was not enough to return. Jacob must return *beshalom,* in peace. Jacob was willing to take on a historic mission and the continuity of his family's purpose but only if, Shalev observes, "his personal needs in the here and now" were accommodated, because he had "pressing problems of his own."[20]

Now back to the dream. Angels going up and down a ladder vertically represent the relationship Jacob tried to establish with God: a continuous ascent and connection between heaven and earth. Jacob's vow emerged from his understanding of a covenantal commitment. True partnership is the result of both sides articulating needs and having them met. God demanded much of Abraham and Isaac personally, but neither of them made great demands of God. Jacob, with his requests, created a more intimate partnership of mutual obligation.

In his book *The Home We Build Together,* Rabbi Jonathan Sacks describes the intimacy of a covenant: "Those bound by a covenant voluntarily undertake to share a fate. They choose to link their destinies together. They accept responsibilities to and for one another."[21] Perhaps this is why we as a nation are referred to as Israel, the children of Jacob. After Jacob wrestled with an angel, the angel renamed him Israel – the one who struggled with God. One man carried two names. The first, Jacob, means a heel, representing the connection he had to his twin brother coming out of the womb. The second, Israel, represents the connection Jacob had with God. Abraham was a knight of faith. Isaac was almost sacrificed for that faith. It was Jacob who wanted that faith to be bound up in the mutuality of a relationship.

Jacob's dream in our *sedra* was his most famous one but not his only one. Later, in Genesis 31, Jacob was tending his flocks when an angel – perhaps one of the angels on the ladder – appeared to him and called out: "Jacob!" Jacob responded with "*Hineni,*" "I am here." The angel had been watching Jacob these long years and saw the way Jacob suffered in his father-in-law's home. Jacob's dream of heaven and earth morphed, over time, into a dream about sheep. Incrementally, Jacob's life became one of a physical rather than spiritual existence. Before it changed Jacob, the angel set him free: "I have noted all that Laban has been doing to you. I am the God of Bethel, where you anointed a pillar and where you made a vow to Me. Now, arise and leave this land and return to your native land" (Gen. 31:13).

It was time to fulfill the words of Jacob's first dream that spoke of God's sheltering love: "I will protect you wherever you go and will bring you back to this land." Jacob was to go back to his land.

Jacob now had food and clothing. But he needed a reminder to make good on the vow made long ago as a result of a dream. It was finally time to go home. In *Leaders: Dreaming Matters,* Susanne Biro, of the Forbes Coaches Council, writes that "inside each of us is a negative internal voice that narrates, judges, and critiques what we do."[22] But there is also a dreaming voice that fills us with longing, inspiration, and ambition. "Mastering the ability to dream," she argues, "is the essence of truly great leadership." It is our dreams that stimulate our energies and our ability to focus on larger, higher ambitions. Sharing those big dreams catalyzes the excitement of others.

Leaders cannot afford to let go of dreams, because dreams represent the part of us we often admire most or are most afraid of – the demons that come out at night. Sigmund Freud, in his research on the subject, cites thinkers who contend that a dream "is the liberation of the spirit from the pressure of external nature, a detachment of the soul from the fetters of matter."[23] Jacob asked God to relieve him of the fetters of matter. Then Laban chained Jacob to material servitude. An angel finally liberated him. And all because of a spiritual dream not forgotten.

Personal Leadership Reflection

What dream are you holding onto that awaits realization?

פרשת וישלח • *Parashat Vayishlaḥ*

The Gift

In one of the most tender scenes in all of Genesis, Jacob and Esau reunite. Much has happened in the intervening years since they lived under the same roof as brothers. Jacob left his parental home alone and as a fugitive from his raging brother. He returned with a large retinue of wives, children, and sheep. Esau left for Mount Seir to become a nation of his own. When the two meet again, the Torah invites us into this exchange of high emotion: "Esau ran to greet him. He embraced him and, falling on his neck, he kissed him; and they wept" (Gen. 33:4).

After they separated and Esau surveyed Jacob's household and the many gifts Jacob brought for him, Esau sought clarification: "'What do you mean by all this company which I have met?' He answered, 'To gain my lord's favor'" (33:8). Jacob was so nervous about this meeting that he tried to mollify Esau with presents. Jacob may have tried to compensate Esau with these gifts for stealing Esau's birthright. Perhaps Jacob tried to impress Esau that he was a changed man, a man of wealth and stability.

But Esau was interested in his brother, not his brother's offerings: "Esau said, 'I have enough (*yesh li rav*), my brother; let what you have remain yours" (33:9). *Yesh li rav* can also be translated as, "I have a great deal," as if Esau was stating that he, too, had accumulated wealth since the two last met. He no longer needed the largesse of an inheritance. Jacob was insistent: "But Jacob said, 'No, I pray you; if you would do me this favor, accept from me this gift; for to see your face is like seeing the face of God, and you have received me favorably. Please accept my present which has been brought to you, for God has favored me and I have plenty.' And when he urged him, he accepted" (33:10–11). The face of a potential murderer had softened, for Jacob, into an image of God. Esau understood that rejecting Jacob's gifts was a way of rejecting him. Accepting these gifts was an acknowledgment that time had changed these brothers.

The expression "I have enough" was understood by biblical commentators in a variety of ways. Rashi, basing himself on a midrash, states that "with these words, he [Esau] admitted his [Jacob's] right to the blessings." In other words, Esau had made peace with the past and accepted Jacob's place as Isaac's spiritual heir. Rabbi Ovadia Sforno interprets Esau's answer as being sharper: "I most certainly do not need this gift," as if Esau were telling Jacob that he needed no handouts from a rich younger brother. *Haamek Davar* states that with these three words, Esau was communicating two messages. Esau had plenty and did not need more, and Jacob was his brother, not his master, and therefore did not need to give him a tribute. Radak, Rabbi David Kimchi, may offer the most emotionally intuitive interpretation of this statement: "After all these years, Esau finally acknowledged that he had not suffered as a result of Jacob being blessed, so he was able to say, 'Keep what is yours!'"

This brief and poignant exchange makes us wonder about the purpose of gift giving more generally. In 1925, Marcel Mauss, a philosopher and sociologist, wrote an important and oft-cited article, "Essay on the Gift."[24] He combed ancient cultures and ethnographic data from America's Pacific Northwest and Polynesia to understand the role that gift giving plays in societal structures. Giving a gift is perceived as an outward expression of generosity that emerges from the giver's own volition, will, and desire. But Mauss concluded from his research that gift giving represents a "strict accounting system" that reflects rights and duties. Gift economies are those in which there is an obligation to give, an obligation to accept, and an obligation to reciprocate. Just think of gift giving within peer groups and the bottle of wine that gets transferred from house to house as a Shabbat gift.

The intricate system of reciprocity and expectation in gift giving changes it from a magnanimous gesture to an expectation freighted with the anxiety of rejection. In a gift exchange, there is always the worry that the gift of one party will not match, in cost or extravagance, the gift of the other. Consider, for example, diplomatic gifts and what they symbolize. Or think of the difficulty of purchasing a gift for a superior. I dropped a question into a search engine: "What should you buy your boss as a gift?" The screen was littered with *tchatchkes,* like an "Essence of Leadership" pen holder and "Great Boss" T-shirts. Coasters, key chains, and posters were all flush with inspirational quotes. But it's hard to imagine any boss happily wearing one of these shirts or hanging up such posters. The gifts then go into storage to be regifted to someone else who also doesn't want them.

Cultural critic and essayist Lewis Hyde wrote a book about gift giving that I once purchased at the J. Paul Getty Museum gift shop and could not put down. There he writes that common to each notion of a gift is "that a gift is a thing we do not get by our own efforts. We cannot buy it; we cannot acquire it through an act of will. It is bestowed upon us."[25] Thinking of Hyde's words, we turn back to the Esau and Jacob encounter and realize that when Esau said to Jacob, "I have enough," he was not rejecting Jacob's gifts but bestowing upon Jacob the most potent gift of all and one that could not be purchased: his forgiveness.

Jacob came armed for this tense moment with an impressive cache of presents. Esau had none. There was no gift exchange or false attempt at superficial reciprocity. Esau gave Jacob the raw gift of his embrace and his tears. He gifted Jacob with a long-absent sense of fraternal feeling. With his three words, "I have enough," Esau told Jacob that he no longer needed a birthright. All of the gifts before him were meaningless. All he needed and wanted was a brother. When Jacob declared that seeing Esau was like seeing God's face, Jacob, too, acknowledged the immensity of the moment. He, too, needed a brother. Jacob could never see God's face, but, if he could, it would be the face of acceptance and relief.

Rabbi Jonathan Sacks questions why the Torah states that Isaac loved Esau even with all of his flaws, and he shares another gift from the *parasha*: "Sometimes love can do what rebuke cannot. It may be that the Torah is telling us that Isaac was anything but blind as to his elder son's true nature. But if you have two children, one well behaved, the other liable to turn out badly, to whom should you devote greater attention? With whom should you spend more time?"[26] Forgiveness and unconditional love may be the greatest gift a parent can give a child and a child can give a parent.

Personal Leadership Reflection

Leaders can bestow many gifts on others, but no gift is greater than emotional validation. When have you received this gift? Who in your life needs this gift? How will you pass it on?

פרשת וישב • *Parashat Vayeshev*

Wait For It

Joseph, Jacob's favorite son, was thrown into prison for a crime he never committed. We know as readers that he will find a way out of confinement and grow in his leadership as a result. Joseph got out of a pit, and he will also get out of a jail.

Yet, despite Joseph's suffering, or because of it, his struggle in prison sensitized him to the suffering of others. He noticed that two other courtiers in prison were deeply troubled: "He asked Pharaoh's courtiers, who were with him in custody in his master's house, saying, 'Why do you appear downcast today?' and they said to him, 'We had dreams, and there is no one to interpret them.' So Joseph said to them, 'Surely God can interpret! Tell me [your dreams]'" (Gen. 40:7–8). Having dreams and sharing them got Joseph in trouble. Interpreting dreams saved Joseph and got him promoted.

Joseph was a problem solver and, giving all the credit to God, told the baker and cupbearer imprisoned with him that he had a solution. At first, he did not say he could interpret their dreams; he simply asked them to share their night terrors, knowing that unburdening themselves of their dreams could itself be healing. After giving one courtier an unhappy interpretation and the other a joyous one, Joseph was hoping that some future reciprocal kindness would be thrown his way. He then unburdened himself: "Think of me when all is well with you again, and do me the kindness of mentioning me to Pharaoh, so as to free me from this place. For in truth, I was kidnapped from the land of the Hebrews; nor have I done anything here that they should have put me in the dungeon" (Gen. 40:14–15).

Not only did Joseph ask for a favor, he also explained that his current jail term was not the beginning of his woes. He did not identify himself as a Hebrew but told them he came from a distance. He mentioned nothing of the harm he experienced at the hand of his brothers. He was bewildered at his prison sentence. His prospects looked bleak. Jailed together and sharing, for the moment, the same grim fate, the courtier with the positive dream interpretation made a promise to seek Joseph's freedom should he ever gain his own.

The moment did arrive, but, as so often happens in life, with the climb out of difficulty, the newly liberated erase their past: "Yet the chief cupbearer did not think of Joseph; he forgot him" (40:23). Joseph wasn't even a thought. Rashi explains that "because Joseph had placed his trust in him that he would remember him, he was doomed to remain in prison for two years."

Hanging onto hope for two long years, Joseph could not see any other way out. Rabbi Abraham ibn Ezra defines "remember" in this verse as "mention," citing many biblical prooftexts to support this reading: "He did not verbally mention him to Pharaoh."

The cupbearer may have remembered Joseph in some vague and distant way, but he never repaid the favor by speaking to those in power. Rabbi Joseph Bekhor Shor adds that the cupbearer never really intended to speak up in the first place. This was not a malicious act; it was just plain forgetfulness. That which is unimportant to us can be easily forgotten. Ḥizkuni also mentions the passage of time. Since the cupbearer did not bring Joseph's plight to Pharaoh's attention as soon as he had been released, "he forgot him totally, erased him from his memory." This reading reminds us that when we don't act on our compassionate impulses immediately, we risk forgetting them.

Joseph thought the solution lay in human intervention. Instead, he found himself disappointed and on the brink of despair. Only God and time would come to Joseph's rescue.

A stunning midrash from Genesis Rabba 88:7 reviews our story from God's perspective. Allow me to paraphrase: "The cupbearer forgot, but I did not forget. Who waited with Abraham and Sarah when they were old until they had a son? Who waited with Jacob until he crossed the Jordan River and attained wealth? Who waited with Joseph to overcome all of his difficulties until he became a royal? Who waited when Moses was thrown into the Nile to become who he became? Who waited with Ruth the convert until she returned monarchy to the Israelites?" The midrash continues to name other figures in biblical history who required God's steady presence over long swaths of time to aid in the realization of their futures. Our midrash teaches us: Hold fast to your conviction and strategy until it's the right time.

Leadership books and articles often recommend action, not waiting. Don't wait for approval. Don't wait to get things done. Don't wait for exactly the right moment. Become who you want to become now. But now may not be the right time. Dan and Chip Heath write that, "because day-to-day change is gradual, even imperceptible, it's hard to know when to jump."[27] It is not always easy to know when to jump. Should we wait or should we leap? Sometimes waiting is costly. Rabbi Jonathan Sacks, observes that "when bad things happen, some avert their eyes. Some wait for others to act. Some blame others for failing to act. Some simply complain. But there are people who say, 'If something is wrong, let me be among the first to put it right.' They are the leaders."[28] The moment a leader sees wrongdoing, he or she tries to stop it. Joseph was such a leader.

The musical *Hamilton* contrasts the impetuousness and speed of Alexander Hamilton with the slow, intentional, and considered pace of Aaron Burr. In the second half of the musical, Burr sings the song "Wait for It" as a testament to his strategy and as a criticism that Hamilton lacked restraint:

> We rise (and we fall) We fall (and we break)
> (And we make our mistakes)

> And if there's a reason I'm still alive When so many have died
> Then I'm willin' to – Wait for it.

Joseph rose and fell, rose and fell. But he was not broken. He held fast to his childhood dreams. He used dream interpretation and problem solving as a strategy to rise again. He learned to wait.

Personal Leadership Reflection

What are you waiting for?

פרשת מקץ • *Parashat Miketz*

Attracted to Problems

Sometimes it's hard to understand what activities and traits distinguish a leader from a follower. This is especially true because the word "leader" is used today to describe someone who runs a country and also someone who volunteers to run a bake sale. This indiscriminate range can lead to cynicism. If everyone's a leader, then maybe no one is.

In the years I've been working in leadership development, I've noticed anecdotally an unmistakable character trait that runs deep in high-impact leaders and is, I believe, a defining feature of leadership. Leaders are attracted to problems. They view issues and conflicts that impede and repel others as interesting puzzles to be solved. They lean into dilemmas rather than lean back. Such attraction doesn't mean leaders can solve problems instantly, but they aren't intimidated by them. They don't experience despair or helplessness when they encounter a difficult problem or regard it as intractable.

Doris Kearns Goodwin describes Franklin Delano Roosevelt's polio and how this illness taught him to overcome adversity and meet it with strength and optimism: "When asked during his presidency how he dealt with continuing problems, he half-jokingly observed: 'If you spent two years in bed trying to wiggle your big toe, anything would seem easy!'"[29]

Eleanor Roosevelt said this of her husband: "I have never known a man who gave one a greater sense of security. I never heard him say there was a problem that he thought it was impossible for human beings to solve." This is the first quote to appear at the FDR Memorial in Washington, DC. In his four terms as president, FDR faced problems on the national and international stage that might have toppled those less self-assured. (FDR's relationship with the Jewish community was, of course, a more complex issue. His relationship to the Jewish community has been the subject of a recent book,[30] as has his knowledge of what was taking place in Europe during World War II.)[31]

Parashat Miketz offers us a glimpse of this problem-solving capacity in Joseph. Joseph was a dreamer, but his salvation and that of his family actually came through dream interpretation. No one else had the confidence, expertise, or temerity to help Pharaoh understand his inner confusion. "And Pharaoh said to Joseph, 'I have had a dream, but no one can interpret it. Now I have heard it said of you that for you to hear a dream (*tishma ḥalom*) is to tell its meaning'" (Gen. 41:15).

Word traveled quickly about Joseph's abilities. Simply hearing a dream revealed its significance to him. Rashi focuses on the verb "to hear" or "to listen," translating it as "to pay attention." The word implies more than simple hearing; it suggests listening for understanding. Rashi cites two other prooftexts to support his reading, Genesis 42:23 and Deuteronomy 28:49. Sforno suggests that Joseph did not guess or speculate but thought carefully about Pharaoh's words, the context in which they were said, and their larger import and significance. Joseph interpreted Pharaoh's dream on a national economic scale, thinking about the dream in political rather than personal terms.

Joseph's talent makes an appearance in another story about the ruler of a large empire and a Jewish courtier: Nebuchadnezzar and Daniel. Chapter 4 of the book of Daniel opens with Nebuchadnezzar in a similar state to Pharaoh, one of confusion and fear: "I had a dream that frightened me, and my thoughts in bed and the vision of my mind alarmed me. I gave an order to bring all the wise men of Babylon before me to let me know the meaning of the dream" (Dan. 4:2–3).

Nebuchadnezzar was desperate to have someone explain his own mind to him. When none of his own dream interpreters, magicians, or exorcists could help, he turned to Daniel, regarding him as a person of deep intelligence and intuition. He said to him, "Tell me the meaning of my dream vision that I have seen" and said of Daniel that "the spirit of the holy gods" rested in him and that "no mystery baffles him" (Dan. 4:6). Daniel was able to explain the dream successfully.

Deborah Ancona and Hal Gregersen studied leaders who were problem solvers to identify common threads in their behaviors and dispositions. "Most striking," they conclude, "is that none of these leaders has any expectation that they will attract 'followers' personally – by dint of their charisma, status in a hierarchy, or access to resources. Instead, their method is to get others excited about whatever problem they have identified as ripe for a novel solution."[32]

These leaders pursue "their own deep expertise" and bring others along for the ride, seeking out talent and the kind of team that can take on complex issues. They became more proficient leaders by engaging in increasingly complicated work. Joseph's skill at dream interpretation later spilled over into governance, where many of the same tools were required: careful observation, listening, analysis, strategic vision, and execution. These bundled talents could easily have led Joseph to flaunt his own abilities. But as Joseph matured and his influence grew, he did not take credit for his problem-solving skills: "Joseph answered Pharaoh, saying, 'Not I! God will see to Pharaoh's welfare'" (Gen. 41:16). Commenting on this verse, Rashi explains that Joseph was telling Pharaoh, "The wisdom to interpret dreams is not my own, but God will answer. He will put in my mouth an answer that will be for Pharaoh's welfare."

Joseph answered to a higher authority than Pharaoh and therefore felt confident in summoning the God of the Hebrews into his conversation. In *Not in God's Name,* Rabbi Jonathan Sacks writes, "Every text needs interpretation. Every interpretation needs wisdom. Every wisdom needs careful negotiation between the timeless and time."[33] Joseph brought wisdom into his interpretation, and, because of his intimacy with God, his insights became timeless. Joseph became more than a shrewd and capable vizier; he eventually became, in the court's eyes, a widely respected man of conviction, because he was more than a problem solver. He was a problem solver who gave God the credit.

Personal Leadership Reflection

What's the hardest problem you've ever solved? How did you solve it, and who got the credit?

פרשת ויגש • *Parashat Vayigash*

The Anxiety of Approach

We all have moments on our way to a difficult encounter or conversation when all we want to do is withdraw, turn around, or run away. It's the walk into the doctor's office to get the results of a biopsy, or the agonizing moments before a break-up. It's the march into the boss's office to resign or request a raise, or the quick inhale of breath before a tough conversation with a child, a spouse, or a friend.

Feelings are high. Outcomes are unpredictable, and we fear the worst.

The name of our Torah reading is taken from its very first word, *vayigash*, from the Hebrew root *nagash*, meaning "to bring close" or "to draw near." The setting is high drama. Judah approached Joseph with trepidation after Joseph accused his brothers of theft: "Then Judah went up to him (*vayigash*) and said, 'Please, my lord, let your servant appeal to my lord, and do not be impatient with your servant, you who are the equal of Pharaoh'" (Gen. 44:18). The simple translation of *vayigash* here fails to communicate the tension implied in the Hebrew. But a review of the root word as it appears throughout Genesis reveals that this verb is used very specifically to describe the beginning of potentially fraught encounters, what I call the anxiety of approach. *Nagash* is not merely "to come close," but to do so when the situation is highly charged or emotional.

Abraham boldly approached God in defense of any pious person in Sodom: "Abraham came forward (*vayigash*) and said, 'Will You sweep away the innocent along with the guilty?'" (18:23). The same verb is used when Jacob deceptively approached his father disguised as Esau: "So Jacob drew close (*vayigash*) to his father Isaac, who felt him and wondered. 'The voice is the voice of Jacob, yet the hands are the hands of Esau'" (27:22). The tremulousness conveyed by this word is apparent immediately before this verse (27:21) and again a few verses after it (27:25). The verb communicates obvious discomfort, the kind of uneasiness that can make one's own brother an enemy. Such uncomfortable feelings can lead to poor choices, as Rabbi Jonathan Sacks observes in Not in God's Name: "Religious people in the grip of strong emotions – fear, pain, anxiety, confusion, a sense of loss and humiliation – often dehumanise their opponents with devastating results."[34]

Further on in the Jacob and Esau narrative, when the two brothers met up years later, Jacob's family approached Esau hesitatingly, understanding the possible danger and vulnerability of their position. The verb appears twice in these verses: "Then the maids, with their children, came forward (*vatigashna*) and bowed low; next Leah, with her children, came forward (*vatigash*) and bowed low; and last, Joseph and Rachel came forward and bowed low" (33:6–7). When Joseph's brothers were brought into his house and accused of theft, they protested to a member of his retinue: "So they went up (*vayigshu*) to Joseph's house steward and spoke to him at the entrance of the house" (43:19).

My personal favorite example of this verb are the two times it appears immediately after Joseph reveals himself in Genesis 45, surely one of the most dramatic and traumatic of biblical moments: "Then Joseph said to his brothers, 'Come forward (*geshu na*) to me.' And when they came forward (*vayigashu*), he said, 'I am your brother Joseph, he whom you sold into Egypt'" (45:4). In our mind's eye, we imagine Joseph dressed regally and sitting upon a throne, towering over his poor brothers. He curls his index finger toward then as he says words that could only, in the brothers' hearing, signal a death threat. They inch forward as he says something they never, ever expected to hear. Joseph was alive. There would be a steep price to pay now. Yet Joseph embraces Benjamin instead and speaks with kindness to his shocked brothers. Joseph saw divine intervention in his strange and difficult path and opened an unexpected portal to reconciliation.

What we find in example after biblical example is that even though each confrontation was potentially treacherous and even explosive, the risky encounter took place and often yielded unanticipated positive results. That's because these individuals were extraordinary leaders who understood what was required of them in the moment. One behavior that distinguishes leaders from followers is the willingness to take an uncomfortable risk to achieve a new state of relationship or negotiation, a risk others would rather not take, even if it might result in a larger platform of influence, a better, more honest relationship, or a larger salary.

Susan Scott, in her important book, *Fierce Conversations*, writes, "Never be afraid of the conversations you are having. Be afraid of the conversations you are not having." She is concerned that we entertain high levels of denial about problems that prevent us from discussing them with authenticity and integrity. She challenges us to look in the mirror and ask, "When was the last time I said what I really thought and felt? What are the leaders in my organization pretending not to know? What are members of my family pretending not to know? What am I pretending not to know?"[35]

She uses a creative and extreme example to illustrate the point within organizational life. A friend of hers who is a high-level executive told Scott that a brave employee came into his office with a large bucket of sand and poured it on the rug.[36] The executive couldn't believe it and asked what prompted this outrageous behavior. The employee replied, "I just figured I'd make it easier for you to bury your head in the sand on the topic I keep bringing up and you keep avoiding."[37] Rather than fire him, the executive admired his courage and promoted him.

Scott is not suggesting that you try the bucket trick with your boss, but she is suggesting that fierce conversations are unavoidable and usually necessary. To that end, she offers some helpful tips and a seven-step formula for navigating them with less emotion and more control to achieve better outcomes. Most importantly, she cajoles her readers to become truth tellers: "Everyone wants one person in the world to whom they can tell the truth and from whom they will hear the truth. Become that person." This isn't because it's easy. It's because, as she writes, "There is something within us that responds deeply to people who level with us."[38]

Personal Leadership Reflection

Can you describe your own "vayigash" moment? Is there a difficult conversation you need to have that you're avoiding? Whom do you trust to tell you the truth?

פרשת ויחי • *Parashat Vayeḥi*

Leading Through Darkness

After decades of difficulty on the way to leadership greatness, Jacob breathes his last in *Parashat Vayeḥi*: "When Jacob finished his instructions to his sons, he drew his feet into the bed and, breathing his last, he was gathered to his kin" (Gen. 49:33). Joseph, perhaps aware of all the lost years between them, was understandably bereft: "Joseph flung himself upon his father's face and wept over him and kissed him" (50:1). But the real summation of Jacob's last years emerges in a conversation he has not with Joseph, but with Pharaoh in last week's Torah reading. We've all participated in or witnessed unusual, almost inexplicable conversations that leave us baffled. This is one of the strangest conversations in all of Tanakh. I've written about this conversation at length and am still bewildered by it every year.

Jacob speaks to Pharaoh and tells this powerful leader and stranger of his woes: "Joseph then brought his father Jacob and presented him to Pharaoh, and Jacob greeted Pharaoh. Pharaoh asked Jacob, 'How many are the years of your life?' And Jacob answered Pharaoh, 'The years of my sojourn [on earth] are one hundred and thirty. Few and hard have been the years of my life, nor do they come up to the life spans of my ancestors during their sojourns.' Then Jacob bade Pharaoh farewell and left Pharaoh's presence" (47:7–10).

Pharaoh asks an odd question about Jacob's age. Jacob responds by telling Pharaoh something he never revealed to his sons. His life has been punishingly hard and is soon to be over. How Jacob knows this is never explained. After this upsetting outpouring of misery, Pharaoh says nothing. He offers not a word of solace or consolation. Jacob then exits the scene. The story progresses with no further mention of the encounter.

Before we look at the content of this dialogue, it is important to note the context for this conversation that appears a few verses later: "Joseph sustained his father, and his brothers, and all his father's household with bread, down to the little ones. Now there was no bread in all the world, for the famine was very severe; both the land of Egypt and the land of Canaan languished because of the famine" (47:12–13). Jacob, the inheritor of the legacy of Abraham and Isaac, had to be supported by his son, in a land not his own, at the point of starvation.

Any leader would be humiliated and ashamed in this desperate situation. How could it be that Jacob began his leadership with a magnificent dream of a ladder covered with angels and many divine promises, and now he was bereft, untethered from his homeland, and virtually penniless?

Nahmanides, the thirteenth-century Spanish commentator known by the acronym Ramban, explains that it was Pharaoh who requested the meeting, not Joseph. Pharaoh was so impressed by Joseph's many talents that he, understandably, wanted to meet Joseph's father. Nahum Sarna, in his JPS commentary on Genesis, observes that it would be undignified for Jacob to appear with his sons as humble petitioners, so Joseph set up a separate meeting to preserve his father's dignity.

Pharoah then asked Jacob a puzzling question, one that sounds out of place, even rude: Why have you lived so long? Yet some understand this as a question that emerges out of respect. Many Pharaohs on the throne were young. This Pharaoh may have been shocked by Jacob's longevity and regarded it as a blessing. Pharaoh was asking Jacob to tell him the secret to a long life. But if this was Pharaoh's intent, why did Jacob answer that his life was actually short and soon to end? Jacob was 130 at this time, but his grandfather Abraham died at 175. His father Isaac died at 180.

Because of Jacob's many disappointments – the theft of his brother's blessing, the switching of wives on the marriage altar, Laban's exploitation, the disappearance of Joseph, the rape of Dinah, the famine in Canaan – he felt that death was fast approaching, even if he was unable to predict it. The French medieval exegete Rabbi Hezekiah ben Manoah takes this view when he explains Pharaoh's perception of Jacob: "You look old and at the end of your days." Life has worn Jacob down. On the expression Jacob uses in response – that the years of his life did not equal those of his ancestors during their sojourns – Rashi explains Jacob's confession: "All my life, I have lived in the country of others." He did not want to spend his old age in someone else's land.

All leaders have dark days, even dark years. Two great leaders in more recent world history – Abraham Lincoln and Winston Churchill – suffered terrible depression. Lincoln called it melancholy. But rather than seeing these difficult periods as obstructions, they may have held the key to their respective greatness. They were able to harness the darkness they experienced to become more empathic to the suffering of others and more willing to take risks to solve problems than others. Writer J. W. Shenk believes that, "Whatever greatness Lincoln achieved cannot be explained as a triumph over personal suffering. Rather, it must be accounted as an outgrowth of the same system that produced that suffering.... Lincoln didn't do great work because he solved the problem of his melancholy; the problem of his melancholy was all the more fuel for the fire of his great work."[39]

Churchill called his dark days the "black dog." A black dog is an interesting image – a hovering, gloomy shadow that stays close but can walk away. In a letter to his wife Clementine in 1911, Churchill wrote that he heard about a German doctor who treated depression: "I think this man might be useful to me – if my black dog returns. He seems quite away from me now – it is such a relief. All the colours come back into the picture."

Jacob struggled in this melancholic moment in last week's Torah reading, but there is a small, redeeming detail that is often ignored in this conversation. It is bookended by Jacob blessing Pharaoh on his way in and on his way out. Sforno regards the blessing as a small act of defiance. Jacob "did not bow to him [Pharaoh], neither when he arrived nor when he departed." Rashi deems the blessing as a "greeting of peace, as is usual in the case of all who are granted an interview with kings at long intervals." We find a similar usage in II Samuel 16:16.

Nahmanides disagrees with Rashi. This was not a polite, inconsequential gesture, the ancient equivalent of a curtsy or bow before royalty. Ramban believes that Jacob was truly blessing Pharaoh. Jacob may not have had bread. He may have been far from home, and his last years were characterized by difficulty, but Jacob always carried with him the capacity to bless. Even when he struggled with an angel, Jacob was injured but asked for a blessing. More than any other biblical leader, Jacob understood the secret of Jewish continuity and leadership: the ability to find the blessing in the struggle.

In his essay "Staying Young" on *Parashat Vezot Haberakha,* Rabbi Jonathan Sacks offers us advice that could have been lifted straight from Jacob's story: "Never compromise your ideals. Never give in to defeat or despair. Never stop journeying merely because the way is long and hard. It always is."[40] It is easy to give in to dejection and misery and to give up. It is always harder to plow on and to seek the light. It is even harder to make the light by finding the blessing in the struggle.

Our longevity as a people is nothing short of a miracle. It can only be explained by the capacity to be a blessing and to bless others even and especially when oppressed and downtrodden. This is leadership. This is Jacob. This is the people Israel named after Jacob.

Personal Leadership Reflection

What difficulty are you facing right now that needs a healthy dose of blessing?

Leadership in the Book of Exodus

פרשת שמות • *Parashat Shemot*

Making It Good

As we open up the book of Exodus, we find ourselves in a time of transition. Joseph's death is recorded at the end of Genesis. A new Pharaoh is put in power. Leadership transitions are always concerning. Joseph's meteoric success and contributions are suddenly eclipsed by fear that the Israelites will become a fifth column. The new Pharaoh took desperate and despotic measures to reduce, quite literally, what he saw as a security threat: "Then Pharaoh charged all his people, saying, 'Every boy that is born you shall throw into the Nile, but let every girl live'" (Ex. 1:22). Forced labor was not enough. Murder was the next step in eradicating our people.

In this oppressive climate, we are introduced to two unnamed individuals as chapter 2 opens: "A certain member of the house of Levi went and took a woman of Levi. The woman conceived and bore a son; and when she saw how beautiful he was, she hid him for three months" (2:1–2). The child is also not given a name. All we know is that the couple both have a noble tribal affiliation that will make an imprint on their baby. The Levites will soon emerge as spiritual leaders of their people.

When this Jewish mother saw her Jewish son right after Pharaoh promulgated his decree, her first two words should have been, "*Oy vey.*" Instead they are, "*Ki tov*" – translated here in English as "she saw how beautiful he was." Literally, the expression means he is good, or it is good. But nothing could have been further from the truth. Having a male child at this time was a death sentence.

Rashi's grandson, Rashbam (Rabbi Samuel ben Meir), simply directs readers, without any explanation, to the first chapter of Genesis, where the expression "*Ki tov,*" "It is good," appears multiple times. The first is when God created light from darkness: "God saw that the light was good, and God separated the light from the darkness" (1:4). Creating light from darkness is good. "*Ki tov*" is used another five times in this chapter, culminating in a superlative state of goodness, "*Tov meod,*" "It was very good": "And God saw all that had been made, and found it very good. And there was evening and there was morning, the sixth day" (1:31). Although not everything God creates is labeled good, altogether "*tov*" appears seven times in the chapter, paralleling the days of creation and the idea of seven throughout the Bible as a state or cycle of completion.

It's easy to say that if God creates, the result is good, until we arrive at chapter 2, when God is not satisfied with divine creation: "God said, 'It is not good for the man to be alone; I will make a fitting counterpart for him'" (2:18). The *New York Times* critic A. O. Scott, in his book *Better Living Through Criticism,* claims that God's assessment here makes God the first critic! Scott cites the biologist E. O. Wilson, who contends that "the creative arts became possible as an evolutionary advance when humans developed the capacity for abstract thought." Scott then compares the work of critics today to the "original critic" of Genesis, "who cast his eyes over what he had made and decided it was good."[1] Rashbam, in simply directing us from the beginning chapters of Exodus back to the beginning of Genesis, may be asking the reader to make comparisons between the world God created out of chaos and the nation that the Israelites had to build out of chaos. The ability to look at a situation that on the surface looks terrible and be able, despite the anguish, to recast it as something with the potential for goodness is a hallmark of leadership.

The recognition of goodness and the ability to label it as such is one of the key ways we act in imitation of God. "To see that someone is good and to say so is a creative act, one of the great creative acts," writes Rabbi Jonathan Sacks in "The Three Stages of Creation." He continues, "Within almost all of us is something positive and unique, but which is all too easily injured, and which only grows when exposed to the sunlight of someone else's recognition and praise. To see the good in others and let them see themselves in the mirror of our regard is to help someone grow to become the best they can be."[2]

In leadership, recognizing and naming the good is essential for hiring talent, keeping talent, and sustaining reliable growth. In *Forbes*, Joyce E. A. Russell concludes, "Positive leadership has been shown to be related to better organizational outcomes (e.g., job satisfaction, job performance, going above and beyond at work, psychological well-being, organizational commitment, creativity) than negative leadership styles (which have been shown to be related to turnover intentions, stress, anxiety, absenteeism, job burnout, retaliatory behaviors). In short, leaders set the tone for their team and/or organization."[3]

Emma Seppälä and Kim Cameron, in their, article "The Best Leaders Have a Contagious Positive Energy," call such leaders "positive energizers" and identify qualities associated with positive energizers: "Energizers' greatest secret is that, by uplifting others through authentic, values-based leadership, they end up lifting up both themselves and their organizations. Positive energizers demonstrate and cultivate virtuous actions, including forgiveness, compassion, humility, kindness, trust, integrity, honesty, generosity, gratitude, and recognition in the organization. As a result, everyone flourishes."[4]

In Jewish law, we bless on the bad as we bless on the good – but use two different blessings to mark these moments. This is how we demonstrate acceptance of that which is beyond our control. It is also a way we imitate God. That which is good can become bad in our eyes, and that which is bad can become good. If our subjective analysis can go in either direction, we have a choice: Will we be able to see the good in what is bad and make it so, or will we see the bad in what is good?

This is a divine task of immense proportions and the challenge of living in a broken world. God models it and invites us to do the same.

Moses's mother models it and invites us to do the same. She was able to see beyond Pharaoh's awful decree by looking at the exquisite innocence of her son and naming the unvarnished beauty and goodness she saw in front of her. Her optimism and fierce commitment at this difficult time had a prophetic impact on the Jewish future. She gave birth to Judaism's greatest hero: "Never again did there arise in Israel a prophet like Moses" (Deut. 34:10).

Personal Leadership Reflection

What goodness is in front of you right now that you need to see and name?

פרשת וארא • *Parashat Va'era*

When You Discover You're Like No Other

Imagine your world suddenly covered with frogs jumping on every surface: "Aaron held out his arm over the waters of Egypt, and the frogs came up and covered the land of Egypt" (Ex. 6:10). It would be absolutely revolting. The God of this slave people was capable of much aggravation and destruction, the Egyptians finally realized. Nevertheless, Pharaoh set his magicians the task of replicating this plague, ironically creating even more amphibian havoc: "But the magician-priests did the same with their spells, and brought frogs upon the land of Egypt" (8:2).

Although the replication worked, something else was not working. Pharaoh's magicians clearly had no idea how to stop the problem they themselves created. In desperation, Pharaoh called Aaron and Moses: "Plead with God to remove the frogs from me and my people, and I will let the people go to sacrifice to God'" (8:4). Pharaoh was willing to make a concession if the plague stopped. Moses approached this request wisely. He did not cave in to Pharaoh's demands immediately.

Moses wanted to raise the stakes by showing Pharaoh the degree to which the Israelites had the upper hand. Moses asked Pharaoh exactly when to stop the plague: "And Moses said to Pharaoh, 'You may have this triumph over me: *For what time shall I plead on behalf of you* and your courtiers and your people, that the frogs be cut off from you and your houses, to remain only in the Nile?'" (8:5). Unlike the magicians, who could create a mess but not extricate themselves from it, Moses's God had such control that the very hour to stop the plague could be determined in advance.

Pharaoh strangely did not ask for the frogs to disappear immediately. "'For tomorrow,' he replied. And [Moses] said, 'As you say – that you may know that there is none like our God.'" Moses added a flourish that offered the reason for the plagues in the first place: to show Pharaoh who was really in control. It was not enough to name God. Pharaoh had to know God. He could even set his watch to God's signs and wonders. Sforno sums it up neatly: "In order that you will recognize the difference between what your sorcerers are able to do and what God is capable of doing."

There is no one like God and nothing but God – *Ein od milvado*. That is made clear in *Va'era*. I only truly understood the significance of this statement when I visited Egypt myself at the tender age of nineteen. Walking through the Temple of Karnak near Luxor and the acres of ancient ruins that were a testament to the power of polytheism was the first time I glimpsed what the ancient Israelites were up against. The statues towered over me. I pondered how difficult it must have been to erect all these altars and prayer spaces and how hard it was to believe in an alternate spiritual reality. Was it my people, I wondered with each step, who were forced to construct these buildings to honor visible gods, all the while holding on to an invisible God whom Pharaoh failed to acknowledge?

The statement of God's singularity and uniqueness appears elsewhere in Tanakh. In Jeremiah, we read, "There is none like You, O Lord; You are great, and great is Your name in might" (Jer. 10:6). In the first book of Samuel, Hannah intones a prayer upon delivering Samuel to Shiloh: "There is no one holy like the Lord; indeed, there is no one besides You, nor is there any rock like our God" (I Sam. 2:2). In difficult times and in times of great joy, our people have held steadfastly to a belief in monotheism even when we suffered for it, even when no one around us believed in one God.

I believe that this iconoclasm – the capacity to challenge cherished beliefs and reigning institutional norms – rubbed off on the Jewish people as well. Believing something no one else believes and challenging existing ways of thinking and being can also help mold the way we generate new ideas, invent new medicines, and chart new pathways in science and the arts. Could belief in a God who is like no other extend to a belief in personal human singularity as well? There is no other God. God is unique. There is no one else like me. I am unique.

Rabbi Jonathan Sacks, in *Radical Then, Radical Now*, reminds us of this singularity: "We are not insignificant, nor are we alone. We are here because someone willed us into being, who wanted us to be, who knows our innermost thoughts, who values us in our uniqueness, whose breath we breathe and in whose arms we rest; someone in and through whom we are connected to all that is."[5] Uniqueness can be uncomfortable rather than reassuring. We do what others do to belong. It takes courage to imitate God by being who we were uniquely meant to be.

Gregory Berns, a professor of neurology at Emory University, demonstrated the brain's plasticity and ability to challenge ideas long accepted. The iconoclast, he contends, is the ultimate leader, because the iconoclast allows himself or herself to think and act differently. "We take for granted that our perceptions of the world are real, but they are really specters of our imagination, nothing more than biological and electrical rumblings that we believe to be real." Berns argues that the iconoclast's brain works on another register in three central and defining ways:

> Perception: The iconoclast sees differently than others.
> Fear response: The iconoclast can tame stress responses to better control fear.
> Social intelligence: The iconoclast connects differently with others.[6]

Berns further reminds us that when we create something novel, we are also destroying what once existed. Fear can quickly deaden the willingness to do something new. We fear ambiguity and staying in spaces that are uncertain, so we rush to convention and routine. We fear failure; if we do things the way they've always been done, we will minimize disappointment. We fear looking stupid or incompetent, so we take no chances.

Moses, the iconoclast of Exodus, saw freedom where others saw slavery. He was able to control his fear response time and again under Pharaoh's threats, and he was able to connect his message of salvation and justice to the people he led. Moses was initially cowed by fears of his own inadequacy. He repeatedly rejected a job he never signed up for. But then, in Pharaoh's own chambers, Moses stood up and declared, "There is none like our God." And in this empowering and dangerous moment, perhaps Moses discovered his own singular voice, leaving us with the gift and invitation to discover our own.

Personal Leadership Reflection

When have you challenged prevailing norms and discovered your uniqueness?

פרשת בא • *Parashat Bo*

Leadership and the Prayer Community

Crisis makes leaders and breaks leaders.

In *Parashat Bo*, the very mention of a locust plague sent Pharaoh and his courtiers into a tailspin. A swarm of locusts is not only unsightly; it can ruin crops for an entire harvest season, decimating an economy and heightening starvation. I learned from a *National Geographic* website that locusts in the ancient world were both feared and revered. Locusts can travel up to eighty-one miles in twenty-four hours and can stay in the air for days at a time. No wonder that when Moses and Aaron threatened Pharaoh with a plague of locusts, Pharaoh was initially willing to accommodate their request to go to the desert and worship their God.

Moses and Aaron were brought back to Pharaoh and he said to them, "Go, worship your God! Who are the ones to go?" Moses replied, "We will all go – regardless of social station, we will go with our sons and daughters, our flocks and herds; for we must observe the Lord's festival" (Ex. 10:8–9). Moses, who had the upper hand in this negotiation, pushed his luck and asked that everyone be allowed to leave. Pharoah was having none of it. He permitted only the Israelite leaders to leave.

> But he said to them, "God will be with you – the same as I mean to let your dependents go with you! Clearly, you are bent on mischief. No! You gentlemen go and worship God, since that is what you want." And they were expelled from Pharaoh's presence. (Ex. 10:10–11)

Nahmanides explains Pharaoh's ire. Moses asked for too much, so he was left with nothing: "Pharaoh's anger was then kindled on account of the sons and daughters, and he said that under no circumstances will he send the little ones, for they take no part in the offerings. Instead, he would send all the adult males because of the feast which Moses mentioned, while the little ones and the women will remain [in Egypt]." If Moses and Aaron led all the Jews out of Egypt, they would have no intention of coming back.

The *Midrash Lekaḥ Tov* on Exodus 10:9 explains Moses's request as an expression of justice: "Just as we all serve you, so must we all serve our God." The Hebrew word for slave is also the word for a worshipper, a servant of God. If Pharaoh had the audacity to enslave children, the elderly, and cattle toward his ends, this same group should be allowed the freedom of worship. It seemed only fair.

Rabbi Samson Raphael Hirsch on the same verse explains Moses's words:

> We have no intermediary, no priests, no representative before our God. If we are to go, we must all go; the tiniest baby in the cradle, the last sheep of our possessions. Each and all are integral parts of our community. None and nothing may remain, for we are all to form a "circle about God." God calls us together around Him, and when God calls us, He wants to see us with every member of our family and with all our possessions, about Him.

Moses needed to explain to the head of a spiritually hierarchical Egyptian society that the nature of a Jewish worshipful community is not based on the intercession of a high priest alone but on the tears of a child, the pleas of a young mother, the requests of a farmer, and the petition of an old woman. To deny them the right to pray is to deny them a basic human need. In that communal space filled with the diversity that travels across ages and gender, the Israelites could articulate their pain to God while in the presence of each other.

Rabbi Jonathan Sacks captures this beautifully when he describes why we pray in the plural:

> Prayer is like a protective wall, and praying together is more powerful and effective.
>
> We do not need superhuman piety – merely enlightened self-interest – to realise that our destinies are interconnected. When we are blessed, we are blessed together. Prayer is community made articulate, when we delete the first-person singular and substitute the first-person plural.[7]

Moses understood the protective wall that is prayer. Today, as we try to rebuild community post-Covid, we do not always focus on bringing everyone back to our prayer spaces. In some communities, the emphasis is on a *minyan* of men. In others, attention is paid to youth and not to seniors. We had become experts at fragmenting our communities of worship long before Covid. We have teen experiences, beginners' services, and tot Shabbatot. While these are all important ways we serve different communal needs, we risk doing what Pharaoh wanted and what Moses decried: We limit prayer to one segment of society instead of creating sacred spaces where all have a voice.

Because we suffer together, we must celebrate together. Because we share a world, we have to see each other. No one can be invisible. Everyone is integral.

I once asked each member of a group of leaders to write a prayer for his or her leadership. Not one person in the room had ever done such an exercise. Many neither attended synagogue regularly nor prayed alone with any frequency. The very word "prayer" seemed alien and archaic to some leaders in the room. But as they sat in silence with pens in hand, I watched their faces soften as they wrote diligently. The results were stunning. People asked for wisdom to make good decisions. They asked for patience. They wanted the fortitude to handle difficult situations that required them to stretch and grow. They wanted comfort for the lonelier moments and help when they struggled to delegate. They prayed that when they were done with their work, they would be succeeded by people who could carry on what they built with responsibility and integrity. They prayed for those they led. And they realized, in processing the activity, that when you're a leader, there is an awful lot to pray for.

As we turn back to our Torah reading, Pharaoh denied Moses's demand, so God told Moses to lift his staff, and with that sweeping gesture, the locusts came on an east wind and covered the land. "Locusts invaded all the land of Egypt and settled within all the territory of Egypt in a thick mass; never before had there been so many, nor will there ever be so many again" (Ex. 10:14). I learned something else about locusts. When the rainy season returns and the earth is moist, locusts reproduce rapidly. They then shift from solitary insects to group behavior – they have greater endurance, and their brain size actually increases.

In Exodus 1:7, when the Israelites grow prodigiously, the term "swarming" is used. Perhaps Pharaoh saw in this plague of locusts a metaphor for the Israelites themselves – a small but mighty nation who covered the land. They endured and became wiser with time until they posed an actual threat that would only be relieved when they could travel home together as a worshipful community.

Personal Leadership Reflection

What do you pray for as a leader? What do you hope your leaders pray for? Take a few minutes to formulate your own leadership prayer.

פרשת בשלח • *Parashat Beshallaḥ*

Confusion and Control

Confusion is a technique leaders can use to maintain control. Confusion can create dependency on leaders because their followers simply do not understand what is expected of them or fail to comprehend the situation they are in. In this scenario, such leaders augment power, because followers continue to look up to the leader for explanation and guidance.

Liz Wiseman, author of the book *Multipliers: How the Best Leaders Make Everyone Smarter*,[8] divides the leadership personality into multipliers and diminishers. Multipliers debate ideas and decisions with those around them. They don't provide easy answers and instead try to coax direction out of others and empower them. They challenge others to create an intense atmosphere that helps bring out people's best efforts. Multipliers also hold people accountable as a way to create ownership.

They give others the credit and take the blame.

Diminishers are often tyrants or micromanagers who always know better than everyone else. But, as Wiseman discovered, many well-intentioned leaders can become diminishers unintentionally by "thinking too big" and expecting their teams to live up to their grandiose plans and vision without connecting the dots on how to actualize their dreams. Teams can feel disempowered and confused and lose enthusiasm. Diminishers can suffer from brainstorming too much without seeing things through, or they may involve themselves in every decision, creating dependency. Wiseman brings many examples of such individuals, who often make abrupt and centralized decisions – because they have the authority to do so – and leave people confused and frustrated.

What diminishers fail to understand is that, psychologically speaking, everyone needs to feel some degree of autonomy and control. Rabbi Jonathan Sacks, in *The Dignity of Difference*, helps us understand what happens when we have little control:

> At the core of our culture is the knowledge that too much of what happens to us is beyond our control, the result of economic choices or political decisions taken far away by people we will never meet nor be able to identify. Beyond the narrowing circle of the self lies a world in which we are not the makers but the made.[9]

This is the genesis of despair.

In *Beshallaḥ*, we find yet another example of a diminisher-in-chief: Pharaoh. He was a tyrant who made abrupt, centralized decisions to augment power, ignoring the welfare and safety of his people. He also thought that by exerting control, he could create the kind of confusion that would make the Israelites dependent on him. In a moment of curated magnanimity, Pharaoh finally allowed the Israelites to leave. The plagues were taking their toll. But he never believed they would find their way. As the Israelites were getting to the edge of the Reed Sea, God told Moses exactly what Pharaoh was thinking: "Pharaoh will say of the Israelites, 'They are astray (*nevukhim*) in the land; the wilderness has closed in on them" (Ex. 14:3).

Rashi defines the word "*nevukhim*" as shut out or sunken and brings prooftexts from Job (28:11, 38:16) and Psalms (84:7) that utilize water imagery. This makes sense, because the Israelites were about to face a sea they could not cross; all their dreams of freedom would only take them to the bottom of an unforgiving ocean. Rashi continues to describe the confusion: "They are shut up in the wilderness, so they do not know how to get out or where to go." Rabbi Abraham ibn Ezra defines "*nevukhim*" as entangled and perplexed and cites his own prooftexts to support his reading. Perhaps the most famous example is in Esther 3:15, when Haman suggested that King Ahasuerus enact a decree to kill one nation among the 127 in his empire. This is yet another example of an abrupt, centralized decision that makes no sense and results in an expected consequence: "The city of Shushan was confused." Ibn Ezra explains the tension in the word: Those who suffer this confusion are "like a person who cannot find anyone to advise him and does not know what to do."

Rashbam, Rashi's grandson, cites his grandfather's explanation and puts us in the heads of the Israelites at that terrifying moment. They were confused by the sea in front of them and a desert filled with scorpions and wild animals behind them. So they set up a camp where God told them to, but they had no sense of a pathway forward: "Tell the Israelites to turn back and encamp before Pi Hahirot, between Migdol and the sea, before Baal Zephon; you shall encamp facing it, by the sea" (Ex. 14:2). God had them face the terror of the future in a state of confusion. Rashbam says that the word "*nevukhim*" describes the hopelessness they felt at having no options. "It describes people faced by insurmountable obstacles to their continued progress." Confusion like this could have fed straight into Pharaoh's unchecked power. The Israelites would have to turn back to Egypt and re-enslave themselves under worse conditions or die trying to leave. Their confusion fed into Pharaoh's control.

The people cry out, and Moses tries to quiet them, relying on the technicolor miracles and God's salvific powers: "But Moses said to the people, 'Have no fear! Stand by and witness the deliverance which God will work for you today; for the Egyptians whom you see today you will never see again. God will battle for you; you hold your peace!'" (14:13–14). All the verbs Moses uses are passive. The people are told to stand, to witness, to observe. God will fight every battle.

God, the ultimate Multiplier, has different plans, however. He empowered Moses and his followers so that they could learn that when facing confusion, they had to take control and charge forward: "Then God said to Moses, 'Why do you cry out to Me? Tell the Israelites to go forward. And you lift up your rod and hold out your arm over the sea and split it, so that the Israelites may march into the sea on dry ground'" (14:15–16). The rest is history. One of the greatest stories of all time pits a Multiplier against a diminisher. The Multiplier's victory is a victory for every one of God's followers. The diminisher's loss turns into a death warrant for his followers.

Every one of us has multiplier and diminisher tendencies in life and in leadership. The *parasha* reminds us to be multipliers and to apply that mindset when we're stuck, confused, and unsure.

Personal Leadership Reflection

Are you more of a diminisher or more of a multiplier?

פרשת יתרו • *Parashat Yitro*

Celebrating Success

Yitro might best be described as recorded history's first consultant. He is an outsider who pays a visit, observes Moses, and tells his son-in-law that he's going about his business all wrong. Moses spends all day adjudicating issues and answering questions for the long line of people waiting for him. Yitro watches the spectacle in disbelief. The dialogue between these two leaders of different faiths and generations is fascinating:

> "What is this thing that you are doing to the people? Why do you act alone, while all the people stand about you from morning until evening?" Moses replied to his father-in-law, "It is because the people come to me to inquire of God. When they have a dispute, it comes before me, and I decide between one party and another, and I make known the laws and teachings of God." But Moses's father-in-law said to him, "The thing you are doing is not right; you will surely wear yourself out, and these people as well. For the task is too heavy for you; you cannot do it alone." (Ex. 18:14–18)

Yitro, it seems, cares about Moses and tells him to take care of himself. This is, on its own, a critical leadership behavior. Leaders with compassion fatigue, who are depleted and running on fumes, will soon run out of the energy to lead. But before Yitro gives this message, knowing that Moses could easily push aside his own health and well-being, Yitro draws Moses's attention to how his behavior is affecting others who are dependent upon him. He feels sorry for all the people who suffer while waiting for Moses.

But when Yitro questions Moses, Moses has a ready answer. It's not his fault. He is the human face of God's law. This is his divine assignment. There is no one else to whom he can delegate the work to relieve him of his responsibilities. Perhaps because Yitro was an outsider to Judaism, he did not accept Moses's reply. "The thing you are doing is not right." It may seem right to you, but it will eventually impoverish you and your people of vital energy and efficiency. Yitro appealed to Moses's concern for others by mentioning the people first. Moses might have dismissed his own burden, but he could not ignore what his overworking was doing to those around him.

Yitro, in effect, tells Moses he is suffering from compassion fatigue, a common problem for mission-driven leaders. The mission never ends, so the work never ends, so the leader never stops. This has a modern-day correlate. We live in an age in which technology has allowed us to be more productive than ever but has led to people feeling more overwhelmed than ever. The day seems to never end. There are no boundaries between work and home life. Exhaustion is high. Satisfaction is low. Energy ebbs.

> You feel it every day when you come home frazzled, uncertain if you accomplished what you needed to, worried about things you've left undone, and dreading the day ahead.... You feel it when you think of your potential and the great goals you have, but then feel battered and bruised by all the incoming tasks and demands that seem to always keep you from focusing on more important things.[10]

What's a hardworking person to do? We turn back to our Torah reading. Often, when we read *Parashat Yitro*, we focus on the above dialogue and Yitro's recommendations. But what we miss in doing this is something Yitro taught Moses that may have been even more important than delegation: celebration. When Yitro showed up at Moses's tent door from Midian, Moses welcomed Yitro in, and the two began a crucial conversation about what had happened since they were last together: "Moses then recounted to his father-in-law everything that God had done to Pharaoh and to the Egyptians for Israel's sake, all the hardships that had befallen them on the way, and how God had delivered them" (Ex. 18:8). Moses never recounted this information to Aaron and Miriam or to the people. They all had the experience together. There was no need.

Or was there?

The visit of an outsider enabled Moses to look back. Yitro's presence and his curiosity empowered Moses to reflect on his immense leadership accomplishments. When you lead people, you always look forward to the next stop, the next project, the next marker of success.

The drive of ambition keeps driving non-stop. But this leadership engine and the intensity it generates can resolve itself in exhaustion and self-recrimination. Why am I not doing more? CEO and author, David Villa, observes that "often we are so busy and so consumed with trying to reach our goals that when we finally do, we simply say, 'What's next?'"[11]

Yitro, however, helped Moses pause, savor, and celebrate all that Moses had done; the young man who believed he was inadequate to the task had realized a dream: "And Yitro rejoiced over all the kindness that God had shown Israel when delivering them from the Egyptians" (Ex. 18:8–9). This rejoicing was followed and enhanced by a festive meal: "And Yitro, Moses's father-in-law, brought a burnt offering and sacrifices for God; and Aaron came with all the elders of Israel to partake of the meal before God with Moses's father-in-law" (18:12). "Celebration is an essential part of motivating," writes Rabbi Jonathan Sacks in his essay "Celebrate."[12] "When we celebrate the achievements of others, we change lives." When we stop to celebrate, it allows us time to recognize all of the people involved in each accomplishment. Leaders never work in a vacuum. As a leader, you may believe that you don't need recognition or celebration and, thereby, deprive others who need to feel valued and want to celebrate.

Celebrating success is more than sending out an email or giving people a few hours off. It's a conscious, detailed recognition of the meaningful contributions of each member of a team that is followed by rejoicing. Rabbi A. J. Heschel once wrote, "People of our time are losing the power of celebration. Instead of celebrating, we seek to be amused or entertained. Celebration is an active state, an act of expressing reverence or appreciation."[13]

Personal Leadership Reflection

What do you need to celebrate right now, and who would benefit from more celebration?

פרשת משפטים • *Parashat Mishpatim*

Cursing the Leader/ Blessing the Leader

In "How Leaders Should Handle Public Criticism,"[14] Ron Carucci argues that the more public your role is and the more decisions you make, the more likely you are to get things wrong and the more people will critique you in ways that are not always just or fair. "The cruel reality of leadership is that when things go wrong, you take a disproportionate amount of the blame." This can be a hard burden to carry, because the rumor mill works overtime. "When you make mistakes, the scrutiny from the broader organization is intensified. Remember, the farther people are from the problem, the less context and understanding they have. They will fill in the blanks with conjecture, projection of their own trauma, and perceived motives for why you did what you did." Carucci advises leaders to accept this reality and, as hard as it may be, try not to get sidetracked by the noise. Play the long-game of impact.

At the same time, respond with humility and transparency and, when necessary, set the record straight with facts rather than emotions.

Respond to the kernels of truth in what you hear, take action, and report back your results. Don't let snarky or malicious feedback make you thick-skinned or cold-hearted, Carucci warns. Be your best self even and especially when you feel crushed: "You have to be true to the values you want people to remember you by. If you don't want this moment to define you, then make sure it reveals who you intend to be." Moments of intense criticism can also be opportunities to share your deepest convictions.

I thought of Carucci's recommendations when reading a verse in *Mishpatim*: "You shall not revile God, nor put a curse upon a leader (*nasi*) among your people" (Ex. 22:27). Cursing the leader is mentioned in the same breath as cursing God because these are two sources of authority: divine and human. The natural tendency to question or rebel against those who have control over us or constrain us is constant. The Torah reminds us to keep it in check.

On a surface level, this may be prudent advice. Cursing those in positions of influence can have unpleasant personal consequences, to say the least. Cursing someone in the ancient world (and in some parts of the modern world today) was taken very seriously, which explains the many prohibitions throughout Tanakh that warn against it. Ecclesiastes recommends that we silence negative thoughts against the king because the walls have ears; any public criticism may come back to bite the one who questions authority: "Do not revile a king even among your intimates. Do not revile a rich man even in your bedchamber; for a bird of the air may carry the utterance, and a winged creature may report the word" (Eccl. 10:20). You don't know whom you can trust or where anyone's ultimate loyalties are.

Who are the leaders the Torah tells us not to curse?

Rabbi Abraham ibn Ezra mentions judges, priests, and Levites – all positions, he contends, that represent Torah. When you curse those who uphold the Torah, he is suggesting, you are, on some level, criticizing the Torah and God who gave us the Torah. Ibn Ezra adds that this law applies to speaking in secret or in public. In other words, the one who curses should try to shift his or her very mindset about the current leadership. Ibn Ezra also helps us understand the context of this law, which appears immediately after the law that one who lends money must return at night the garment that a poor person gave as collateral and an enigmatic line of compassion amidst a listing of laws: "In what else shall [your neighbor] sleep? Therefore, if that person cries out to Me, I will pay heed, for I am compassionate" (Ex. 22:26). Ibn Ezra examines this juxtaposition and concludes: "The poor man, while in pain during the night, might revile the judge who ruled that the lender should take the pledge."

Sforno takes this prohibition in a different direction: "Even though you may feel that the judge has judged you unfairly, you must not curse him. The reason is that no individual can judge his own guilt or innocence objectively." Before we curse a leader, we have to look in the mirror to check if we judge others more harshly than we judge ourselves. We should interrogate our own subjectivity. The medieval compilation of mitzvot *Sefer HaḤinukh* (71:1) adds that this law applies not only to a king but also to the head of the Sanhedrin, the ancient assembly of sages who determined Jewish law, "since the intention of the verse is about anyone who is the head authority over Israel, whether it is the government of the kingdom or whether it is the government of the Torah." The *Sefer HaḤinukh* extended the application of this law beyond those in political positions of power to include the authority of scholars.

So seriously was this law observed that the Talmud includes the strange and gruesome story of the sage Bava ben Buta to illustrate. King Herod called upon Bava ben Buta and placed a porcupine hide on his head to prick his eyes out. Herod sat before this blind scholar and cursed *himself* to see Bava ben Buta's reaction. He goaded the sage to join him. Bava ben Buta quoted our verse in Ecclesiastes – "Do not curse the king, not even in your thoughts" – but Herod pushed him further: "He is not a king, since he rules illegally." Still Bava ben Buta would not concede. "And even if he were merely a rich man, I would not curse him, as it is written: 'And do not curse a rich person in your bedchamber' (Eccl. 10:20). And even were he only a leader, I would not curse him, as it is written: 'And you shall not curse a leader among your people' (Ex. 22:27)" (Bava Batra 4a). Bava ben Buta suffered greatly under Herod's rule, yet he still observed this commandment.

Here it is important to make a distinction between criticizing and cursing. One is not forbidden to question a leader's rulings, policies, or character to maintain the integrity of the office. Most ancient Israelite kings had a prophet to guide and chastise them, precisely to keep the king's power in check and remind him to answer to the King of Kings. Saul had Samuel. David had Nathan. But there is a difference between the legitimate critique of power and a coarse, emotional, and blasphemous challenge that invokes supernatural powers against the leader.

The word for leader in our verse is "*nasi*," and it is in defining this term that we may better understand the prohibition. The infinitive "*laseit*" is used throughout Tanakh to refer to shouldering a burden, sometimes a very heavy one. Those who curse a leader add weight to an already heavy burden. Sometimes, in our anger or indignation, we fail to see all that a leader may be carrying. When adding to the load, we may inadvertently become the reason a leader walks away from the position. "What do I need this for?" Look around to see how many volunteers are *not* signing up for senior leadership roles because they don't want the constant criticism without much recognition or praise. It is a lot to carry.

Nahmanides, in his interpretation of our verse, adds that the root of "*nasi*" also means to lift up. The role of the leader is to lift up the follower. Perhaps the word also reminds us that leaders themselves need to be uplifted. If we lift up leaders, and they lift us up, maybe more people would sign up for these unpopular jobs. When leaders make mistakes, it is incumbent upon us to bring them to public attention, but there is a difference between constructive solutions and reckless gossip, between offering respectful feedback and cursing the leader.

In his book *Judaism's Life-Changing Ideas*, Rabbi Jonathan Sacks shares a personal story that may provide a small window into this complex issue. At the beginning of his rabbinical career, he sought the approval of a senior rabbi and waited for a word of encouragement. He was working hard and taking risks. "You need support at such moments, because taking risks and suffering the inevitable criticism is emotionally draining. The encouragement never came. The silence hurt. It ate, like acid, into my heart." It was then that he had a shift in strategy. Instead of waiting for praise, he praised the rabbi he sought praise from. "I began to formulate it as an ethic. Don't wait to be praised: Praise others. Don't wait to be respected: Respect others. Don't stand on the sidelines, criticising others. Do something yourself to make things better."[15]

Personal Leadership Reflection

Consider ways you may have "cursed" a leader. What praise could you offer to lift up a leader who is lifting you?

פרשת תרומה • *Parashat Teruma*

Sacred Work

"Leaders," writes Rabbi Jonathan Sacks in *Lessons in Leadership*, "do not do the work on behalf of the people. They teach people how to do the work themselves."[16] These words offer an important perspective in *Parashat Teruma*, and it follows until the end of the book of Exodus.

To understand the nation's work, we have to look at the entirety of the book of Exodus. It can be divided into three distinct sections: (1) chapters 1–15 tell the Israelite story from slavery to freedom, (2) chapters 16–24 tell the movement to and from Sinai and the giving of the law, and (3) chapters 25–40 list the instructions for and execution of the construction of the *Mishkan*, our portable Temple in the wilderness. The order makes sense. First, we have a shared story of our anguish, God's salvation, and Moses's leadership. Without freedom, we cannot receive and observe the laws that unite us. Once we have laws, we move from a shared past to shared values and behaviors.

Our shared history and values enable us to build a holy community; the *Mishkan* represents the centerpiece of the camp, literally and emotionally, as a way to access the sacred. We needed more than freedom. We needed transcendence. And to achieve this as a community, we needed to build the *Mishkan* as a community. The Israelites were called upon to each contribute a half-shekel and to give the best of what they owned and their individual talents as artisans: "Tell the Israelite people to bring Me gifts; you shall accept gifts for Me from every person whose heart is so moved" (Ex. 25:2). Everyone's heart, it seems, was so moved. But what can a rag-tag group of former slaves possibly have to contribute to the grandeur of the project? Certainly not the list of expected contributions:

> And these are the gifts that you shall accept from them: gold, silver, and copper; blue, purple, and crimson yarns, fine linen, goats' hair; tanned ram skins, dolphin skins, and acacia wood; oil for lighting, spices for the anointing oil and for the aromatic incense; lapis lazuli and other stones for setting, for the ephod and for the breastplate. (25:3–7)

It is clear what some of these Hebrew terms mean. What is less clear is how any of the Israelites obtained precious metals, rare skins, and expensive dyes. Rashi, who offers a definition of almost every item, shares no wisdom on where these came from. Rabbi Abraham ibn Ezra suggests that some of these goods came into Israelite hands because the people were told three times to take dresses and finery from the Egyptians before they left. He also suggests that either the Israelites planted acacia trees when they were in Egypt and took the wood with them or there was a forest of acacia trees near Sinai.

Sforno suggests that only the gemstones that were described in Moses's instructions should be contributed. Other items were rejected. Underlying his reading may be the notion that people, in their generosity, want to give of themselves but often donate objects because they have them and not because they are needed. The right way to give, suggests Sforno implicitly, is to understand first what the needs are. The way in which the Israelites obtained these materials is secondary to the fact that giving something of value helped them value the *Mishkan*. All of this activity was to fulfill God's mandate: "And let *them* make Me a sanctuary that I may dwell among *them*" (25:8).

Commentaries on this verse emphasize the second "them" – when they build this portable sanctuary, God will live in the people, rather than in the building. But the first "them," I believe, explains the second. God will live in them because each one of them made a personal contribution to a joint project of holiness. As slaves, the Israelites were involved in building the edifices of the Egyptian empire. The backbreaking work did nothing to advance themselves as a people. Finally, they were able to build something extraordinary themselves.

This work was a labor of love. *Avot DeRabbi Natan* (11:1), an ancient rabbinic collection of sayings, states, "A person should love work and not hate work. For just as the Torah was given in a covenant, so work was given in a covenant, as it says (Ex. 20:10): 'For six days you shall labor and do all your work, and the seventh day is the Sabbath of the Eternal your God.'" Work, according to this, should represent a fulfillment of our purpose on this earth. Just as the Sabbath is joyous and restorative, so should the right work be purposeful and energizing.

To illustrate, the text continues with an example from the building of the *Mishkan*. According to R. Natan, Moses led the building charge while his chiefs sat silently observing him and waiting for direction. Then, when they heard a call throughout the camp that the work was complete, they bemoaned the fact that they had made no contribution. This explains, according to R. Natan, the verse, "And the chiefs brought the *shoham* stones [for the breastplate of the high priest] (Ex. 35:27)." Of their own volition, they wanted to take part in the *Mishkan*'s construction. No one wanted to be left out.

One of the most important functions leaders have is bringing people together, especially those with disparate interests and backgrounds, to work toward a common purpose using their God-given talents. Leadership expert Patrick Lencioni believes that such projects serve another function: They help minimize the differences that prevent people from getting the work done. In *Silos, Politics and Turf Wars: A Leadership Fable About Destroying the Barriers That Turn Colleagues into Competitors*, Lencioni identifies silos as barriers that exist within an organization that cause people who should be working with each other to inadvertently work against each other. He blames leaders for this, saying that many executives fail to coordinate talent and bring their teams into alignment.

The consequences of siloed behavior are not insignificant; in Lencioni's view, they can create profound pain, hurt institutions internally, and lead to unnecessary turnover and low organizational morale.

Lencioni suggests that the best way to bring people together is to create projects that everyone in a company or team can work on together for a limited period of time to generate connections and give people a sense of pride and solidarity. The leader has to provide a unifying sense of purpose that highlights everyone's contribution and gets people moving in the same direction.

Moses made this happen under God's direction. Every person who labored in the construction of the *Mishkan* became one of its key stakeholders and felt a profound connection to it and to the God who would one day dwell *in them*. Community is formed ultimately by builders rather than buildings. Leaders lead best when they create a community of stakeholders.

Personal Leadership Reflection

What project can you create that will lower the barriers between people and create genuine stakeholders?

פרשת תצוה • *Parashat Tetzaveh*

Dress for Leadership Success

Fashion icon Ralph Lauren once said, "I don't design clothes. I design dreams." *Parashat Tetzaveh* provides a detailed description of the high priest's garments. To understand the "dream" behind them, we must understand more about the design of this clothing, specifically the tunic:

> On its hem make pomegranates of blue, purple, and crimson yarns, all around the hem, with bells of gold between them all around: a golden bell and a pomegranate, a golden bell and a pomegranate, all around the hem of the robe. Aaron shall wear it while officiating, so that the sound of it is heard when he comes into the sanctuary before God and when he goes out – that he may not die. (Ex. 28:33–35)

This garment alone invites a rich visual and sensory reaction. The gemstone colors appeal to the eyes. The small pomegranates on the hem remind one of taste. The bells between the pomegranates invoke sound.

Rashi and Ḥizkuni add that there were clappers in each bell that would make noise when the high priest walked. Nahmanides maintains that the bells functioned as clappers inside pomegranates. In the Talmud, R. Yitzḥak says, "This teaches that the Divine Presence jangled before him, inspiring him, like a bell" (Sota 9b). In this reading, the bells were not only making noise for the people to sense the close presence of the high priest; they also functioned as a constant reminder to Aaron of his mission.

Whenever the high priest moved, he was aware of his divine service. Rabbeinu Baḥya (1255–1340) elaborates on this: "When a person wishes to receive an audience, he first knocks on the door of the king or prefect from whom he requests the audience. Aaron would announce his intention to pray by means of the chiming of the bells at the hem of his robe. What is customary as a sign of deference to a mortal king must also be observed when one petitions the King of Kings." In the *Mishkan*, the bells were a sign of respect to prepare for meeting God. Each stitch of the priest's clothing also had to be made with proper intention, signaling the care that a spiritual leader must put into clothing choices and the service performed in them.

In the Talmud, R. Yoḥanan makes clear how sartorial choices impact others long after the priestly service stopped: "Any Torah scholar on whose garment is found a stain deserves death, as it says (Prov. 8:36), 'All who hate Me love death.' Do not read it 'who hate Me' but 'who cause [people to] hate Me'" (Shabbat 114a). To bring majesty to an office, one must dress the part. Those who represent Torah must understand that people's impressions are almost always shallow and based on external realities; the leader has to communicate, at all times, the dignity of the position.

In their article "Clothes Make the Leader," Thomas Maran, Simon Liegl, Sebastian Moder, Sascha Kraus, and Marco Furtner seek to understand the impact of clothing on leaders: "While popular media relishes leaders who catch the eye by way of such distinctive fashion, we know little about how this salient daily practice of dress specifically affects perceptions of leaders in their daily business." Their findings? "Leaders' charisma and approval were higher when a person's clothing style contrasted [with] their organization's culture." [17] Lastly, in their study of CEOs of Fortune 1000 companies, they discovered that "leaders can manipulate their style of attire to actively shape their followers' impressions of themselves."

In "Dress for Success: How Clothes Influence Our Performance,"[18] Matthew Hutson and Tori Rodriguez cite multiple studies that correlate behavior with clothing. In the journal *Social, Psychological and Personality Science* (August 2015), researchers asked participants to wear either formal or informal clothes before taking cognitive tests. They discovered that "wearing formal business attire increased abstract thinking – an important aspect of creativity and long-term strategizing. The experiments suggest the effect is related to feelings of power." Other research points to the way that nonconformity of dress can be its own form of status.[19] In a 2012 study in the same journal, subjects made half as many mistakes on a particular task when wearing a white lab coat.[20] Clothing, in this study, not only positively influenced others, it also changed one's own sense of self-worth and performance.

According to one view in the Talmud, the high priest's clothing represented more than mere ceremonial fitness for office: "R. Simon said: Just as sacrifices atone, so the garments of the high priest atone: shirt, trousers, turban, and vest" (Y. Yoma 7:3). The high priest was the intermediary between the human and the Divine. Followers, therefore, needed to see in their spiritual leaders the possibility of getting closer to God. The priest's clothing conferred dignity and authority to the role and inspired repentance in those who observed the high priest's activities. That was the dream behind the design.

Today, even with no centralized worship space, clothing still communicates authority, but you don't have to be a priest for clothing to matter. "To be a leader," Rabbi Jonathan Sacks writes, "you don't need a crown or robes of office. All you need to do is to write your chapter in the story, do deeds that heal some of the pain of this world, and act so that others become a little better for having known you."[21]

Personal Leadership Reflection

How do your clothing choices communicate leadership to you and to those around you?

פרשת כי תשא • *Parashat Ki Tisa*

The Stiff-Necked People

Is there a cure for stubbornness?

Stubbornness is the inflexibility and determination to hold onto a view or belief such that you fail to hear or accept a different position, even a well-reasoned and rational one. Leaders need to be stubborn to succeed, but too much rigidity can get leaders into trouble. Muriel Maignan Wilkins expands our definition:

> You keep at an idea or plan, or insist on making your point, even when you know you're wrong.
> You do something you want to do even if no one else wants to do it.
> When others present an idea, you tend to point out all the reasons it won't work.
> You visibly feel anger, frustration, and impatience when others try to persuade you of something you don't agree with.
> You agree to or commit halfheartedly to others' requests, when you know all along that you're going to do something entirely different.[22]

Wilkins argues that if you're a stubborn leader, you can hurt yourself and your vision for the future. But in leadership, it's hard to know what separates dogged obstinacy from passionate, visionary determination. We don't want leaders to let go of good ideas too soon or not stand up with conviction for what they believe in. Here's how Wilkins parses the issue: "Stubbornness is the ugly side of perseverance."

We find this ugly side in *Ki Tisa*. "I see that this is a stiff-necked people (*am kesheh oref*)" (Ex. 32:9), says God to Moses. This was not a mere observation of a negative collective disposition. It was in response to the Israelite creation and worship of a golden calf. They were unable to see how wrong they were in betraying God and Moses. God was angry. But how are we to understand God's anger? Rabbi Jonathan Sacks writes, "The 'anger' of God, so often expressed in the Hebrew Bible, is actually not anger but anguish: the anguish of a parent who sees a child do wrong but knows that he or she may not interfere if the child is ever to grow, to learn, to mature, to change, to become responsible."[23]

In this *parasha*, we are challenged to grow, to learn, to change, and to become responsible. But it will take a long time. The expression "a stiff-necked people" will make several more appearances in our Torah reading: "Moses went back to the Lord and said, 'Alas, this people is guilty of a great sin in making for themselves a god of gold. Now, if You will forgive their sin [well and good]; but if not, erase me from the record which You have written!'" (32:31–32). Moses, who was tasked with admonishing the people, admits their great wrongdoing but also shows his fidelity to them. They may be sinners, but they are *his* sinners – and his penitents.

A chapter later, we find another appearance of the same expression. God told Moses to make the people's offense clear to them: "God said to Moses, 'Say to the Israelite people: You are a stiff-necked people. If I were to go in your midst for one moment, I would destroy you'" (33:5). Moses was told to give the people language to describe themselves so they could see their own rage and manage it. Rashi cites a verse from Isaiah that presents God's strategy and an effective management technique in the face of anger: "Hide yourself for a short moment, until the indignation passes" (Is. 26:20). Fury is all-consuming. Wait for a few moments and let the vehemence of the emotion subside.

Rashi, on Exodus 32:9, explains what it means to be stiff-necked: "They turn their stiffened necks away from those who criticize them and refuse to listen." Rashi considers the physical movement implied in the term "stiff *neck*" and provides us with a visual image of turning away from important counsel. Rabbi Abraham ibn Ezra similarly explains stiff-necked in this context: "The Israelites refused to do as God commanded, like a person who runs in a particular direction and does not turn his head back to the one who calls out to him." Sforno adds yet another visual cue by describing this kind of neck as an iron ligament that will not allow them the motion to listen to feedback or criticism. He adds that this is a stumbling block to *teshuva*, repentance. In Proverbs, we are told the cost of repeated stubbornness: "One often reproved may become stiff-necked, but he will be suddenly broken beyond repair" (Prov. 29:1). A stubborn person can become broken beyond repair.

Wilkins offers her advice: Listen to others instead of automatically shutting them down. Stay open to possibilities, ones that you may not have considered. Admit when you are wrong. A failure of leadership accountability can lead to more mistake making in the future. Finally, Wilkins advises us to decide what we can live with: "Rather than always pushing for your idea, decision or plan, recognize when it's okay to go with a decision that you can live with even if it's not your top choice." The Torah itself identifies a "solution" to this stubbornness in the book of Deuteronomy: "Circumcise… the foreskin of your heart, and be stiff-necked no more" (Deut. 10:16; this expression is found several more times in Deuteronomy – 9:6, 9:13, 31:27 – because this behavior unfortunately persisted). The opposite of the neck here is the heart. Create an opening in the heart, a small space of humility and vulnerability, and the hard, iron neck of arrogance will soften. We can dig our heels in, or we can pour our hearts out. It's hard, so very hard, to admit a mistake. In the short term it feels like losing. In the long term, however, making that hole in the heart allows the breath and the light in.

Personal Leadership Reflection

What's one stubborn belief that has cost you leadership credibility? How will you improve your life and the life of others if you let it go?

פרשת ויקהל • *Parashat Vayak'hel*

Work and Rest

It seems like everyone today is talking and writing about work: the great resignation, the evolution of office life, and the culture of remote meetings. The empty building is the new symbol of American jobs. We're unsure how to get people back into offices or how to retool work life to accommodate the flexibility that has become a right rather than a privilege. The title of Sarah Jaffe's recent book, *Work Won't Love You Back: How Devotion to Our Jobs Keeps Us Exploited, Exhausted, and Alone*, says it all. Jaffe argues that we have overly romanticized our work lives and created all kinds of unrealistic emotional expectations of what it should be: "We want to call work what is work so that eventually we might rediscover what is love."[24]

Organizational leaders often exploit this need by promoting false images of the fun, mission, or sense of familial belonging attached to work, especially to those with little control of their work day: "The compulsion to be happy at work, in other words, is always a demand for emotional work from the worker."[25] Jaffe warns her readers that this premise is mistaken: "Work, after all, has no feelings. Capitalism cannot love."[26]Families, for example, do not fire people. When families relocate, they take you with them. Jaffe asks that we rethink why we began working in the first place: to pay the bills. Now the dignity of affording one's needs has been eclipsed by a notion of work that is an all-consuming identity. The humble brag about overwork has become a cliché: "The ownership class these days does tend to work, and indeed, to make a fetish of its long hours."[27] The tensions she points out are greater with creative work, which is "based in a different kind of self-sacrifice and voluntary commitment that is expected, on some level, to love you back." This, too, is untrue: "...work never, ever loves you back."

The double Torah reading of *Parashot Vayak'hel/Pekudei* has a lot to say about work and about when to stop work: "Moses then convoked the whole Israelite community and said to them: 'These are the things that God has commanded you to do: On six days work may be done, but on the seventh day you shall have a sabbath of complete rest, holy to God'" (Ex. 35:1–2). If we close our eyes, we might think we are in the early chapters of Genesis, not the closing chapters of Exodus. Our *sedra* opens by mimicking the language of creation about the purposefulness of work and the necessity of rest. We were to build the *Mishkan* for six days and rest on the seventh.

What God declared when the world was created reflected the same pattern in building the portable sanctuary to honor Him. The classic commentators make the connection between Shabbat and the *Mishkan* explicit. Rashi on 35:1, for example, cites *Mekhilta DeRabbi Yishmael's* teaching that God instructed Moses about the Sabbath *before* discussing the building procedures, as if to say no matter how extraordinary the work, we must prioritize the sanctity of the Sabbath. One might easily assume that erecting a sacred space to honor God would trump Sabbath observance. The temptation to keep going – to place one more board, to smelt one more fixture, or to embroider one more stitch – would have been overwhelming. Nahmanides highlights the expression, "These are the things which the Eternal has commanded" as a reference not only to the building's structures but also to the holy vessels made to service God within its portable walls. Busy yourself as artists for six days, but even this special work must come to an end.

The message could not be more clear. The end of all creation is not building but resting. The pinnacle of creation can only be achieved by the cessation of creation. It is ironically the Sabbath, the "cathedral in time," as Rabbi Abraham J. Heschel called it, that is the acme of the process. "To gain control of the world of space is certainly one of our tasks," reminds Rabbi Heschel. "The danger begins when in gaining power in the realm of space we forfeit all aspirations in the realm of time. There is a realm of time where the goal is not to have but to be, not to own but to give, not to control but to share, not to subdue but to be in accord. Life goes wrong when the control of space, the acquisition of things of space, becomes our sole concern."[28]

Parashat Vayak'hel makes the case that for the ancient Israelites to achieve true piety as a community, they needed to combine holy space with holy time. That is why in the midst of all of the instructions for erecting the *Mishkan*, God assures Moses of our spiritual priorities. This break in the work also flattened whatever artisanal hierarchies existed in the *Mishkan*'s construction. Everyone had a distinct role in the building project. Some had tasks demanding a high level of skill and expertise that made their work seem superior. But when everyone stops working to observe the Shabbat, the community sheds itself of titles and talents. Work creates status. Rest is status-free. I'm always moved by the view from the pew: People with impressive business cards sit beside those too young to work, those who are retired, or those who have simple jobs. It does not matter. In this space, we are all spiritual citizens in the eyes of God, judged not by our place in society but by our goodness and piety. There must be somewhere in the world where the first question someone asks you is not what you do but who you are.

"Our Shabbat is a religious institution," writes Rabbi Jonathan Sacks in *A Letter in the Scroll.* Shabbat is "a memorial to creation, the day on which God Himself rested. But it is also and essentially a political institution. Shabbat is the greatest tutorial in liberty ever devised.... One day in seven, Jews create a Messianic society.... It is the day on which all hierarchies, all relationships of power are suspended."[29] Shabbat suspends hierarchy and produces the necessary restoration to keep the holiest of building projects going. Rest is not a weakness. It is our greatest strength.

Jim Loehr and Tony Schwartz, who used to coach Olympic athletes and then began working with corporate leaders, share that one of the most important lessons they learned from extraordinary athletes is the way they build recovery into their routines. In their book *The Power of Full Engagement,* they write, "We live in a world that celebrates work and activity, ignores renewal and recovery, and fails to recognize that both are necessary for sustained high performance."[30]

Personal Leadership Reflection

As a leader, how do you build rest and recovery into your routine to maintain high performance? How can you integrate more of Shabbat's gifts into your life?

פרשת פקודי • *Parashat Pekudei*

Leadership Gems

> There are gems of wondrous brightness
> Ofttimes lying at our feet,
> And we pass them, walking thoughtless,
> Down the busy, crowded street.

These lines from "If We Only Understood," a poem attributed to Rudyard Kipling, discuss all the gems, the beautiful visions, we may pass because we are walking too quickly to notice their radiance or worth. This may help explain why the *kohen gadol,* the high priest, wore gemstones up high on his breastplate during his service in the *Mishkan,* the ancient portable sanctuary. Those stones brought and focused attention on the sacred act of service.

We read all about this stone-studded breastplate, the *ḥoshen* that was worn on top of the apron, the *ephod,* and the specific gemstones embedded in it:

> The breastplate was made in the style of the *ephod*: of gold, blue, purple, and crimson yarns, and fine twisted linen. It was square; they made the breastplate doubled – a span in length and a span in width, doubled. They set in it four rows of stones. The first row

> was a row of carnelian, chrysolite, and emerald; the second row: a turquoise, a sapphire, and an amethyst; the third row: a jacinth, an agate, and a crystal; and the fourth row: a beryl, a lapis lazuli, and a jasper. They were encircled in their mountings with frames of gold. (Ex. 39:8–13)

Nahmanides explains in his commentary on an earlier verse (25:7) that we are familiar with the way gemstones are set to enhance their sparkle: "This is how they also do it today when they set precious stones in rings, in order that they be seen from all angles and that their beauty and splendor should not be hidden in the indentations." Imagine the shine and luster of these gemstones and the way they might have caught the eye of worshippers and sustained their glance. Set against the sun's whiteness and the desert's continuous golden floor, the breastplate imbued divine worship with richness and color.

In addition to their splendor, we are also told that these precious stones have a deeper numerical significance: "The stones corresponded [in number] to the names of the sons of Israel: twelve, corresponding to their names; engraved like seals, each with its name, for the twelve tribes" (39:14). Each stone correlated with a specific tribe. Thus, both the high priest who wore the breastplate and all those who looked at it were reminded of the unity of Israel. All the gemstones were gathered together and worn by Israel's special spiritual leader.

The breastplate must have been a weighty garment that signaled to the one wearing it the responsibility he carried, not only for each tribe but for maintaining a holy community and bringing the tribes together, especially when there were fissures and arguments among them. Not only was it heavy. It also shone brightly, reminding the high priest that as a leader, his job was not only to help maintain unity and bring all the Israelites together but also to see the divine radiance in them all, especially when it might not be obvious. Every tribe is a gem, literally and figuratively.

The classic interpreters are relatively silent on this verse, but the Zohar, a mystical commentary on the Torah, draws us to a statement in Psalms: "…the tribes of the Lord, are a testimony to Israel" (Ps. 122:4). We need every tribe to make up the Israelites. Only together do they form a nation and serve as a witness to what can be done in community when we bring everyone together. We must see their worth and value as separate units and as a majestic whole, much the way that the breastplate looked.

The *Urban Dictionary* defines a tribe as "close friends, group of people who are loyal to you, and care for you like family." Despite its particularistic character or because of it, there has been a revival of the use of the terms "tribe" and "tribal" in healthy and in unhealthy ways. "Are you in the tribe?" one person might ask another to sort out that person's affiliations, associations, and membership. Being part of a tribe creates a sense of belonging and affirmation. But tribalism, especially in politics, can lead to discriminatory behaviors and loyalty without reason. Daniel Shapiro, in his book *Negotiating the Nonnegotiable: How to Resolve Your Most Emotionally Charged Conflicts,* warns that "when a group enters this divisive mindset, they experience the 'tribes effect' in which they view their relationship with the other side as oppositional, claim that legitimacy rests solely with their own perspective, and close off to learning about the other's point of view."[31]

When the tribes are represented together – much the way they are imagined artistically on the breastplate of old and in many synagogue stained-glass windows today – it suggests that Israel is at its best when it functions in community. Rabbi Jonathan Sacks, in his book *Community of Faith,* published in 1995, writes that "Jewish faith is learned and taught, lived and experienced, in community. That is why the integrity of the community, its inner cohesiveness and its loyalty to the founding terms of its existence, matter even more than the learning or piety of individuals."[32] We need each other.

Each tribe needs to be successful for the good of the whole, write Dave Logan, John King, and Halee Fischer-Wright in *Tribal Leadership: Leveraging Natural Groups to Build a Thriving Organization.* They did an eight-year study of about 24,000 people in approximately twenty-four organizations to study the tribal nature of the way we work. They conclude that "you are only as smart and capable as your tribe." They describe organizations as "a set of small towns" and describe a tribe as a cluster of 20 to 150 people that is complex and sometimes irrational: "Tribal leadership focuses on two things, and only two things: the words people use and the types of relationships they form."[33] They advise building triads of such clusters to identify and fix problems, so that people begin to work across departments and with the benefits of interdisciplinary expertise. They don't discourage tribalism. They lean into it. Because we all live within complicated networks, they suggest we strengthen and deepen natural affiliations and then find ways to bring those clusters together to intensify the work and achieve better outcomes.

The *ḥoshen*, the breastplate, was created as a *maaseh ḥoshev*, uniting the garment and the way it was created first through a verbal pronunciation. It was to be "a work of intention or purpose." Everything about it told the story of a brilliance achieved by the uniqueness of each gem magnified by their luminosity together, reminding leaders to see the gem in others and find ways to unify and amplify the beauty through diversity.

Personal Leadership Reflection

What reminders do you need to envision the beauty in others when you are having trouble seeing it?

Leadership in the Book of Leviticus

פרשת ויקרא • *Parashat Vayikra*

The Power of Invitation

Sometimes we wait for a formal invitation only to be told, "You don't need to be invited. You're always welcome." But we don't necessarily feel welcome until someone extends a real invitation to us. This is the way we open the very first chapter of *Sefer Vayikra*, Leviticus. Our *sedra* and our book commence with the power of an invitation: "And God called…" (Lev. 1:1).

The "and" connects this Torah reading to that which preceded it. When we turn back to the last chapter of Exodus, we find Moses in a flurry of activity to complete the *Mishkan*. We find this in the very beginning of the final chapter: "On the first day of the first month you shall set up the Tabernacle of the Tent of Meeting. Place there the Ark of the Pact, and screen off the ark with the curtain" (Ex. 40:1–2).

And we find it in the chapter's continuation: "In the first month of the second year, on the first of the month, the Tabernacle was set up. Moses set up the Tabernacle, placing its sockets, setting up its planks, inserting its bars, and erecting its posts" (40:17–18). This was hard physical labor, and Moses executed it alone.

Fifteen chapters of Exodus are filled with the vision and action necessary to build the *Mishkan*. Many commentators ponder the need for such detailed instructions and the repetition that these instructions were carried out. There is an important leadership lesson embedded in this structure. You can have a vision, an architectural rendering, or a strategic plan, but your ideas are only as good as your follow-through. Your actions reflect your accountability. And if you're the leader, your actions matter most.

Larry Bossidy and Ram Charan, in their bestselling leadership book *Execution: The Discipline of Getting Things Done*, write about the importance of leaders having a granular understanding of the personnel, activities, and directions of their organizations. This is the job. When this kind of close monitoring for accountability is absent, visions fall flat. Strategies die. Results tank. "Execution has to be a part of a company's strategy and its goals," they write. "It is the missing link between aspirations and results. As such, it is a major – indeed, the major – job of a business leader. If you don't know how to execute, the whole of your effort as a leader will always be less than the sum of its parts."[1]

Talk can only get you so far. Only clear goals, measurable performance, and tight operations bring results.

The entire close of the book of Exodus reflects this intense concern for details and execution. Holiness, like love, resides not only in the amorphous cloud but in the small things, the sockets and the planks. Leaders must care about the minutiae of the work because that creates the foundation for everything else, especially when there is much to do and little time to do it in. Bossidy and Charan continue the theme:

> Follow-through is a constant and sequential part of execution. It ensures that you have established closure in the dialogue about who will be responsible for what and the specific milestones for measurement. The failure to establish this closure leaves the people who execute a decision or strategy without a clear picture of their role. As events unfold rapidly amid much uncertainty, follow-through becomes a much more intense process.

Milestones need to be placed closer together so there is less room for slippage, and information needs to flow faster and in more detail so that everyone knows how the strategy is evolving.[2]

Finally, in the very last verses of Exodus, the *Mishkan* was complete. Herein lies the irony. The very leader who ensured the instructions were carried out precisely was then forbidden to enter the space: "Moses could not enter the Tent of Meeting, because the cloud had settled upon it and the Presence of God filled the Tabernacle" (Ex. 40:35). God filled the entire *Mishkan,* and there was no room for human beings.

This is why the word "*Vayikra*" – "And He called" – is so essential to understanding the entire book. God formally invited Moses back into the space after it was infused with the Divine Presence. Only then would the activities taking place there be full of vitality and purpose. Without God's presence, the walls would have been just walls. God's presence made the space a sanctuary. But not until Moses reentered the space did it become a true covenantal center, a meeting place where God and human dwelled together in holy partnership. Without God's invitation, Moses would never have reentered the *Mishkan*. He would have created it and remained outside its boundaries.

An ancient rabbinic text celebrates the importance of invitation (*Kalla Rabbati* 8:11). God called (*Vayikra*) to Moses from Mount Sinai: "God called to him from the mountain" (Ex. 19:3). Just like our opening verse in *Parashat Vayikra,* a momentous occasion calls for a formal invitation. God calls out to Moses, reflecting His active engagement with humanity, as Rabbi Jonathan Sacks notes in his book, *The Great Partnership*: "Far from being timeless and immutable, God in the Hebrew Bible is active, engaged, in constant dialogue with His people, calling, urging, warning, challenging and forgiving."[3] Calling is part of this essential, divine dialogue. Moses, in turn, called out to other leaders at the foot of the mountain: "Moses called (*Vayikra*) the elders of the people and put before them all that God had commanded him" (19:7). Later, in prophetic literature, Isaiah calls the people to attention: "When I call (*korei*) to them, they stand up together" (Is. 48:13). There is a reason we have a term for professions and obsessions that speak to the most alive part of us: a calling. We feel called.

Leaders grow people by inviting them to a task, to a project, or to a new level of service. Calling matters because it lets people know that they matter. "You're always welcome" is not the same invitation as, "I was thinking about you. I'd like to invite you…" Think of a time you were not invited to take on a leadership responsibility. You felt excluded, unimportant, or even rejected. Now think of a time you were invited to assume a significant role. Whether or not you said, "Yes," you still felt special and included. You can gift that gift to others.

Personal Leadership Reflection

What invitation can you extend right now that would grow someone else's leadership?

פרשת צו • *Parashat Tzav*

The Perpetual Flame

Since childhood, I have been mesmerized by the *ner tamid,* the permanently lit ritual lamp in every synagogue that hangs in front of the *aron,* the holy ark. One of my favorite times of the week then and now is right after Friday night services, when everyone congregates in the social hall before dispersing for the night. I often slip back into the sanctuary and sit in the front row for a few minutes by myself. The room is always very dark except for that light. When the synagogue is well lit, it's hard to see that small lamp and the difference it really makes. To this day, I find it among the most meditative of spaces. It's a place where I go to reflect on the week past. I find in that quiet sanctuary, empty of people, a place of clarity.

In *Parashat Tzav,* we have the foundational image that is captured in the *ner tamid* of every synagogue: "The fire on the altar shall be kept burning, not to go out: Every morning the priest shall feed wood to it, lay out the burnt offering on it, and turn into smoke the fat parts of the offerings of well-being. A perpetual fire (*esh tamid*) shall be kept burning on the altar, not to go out" (Lev. 6:5–6). Rashi comments that one who extinguishes its flame transgresses not one but two commandments – that the fire of the altar remain lit and that it also never be extinguished.

Rabbi Abraham ibn Ezra explains the repetition differently. The prohibition is repeated "to add that it shall not go out during the day." Even when you cannot see it, you must know that a flame is always burning. Ḥizkuni, a medieval French exegete, adds that even when the Israelites were journeying through the wilderness, the flame never went out. If you've ever tried walking with a candle, you know how hard it is to travel while holding a flame. One midrash Ḥizkuni cites suggests that a metal cover was used to prevent the flame from going out. If you want to maintain the flame, you have to protect it. According to the Talmud, the eternal flame on the altar was used to light the Menora (Yoma 45b). One light brings more light.

Maimonides, in his philosophical opus *Guide for the Perplexed,* writes about the symbol of a small light as a metaphor for wisdom and the power of parables: "A person let a pearl drop in his house, which was dark and full of furniture. Now this pearl is there, but he does not see it and does not know where it is. It is as though it was no longer in his possession since he can get no benefit from it until… he lights a lamp." We often find ourselves in the dark – I can only speak personally – but we know a solution lies somewhere in the opacity, and one small light in that darkness makes all the difference.

That light that burns perpetually on the altar and in the synagogue reminds us of the flame that burned but did not consume the burning bush, where Moses received his calling. It prompts us to remember the way that Mount Sinai was aflame with God's presence and also brings to mind the Hanukka menora as a symbol of optimism amidst oppression that became the logo of the State of Israel. These holy fires are unlike larger, uncontrolled conflagrations that we associate with darker periods of Jewish history, as Rabbi Jonathan Sacks wrote in a column in *The Times*: "Somehow faith outlives every attempt to destroy it. Its symbol is not the fierce fire that burns synagogues and sacred scrolls and murdered lives. It is the fragile flame we, together with our children and grandchildren, light in our homes, singing God's story, sustained by our hope."[4]

When we think of those fires that tried to destroy us, we can take comfort in an obscure detail of Jewish law. One scholar of the Talmud was concerned that the wine libations offered on the altar might put out the flame, citing our verse: "A perpetual fire shall be kept burning on the altar, it shall not go out" (Lev. 6:6). The novel conclusion is itself telling: "Extinguishing in a partial manner is not called extinguishing" (Zevaḥim 91b). A sprinkle or trickle of wine is unlikely to put out the fire, even if the flames are temporarily diminished. They will soon come back to their full size and provide the same light and heat they did before. This, too, is a pearl of leadership wisdom to treasure. Our light may become temporarily dimmed by circumstance, but we must maintain the still, small flame – watched over and protected – so that it will never go out.

Is that not the ultimate function of the *ner tamid* – to let us know as a small people that we must bring light, be the light, and seek out light, that leaders must take a role in stewarding and protecting this light? Is this not what Isaiah meant when he called upon us to be a light to the nations? He was not posturing with spiritual confidence but making a statement of collective obligation: "I the Lord in My grace, have summoned you, and I have grasped you by the hand. I created you, and appointed you a covenant people, a light of nations – opening eyes deprived of light, rescuing prisoners from confinement, from the dungeon of those who sit in darkness" (Is. 42:6–7). God holds our hands and points us in the direction of darkness, as if to say, "You are My partner. Now go spread your light."

The world can be a dark, dark place. Go to where there is darkness, says the prophet, because one small light can make all the difference. The same was said of Moses as a leader: he was like a candle that provided the flame for other candles (Numbers Rabba 11:17).

Personal Leadership Reflection

What darkness in the world needs your light right now?

פרשת שמיני • *Parashat Shemini*

When Leaders Atone

A new museum just opened in Brooklyn, curated by a licensed psychologist. The Museum of Failure is a collection of projects and products from around the world that flopped. It's easy to ask, "What were they thinking?" with hindsight. It's harder to recognize that some failures turn into innovations. The museum is designed to help people take a meaningful look at mistakes and risks and accept that there is often progress hidden in failure. But not always. Sometimes, failure is just a soul-crushing realization that is relived again and again.

In the ancient world, failure was often acknowledged and atoned for with the giving of a sacrifice. A sacrifice could not reset or erase a mistake but created a ritualized break from it that required a significant loss or renunciation from the giver, let alone the animal. When we use the word "sacrifice" today, we usually mean that someone is ready to give up something of personal importance for a belief or an ideal or to achieve a particular result. On some level, the giving has to hurt to be meaningful.

The laws surrounding all sacrifices in *Vayikra*, the book of Leviticus, are highly detailed. Moshe Halbertal, in his book, *On Sacrifice*, explains that ritual, in the case of sacrifices, "is an attempt to grapple with the inherent unpredictability of rejection."[5] When we give a gift to God, whether out of thanks or guilt, it is not like a human gift cycle. In a human gift exchange, I give a gift to you on the presumption that, when the occasion calls for it, you will do the same for me, as part of a normative social standard. It's an expression of social capital.

But when a person gives a gift to God or to any authority figure, there is no expectation of reciprocity. We give gifts to superiors to seek their approval, to appease them, or to put ourselves in their good graces, not to get a reciprocal token of their affection. With such gifts, we might worry that the gift will be ignored or even rejected, as was the case for Cain early in Genesis: "...to Cain and his offering [God] paid no heed. Cain was much distressed, and his face fell" (Gen. 4:5). Sometimes, as in the story of Cain, no explanation for the dismissal is offered.

To avoid rejection in such gift giving, we do as much research as we can to get it right. Halbertal reasons that all the details and protocols about sacrifices related in the book of Leviticus serve as a "shield for the human approaching God. Any change in the protocol might be lethal.... The one who is offering a sacrifice wished to appear before God, to be made visible.... And yet being in the spotlight before power can be terrifying."[6] Halbertal warns that those sacrificing should not have "wrongly presumed intimacy" with the Divine, the way that two of Aaron's sons did.

In *Parashat Shemini*, "Moses said: 'This is what God has commanded that you do, that the Presence of God may appear to you. Then Moses said to Aaron: 'Come forward to the altar and sacrifice your sin offering and your burnt offering, making expiation for yourself and for the people; and sacrifice the people's offering and make expiation for them, as God has commanded'" (Lev. 9:6–7). This must have been, using Halbertal's explanation, the most terrifying sacrifice of all. Part of Aaron's job as *kohen gadol*, high priest, was to seek expiation for himself and his people.

Failure was assumed with the job description. It's impossible to serve others as a leader and not make hundreds of mistakes, as Rabbi Jonathan Sacks wrote in *Lessons in Leadership*: "Leaders make mistakes. That is an occupational hazard of the role. Managers follow the rules, but leaders find themselves in situations for which there are no rules."[7]

Where there are no clear guidelines or precedents, leaders must rely on common sense, instinct, and experience. It's easy to get it wrong.

Rabbi Abraham ibn Ezra's commentary on Leviticus 9:7 explains Aaron's role here: "There is a divine command that you make atonement for yourself and for all of the people. You will atone for yourself with a sin-offering bullock. Afterward you will atone for the congregation by offering the people's sacrifice, for a person cannot atone for another unless he has been purified from all sin." It's not only that a leader must be cleansed of sin in order to represent others on the altar; in order to achieve atonement, the leader must confess his own sins first. Leaders might complain about or belittle their followers or regard themselves as superior. The atonement sacrifice only worked because the high priest first cataloged his own transgressions, making him humbly aware of his own smallness, before he confessed on behalf of the people.

Imagine, for a moment, if all leaders today – in every field – had a day of atonement, when they had to spend an *entire* day both reflecting on and confessing their mistakes and bearing on their own shoulders the wrongdoing of those they serve so that they might ask forgiveness. Perhaps many of today's scandals involving the narcissistic, even criminal behaviors of politicians, CEOs, celebrity athletes, and entertainers might be kept in better check. Such leaders do not take responsibility for others because they also do not feel accountable themselves. Every day, every newspaper carries such headlines.

In contrast, the high priest is accountable for himself and for everyone else. It's an astonishing model of leadership. Gifford Thomas, in his article, "Leaders Take All the Blame and Give Away All the Credit," writes that leaders "take responsibility...for EVERYTHING. They turn each misstep into an opportunity to learn from the mistake instead of pointing figures; they pull the thumb and ask themselves, 'What could I have done differently?'" In a total shift of mindset, leaders "find a lesson while others only see a problem. They privately address their subordinates' mistakes with them but take the blame publicly without dissent. If someone slipped up, they pick them up, they don't point the finger and pass the blame."[8]

The greatest act of responsibility as a leader is to hold the mistakes of others as your own. On the one hand, leaders cannot be liable for every failure of his or her followers. On the other hand, responsible leaders must always reflect on the problems in a culture that they are ultimately responsible for by asking three essential questions:

- Is there anything I could have done to *prevent* this problem?
- What did I *contribute* to this problem (possibly by ignoring it or not taking it seriously enough)?
- What can I *learn* from the way I handled this problem that might prevent failure in the future?

Ultimately, a leader is always a learner who understands the importance of direction, reflection, and course correction.

Personal Leadership Reflection

When has failure been your greatest teacher?

פרשת תזריע • *Parashat Tazria*

Taking the Lead

Our Torah reading of *Tazria* is among the most challenging in the Torah. It is about a spiritual skin affliction that we erroneously call leprosy, its many variations, and the places it can reach: one's body, one's clothing, and even one's house. Instead of going to the ancient equivalent of a dermatologist, the person infected notifies a *kohen*, a priest. If the illness is spiritual with a physical manifestation, then the doctor, too, must be a spiritual one. Who better than the high priest to diagnose the rash?

> When a person has on the skin of the body a swelling, a rash, or a discoloration, and it develops into a scaly affection on the skin of the body, it shall be reported to Aaron the priest or to one of his sons, the priests. The priest shall examine the affection on the skin of the body: If hair in the affected patch has turned white and the affection appears to be deeper than the skin of the body, it is a leprous affection; when the priest sees it, he shall pronounce the person impure. (Lev. 13:1–2)

The priest has the unenviable job of declaring the sufferer impure and has the more gratifying job of declaring that same person free of *tzaraat* when the inflammation disappears: "...the priest shall pronounce the person pure. It is a rash; after washing those clothes, that person shall be pure" (13:6). In his commentary on 13:1, Rabbi Abraham ibn Ezra writes that "this commandment was directly communicated to Aaron because all human maladies shall be determined according to his pronouncement. Aaron shall declare who is clean and who is unclean." The fate of this sick person was placed on the priest's shoulders.

Referring to the same verse, Rabbi Samson Raphael Hirsch observes that "naming Aaron next to Moses at the introduction to certain laws... is to indicate the quite special importance of these laws, not only for the theoretical understanding of these laws and the establishment of them for practical use in life... but also for the training and education of all the individual people." What education might the community need from Aaron's inclusion in this supervisory role?

When it comes to this diagnosis, we might expect three people to weigh in on the problem, because in most cases of Jewish law, a person presents his or her case before a *beit din*, a Jewish court of three. For more serious crimes, sometimes a court of twenty-three is necessary, and for certain issues a full Sanhedrin had to meet. In two places in the Talmud, however, we learn that only one priest is necessary to determine this malady: "The verse states, 'And he shall be brought to Aaron the priest or to one of his sons, the priests' (Lev. 13:2). Learn from this that even one priest may view leprous marks" (Nidda 50a, Sanhedrin 34b). One priest alone is trusted in this role. Again, our question is why?

One answer may lie in a distinction Rabbi Jonathan Sacks makes in his book *Ceremony & Celebration* between the role of a prophet and that of a priest: "The prophet lives in the immediacy of the moment, not in the endlessly reiterated cycles of time.... The priest represents order, structure, continuity, the precisely formulated ritual followed in strict, meticulous obedience."[9] Assigning the priest the task of identifying *tzaraat*, leprous boils, and then declaring the disease over is a way to reinstate order into a situation of chaos because everything that surrounds the sufferer is at risk of infection. Rabbi Sacks continues his description of the priest's foundational orientation: "For the priest, the key words of the religious life are *kadosh*, holy, and *tahor*, pure. To be a Jew is to be set apart: That is what the word *kadosh*, holy, actually means. This in turn has to do with the special closeness the Jewish people have to God." We can extrapolate from here that because the priest is exquisitely sensitive to purity and can make fine distinctions between what is pure and impure, it only takes one priest to make the designation.

Another approach is to think of the priest in this role as a leader doing a job that others may shun for fear of infection. The declaration was likely humiliating to the individual afflicted, alienating him society and from those he loves. This fear of disease may have also led others to marginalize the leper and refuse to usher him back into the community at the earliest possible time. We can trust that one priest, sanctified and prepared to face the challenge, would do his very best to ensure fair and efficient treatment, because he represents God. Of all people, it is the priest who should see the divine in others and remove any barrier to achieving godliness.

The priest, by modeling these difficult activities, also helped others reintegrate the sufferer. After all, if the holiest person in the community declares a person afflicted safe to return to normal life, then that declaration must be good enough for everyone. The leader sets the standard of care and concern for others. Dr. Tracy Brower claims that "one of the most significant responsibilities as a leader is to model the way."[10] When it comes to managing others, she writes, "People pay attention to you as a manager – perhaps more than you realize – including what you say, how you react, and the decisions you make." She also adds that when leading through hard times, the leader must stay "connected to key information. As leaders rise in the hierarchy, they run the risk of being increasingly insulated from key information because people are taught to bring them solutions, not problems. To be resilient, you must be informed, so do all you can to ask for difficult details as much as you seek solutions." The priest's knowledge of every boil and scale and his intimate involvement with all stations of society in this diagnosis kept him connected to key information and close to those he ultimately served.

Brower makes another striking point. "Sometimes leaders may avoid asking too many questions because they fear being invasive."

She states that in one study about the mental health and wellness of employees, "…employees felt better when leaders checked in and demonstrated they cared. Take cues from people about whether they want to talk through issues, and back off if they don't. But be clear about the fact that you are paying attention." The priest in this *parasha* asked lots of questions. He had to pay attention, and attention is something that followers crave from leaders. The questions he asked the person afflicted were a way of intently focusing on the problem and potential solutions in the life of one person from someone who cared profoundly.

Brower offers another role that leaders play in hard times. They provide psychological safety: "…a feeling that employees are secure, can take appropriate risks and bring their best to their work." Knowing that the high priest had this body of information and would use it to ameliorate the life of any Israelite provided psychological safety to the community.

Personal Leadership Reflection

As a leader, describe how you provide psychological safety and acute concern to those you lead.

פרשת מצורע • *Parashat Metzora*

Where Leadership Lives

The last words of Mercutio, a dying character in Shakespeare's *Romeo and Juliet,* are used to curse the two families embroiled in this romantic tragedy, "A plague on both your houses." So famous is this line that it's become a common idiom to indicate that both sides of an argument are at fault. A plague on a house here refers to those within the house, the unit that contains and holds a family together.

Cursing a home is, in effect, wishing that all that a person holds dear and is most personal is reduced to a state of ruin. This is why homelessness is such a tragedy. There is no place to set down one's life. One of the most impactful books I've read in years and assigned to students is Matthew Desmond's *Evicted: Poverty and Profit in the American City*. I knew almost nothing about the increase in eviction in the United States until I read Desmond's Pulitzer Prize-winning book. There he writes, "It is hard to argue that housing is not a fundamental human need. Decent, affordable housing should be a basic right for everybody in this country. The reason is simple: without stable shelter, everything else falls apart."[11]

The home, he argues, is the center of our lives: "It is a refuge from the grind of work, the pressure of school, and the menace of the streets."

At home, we can be ourselves. "Everywhere else, we are someone else. At home, we remove our masks."[12] Psychically, the home is something else. It is "the wellspring of personhood. It is where our identity takes root and blossoms." The significance of a home changes as we age. It can be the place of our childhood games, our adolescent retreat, our middle-age status, and our senior shelter. A home for most people is an island of own's own identity that keeps the people and objects within it in intimate relation. I once saw a pair of worn clogs nailed onto a front door of a historic home and was told that it signaled to those outside the house that the family finished its journey and finally settled. There must have been immense relief when all the trunks had been unpacked, and the safety of the hearth was established. "Peace in the home," writes Rabbi Jonathan Sacks in *Faith in the Future,* "is where world peace begins."[13]

But what happens to children when the little the family owns is thrown out onto the curb because a parent cannot cover the rent? There is no single place to call one's own. In this book, which depicts the lives of families shattered by eviction and the slum lords who profit from them, Desmond shares the terrible truth: "Eviction is a cause, not just a condition, of poverty." This is not only a matter of people pulling up their bootstraps and holding down a job. Predators exploit the poor, and once a family suffers eviction, it is much harder to rent again, creating a cycle of homelessness. We shield ourselves from much of the havoc that may be taking place around our own neighborhoods, especially to single mothers and children.

Our Torah reading, *Parashat Metzora,* offers us a scenario of internal crisis for the Israelites when they arrive in the Land of Israel and become homeowners: "When you enter the land of Canaan that I give you as a possession, and I inflict an eruptive plague upon a house in the land you possess, the owner of the house shall come and tell the priest, saying, 'Something like a plague has appeared upon my house'" (Lev. 14:34–35). A spiritual malady caused by human failure affects the walls of own's home. A spiritual healer, a *kohen,* must be called for a diagnosis. The homeowner cannot say with any certainty what is wrong, only that something *like* a plague appeared on his walls. Sometimes we know something is wrong in our own houses, but we cannot name it with any clarity. Only an outsider looking in can see what we cannot.

Rabbi Samson Raphael Hirsch in his comments on this unusual plague writes that the plague "does not refer to the building as such, but to the personality of its inhabitant to whom it is evidently addressed. It is not the house which is affected but 'the home,' the domesticity, the sphere which individualizes a human life toward the general community, which a house represents" (Lev. 14:52–53). Among the problems Rabbi Hirsch detects is "selfishness which shuts itself up against being of service in neighborly kindness" and points us to a famous maxim in *Ethics of the Fathers*: "There are four types of character in human beings: One who says: 'What's mine is mine, and what's yours is yours'; this is common, and some say this is a Sodom type of character. One who says, 'What's mine is yours, and what's yours is mine,' is an unlearned person. One who says, 'What's mine is yours, and what's yours is yours,' is a pious person. And one who says, 'What's mine is mine, and what's yours is mine,' is a wicked person" (5:10). Human beings, Rabbi Hirsch writes, "can only begin to have a justified social existence by readiness for self-sacrifice and service to others."

If the problem persists, then increasingly serious measures are taken. First the walls are scraped: "The house shall be scraped inside all around, and the coating that is scraped off shall be dumped outside the city in an impure place" (Lev. 14:41). Whatever is on those walls must come down. If this is insufficient, the whole edifice must be destroyed: "The house shall be torn down – its stones and timber and all the coating on the house – and taken to an impure place outside the city" (14:45). Think of a renovation. Sometimes walls just need a new coat of paint. Sometimes they need to be replastered, but sometimes, if they are in real disrepair, they must be taken down altogether. Sometimes, in the life of family, the home has to be rebuilt.

The purification of the home involves several symbolic ingredients, among them a piece of cedar wood – the most resplendent of trees – and hyssop – a plant with very tiny leaves. The one who was a proud homeowner has been reduced in stature to humility. The priest also mixes blood and water and sprinkles the mixture on the house. He then sets another bird free: "... he shall set the live bird free outside the city in the open country. Thus, he shall make expiation for the house, and it shall be pure" (14:53). Here, Rabbi Hirsch adds that the "bird allows the house to be free from sin" as if to remove "the unsocial past of the house and give it the possibility of a pure future again."

The house – the *bayit* – is always more than a home. It is where holiness resides. The *Mishkan,* our portable sanctuary, means "dwelling." The *Beit HaMikdash* is literally the House of the Holy. The *beit midrash* is the house of study. In this Torah reading, the spiritual leader diagnoses and repairs the home. He understands that home life is a blessing that comes with challenges, and that just as God lives in a house of glory, so must humans. Sometimes that house is broken by misdeeds and dysfunction. Sometimes it is broken by poverty. A leader knows that we cannot make our homes places of true refuge when others live without stability.

Personal Reflective Question

How are the walls of your house doing? What can you do to help repair someone else's home?

פרשת אחרי מות • *Parashat Aḥarei Mot*

Leadership and the Scapegoat

One of the most unusual rituals in the entire book of Leviticus is found in *Parashat Aḥarei Mot*. Aaron is commanded to take two male goats and place lots upon them as a means of expiation. One goat is to be sacrificed, and the other, the mysterious Azazel, is to be sent off into the wilderness.

> Aaron shall take the two he-goats and let them stand before God at the entrance of the Tent of Meeting; and he shall place lots upon the two goats, one marked for God and the other marked for Azazel. Aaron shall bring forward the goat designated by lot for God, which he is to offer as a sin offering; while the goat designated by lot for Azazel shall be left standing alive before God, to make expiation with it and to send it off to the wilderness for Azazel. (Lev. 16:7–10)

The word "*ez*" in Hebrew is a goat, and "*azal*" means to be gone, making the goat in this conjunction an animal that has been banished. Rashi explains that the word "*Azazel*" is a compound of the Hebrew for strong and mighty. He also cites the Talmud, which states that the word means a "precipitous and flinty rock" (Yoma 67b), implying that the goat should meet its death by being cast off a rough, mountainous cliff. The Sages of the Talmud interpret our verses to mean that the goats should be as equal in size and appearance as possible (Ḥullin 11a).

Maimonides explains that on Yom Kippur, the high priest confessed for the sins of all of Israel on this goat, the severe and non-severe transgressions, those intentional and those not intentional, and then sent the goat away (*Mishneh Torah, Hilkhot Teshuva* 1:2). Maimonides also adds an important qualifier: This ritual only worked to atone for certain wrongdoings if the people themselves repented. This unusual goat could not magically carry away sins if those committing them felt neither agency nor determination to change.

This ancient rite had important and potent symbolism for those cleansing themselves of sin. The effects of sin can be crippling. It can lead people to internalize that they are only the sum total of the wrongs they have ever done.

Wrongdoing can make people label themselves as unworthy and lead to a downward psychic spiral of behavior. Externalizing sin and having it be symbolically marched far away into the wilderness may have had a liberating impact, allowing people to begin to truly heal themselves. Wilderness is the perfect location for the goat; it represents a tangle of uncertainty, fear, danger, loss, and risk. Wilderness is a place of both disequilibrium and freedom. Sending this goat into the physical wilderness may have allowed the high priest and those he prayed for to imagine that all the internal chaos of sin fled far away, leaving them cleansed with a sense of returned order and a renewed sense of their own goodness.

This fascinating ritual also gave birth to the word "scapegoat" – someone who is blamed for the mistakes or faults of others, often unfairly, to relieve others of responsibility. When we blame others, we remove the burden of accountability from ourselves. Yet the use of this word today in common parlance is the exact opposite of its ancient meaning, according to Maimonides. The goat was there to help make sin visible and pronounced to all of Israel; it worked as a symbol only when the community was committed to change.

Rabbi Jonathan Sacks, in his book *Judaism's Life-Changing Ideas*, describes the perils of a scapegoat mentality: "It happens whenever a society feels that something is badly amiss, when there is a profound cognitive dissonance between the way things are and the way people think they ought to be. People are then faced with two possibilities. They can either ask, 'What did we do wrong?' and start to put it right, or they can ask, 'Who did this to us?' and search for a scapegoat."[14]

The scapegoat is a common hazard in leadership. Leaders who don't want to take responsibility for problems within their organizations commonly look around for people and conditions to blame. Leadership consultant Suket Gandhi writes that "Scapegoat Leaders" are quick to blame others for their own shortcomings and their inability to achieve expected outcomes. "These leaders have the mindset of finding a scapegoat for everything that has not gone well so that they can protect themselves." He claims the tribe of scapegoats keeps growing and says that the expression "Scapegoat Leader" is itself an oxymoron: "A scapegoat is a victim, and a leader cannot have a victim complex."[15]

Leaders can also become scapegoats for much deeper systemic issues that boards or administrators do not want to acknowledge or treat. Roberto Motta in "Are You a Leader or a Scapegoat?" describes what happens when companies identify a scapegoat for their problems: "The catharsis achieved by firing the unsuccessful company executive serves the important function of bringing relief to the people who remain in the organization, as well as hope that things will improve." It also reinforces "everyone's belief in individual action. These people were fired because they did not do enough. If you work harder and better, you will not be fired. But, in reality, those who are truly guilty for the health and well-being of an organization are not identified or punished. They can then seize control of the chaos for their own ends. The factors contributing to organizations' problems are ignored."[16]

The scapegoat of the Hebrew Bible was meant to achieve the very opposite of what scapegoating does today. It was the high priest himself who was charged with confessing on the day and sending the goat away. In full view of his community, the high priest took responsibility for his sins, those of his household, and for those of all of Israel. When he intoned the words, he understood his responsibility as the leader to own his sins and those of his flock.

Personal Leadership Reflection

Who and what have you blamed for your mistakes? In only one paragraph, rewrite the story of your own accountability to avoid making the same mistakes in the future.

פרשת קדשים • *Parashat Kedoshim*

Thanks for the Feedback

In *Parashat Kedoshim,* the challenging mandate to correct friends and colleagues who have erred or lost their way is sandwiched between a complex cluster of interpersonal emotions: "You shall not hate your friend in your heart. Correct your friend and incur no guilt on his account. You shall not take vengeance or bear a grudge against members of your people. Love your neighbor as yourself: I am God" (Lev. 19:17–18). In only two biblical verses, we mention hate, guilt, revenge, and love.

It's not only the hatred of friends that is prohibited but the hatred of strangers. Rabbi Jonathan Sacks, in a very profound observation, helps us understand why we should never hate the stranger: "If you are human, so is he. If he is less than human, so are you.... Why should I not hate the stranger? Because the stranger is me."[17] We have all been strangers and felt the contempt that people express toward strangers. But not hating a friend, a prohibition in our Torah reading, feels like another dialogical command entirely.

Maimonides, in his "Book of Character Traits," helps us think about what we might call soft honesty when he writes about how to give feedback, wherever relevant, to fulfill this biblical commandment. In the sixth chapter, he advises that the one giving feedback should make clear what's at stake for the person receiving it. These conversations, he recommends, should always take place in private and with patience. The giver must employ gentle language and remind the receiver that it is for his or her own good. Sometimes, in the face of denial or resistance, the person dispensing the criticism must be insistent and even sharp. There are indeed times that call for urgency and persistence to prevent a person from self-harm or from hurting others.

Maimonides concludes with what is at stake for the giver, not only the receiver: "Whoever has the possibility of rebuking [a wrongdoer] and fails to do so is considered responsible for that sin, for he had the opportunity to rebuke [the wrongdoer]." We may opt not to say anything, but, because the Torah believes we are responsible for one another, we each hold some of the wrongdoer's blame if we stay silent. Ultimately, what this communicates is that the culture of any society is dependent on the behaviors of every member of that society.

At the same time, not everyone can handle constructive criticism. Proverbs 9:8 wisely states that we must be judicious when correcting others: "Do not rebuke a scoffer, for he will hate you; correct a wise person and he will love you." People who are defensive cannot grow. It's not worth saying anything because they will not listen. People who are wise, however, thrive on feedback.

If you're a leader, you're likely offering and hearing feedback all the time, so it's important to get good at giving and receiving it. Douglas Stone, in his book on giving and hearing feedback, claims that "receiving feedback sits at the intersection of… two needs – our drive to learn and our longing for acceptance."[18] We want to grow, and to do that effectively we need the observations and recommendations of others. We also want to be recognized and praised. Stone contends that we generally get too much feedback. He warns that before you give him any constructive criticism, "… know this: I've heard it before. I've been graded, rated, and ranked. Coached, screened, and scored. I've been picked first, picked last, and not picked at all. And that was just kindergarten."[19]

Stone reminds us that no matter how carefully one person critiques another, the person on the receiving end has control over what he lets in and how he makes sense of what he is hearing. That's why he believes we need to help people become more skillful listeners, reshaping feedback from an instrument of rejection or criticism to one of curiosity and learning, even when "it is off base, unfair, poorly delivered, and frankly, you're not in the mood." Dr. David Burkus writes that even though good feedback is a gift, it is also a risk. He offers a few helpful steps for those on the receiving end:

- Respond to feedback with a "thank you" first. It can make you aware of your own defensiveness.
- Restate what you heard so that you can check for understanding; let the giver know they've been heard.
- Mention what you are changing. If you don't use feedback to change anything, growth never happens.[20]
- Seek out more feedback. That's how you get better at work and at life.

Turning back to the verses in our *parasha*, we notice the unusual ending to the string of emotions mentioned above: "Love your neighbor as yourself: I am God." I am the God who sees through to the heart where the resentment, revenge, and bitterness lies. I am the God who cuts through the false feelings, the acting, and the superficial attempts to make peace. We might lie to ourselves so profoundly that we don't even realize that our hatreds are hard to conceal. Punctuating these verses with "I am God" also lets us know that because each and every one of us is God's concern, we imitate God when we make others the core focus of our lives. Hate is a poison. Anne Lamott, in *Traveling Mercies: Some Thoughts on Faith*, famously wrote, "Not forgiving is like drinking rat poison and then waiting for the rat to die."[21]

Explaining the connective tissue in these few verses can help us understand why we should correct a friend or colleague at all. When we let wounds fester, we develop negative feelings that risk turning into disgust and resentment if not articulated and healed. The vehemence of these emotions can also turn inward into regret and shame. Hate is forbidden in the Torah. Love is commanded. Honesty lives somewhere in between.

Personal Leadership Reflection

How well do you accept feedback? Name a time that a piece of feedback changed you.

פרשת אמר • *Parashat Emor*

Scrupulous Leadership

I've always loved the word "scrupulous," even though it can be a mouthful to pronounce. It offers the subtle combination of meticulousness, thorough attention to details, and the moral quality of avoiding wrongdoing in the smallest of ways. It communicates the nexus of careful, intentional thought and deed in relationship with honesty, integrity, and righteousness. It describes leadership at its best. Sadly, we don't expect our leaders to be scrupulous today when it comes to ethics. We've lowered the bar so much that some leaders step right over it.

Our *parasha, Emor,* demands that the priestly class, in particular, be very careful about their conduct, especially when with regard to managing donations to the Temple: "God spoke to Moses, saying: Instruct Aaron and his sons to be scrupulous (*veyinazru*) about the sacred donations that the Israelite people consecrate to Me, lest they profane My holy name" (Lev. 22:1–2). Rashi explains that the root of fastidious care – *nezer* – means to distance oneself or set oneself apart. He uses two biblical prooftexts to support his explanation from both Ezekiel 14:7 and Isaiah 1:41. We recognize this word from the *nazir,* the ascetic who refrains from certain behaviors to live a less worldly existence. He sets himself apart. *Nezer* also refers to a crown around the head; the Nazirite does not cut his hair, perhaps to bring attention to the role the mind plays in self-sanctification.

One passage in the Jerusalem Talmud (Shekalim 3:2) explains that scrupulous behavior was also expected of those who collected funds for the *Beit HaMikdash*, our holy Temple, to cover the cost of offerings. The coin gatherer was not allowed to wear clothing with cuffs. He was also not allowed to wear shoes, sandals, tefillin, or amulets, all places where coins might be hidden from view. Having authority and exposure to a lot of money can tempt even the most scrupulous. Avoid suspicion and take every precaution not to arouse it. The talmudic passage concludes with a verse from Proverbs: "Find favor and approval in the eyes of God and humans" (Prov. 3:4).

Speaking of endings, our chapter in *Parashat Emor* ends where it begins: "You shall faithfully observe My commandments: I am the Lord. You shall not profane My holy name, that I may be sanctified in the midst of the Israelite people – I, God, who sanctify you, I who brought you out of the land of Egypt to be your God, I, the Lord" (Lev. 22:31–33). It's not easy to know what it means to sanctify God's name and not profane it. It might all come down to one question: Does every small action of ours reflect uprightness?

Leadership expert Dan McCarthy challenges readers to think hard about this question. McCarthy resurrects the game Scruples to ask leaders how they would handle different scenarios. Here are just five of his twenty questions:[22]

1. Your manager congratulates you for a brilliant suggestion and hints at a promotion. Your employee gave you the idea. Do you mention this to the manager?
2. A colleague is out of his office. You notice his paycheck stub on his desk. Do you glance at it?
3. Your manager demands to know what a coworker is saying behind his back. It's not flattering. Do you tell him?
4. You want to quit a job without notice, but you need a good reference from your employer. Do you invent a family health emergency?

5. You decide not to hire someone because he's wearing a nose ring. When he asks why he didn't make it, do you give the real reason?

We can add lots of questions to McCarthy's list. There are the big questions about leadership scrupulousness, like: "Am I honest in what I say and do? Do I use language that hurts or heals? Do I curse or gossip too much about colleagues?" And then there are the smaller but no less important questions that are the modern-day version of the coin-free charity collector's clothing: "Do I take office supplies for personal use without asking permission or checking on the company's policy?"[23]

At the heart of scrupulous behavior is the understanding that small acts of misconduct can grow over time into larger acts of moral corruption, whereas small acts of honesty can grow a reputation of trust. Who would you hire, the person who takes paperclips home or the person who asks before taking something for personal use? I know my answer.

Our Torah reading this week puts another frame on these questions: Godliness. Sanctification opens our chapter and closes it. If you want to strengthen your relationship with God, care about the details. If you want to strengthen a relationship with others, care about the details. If you want to strengthen your leadership, care about the details. All of the small details add up to a reputation of love, integrity, goodness, warmth and depth.

In his book *Morality*, Rabbi Jonathan Sacks explains that "bad behaviour can easily become contagious, but so can good behaviour, and it usually wins out in the long run."[24]

Personal Leadership Reflection

When it comes to your leadership, how scrupulous are you?

פרשת בהר • *Parashat Behar*

The Eternal Stranger

How we treat strangers is the mark of our humanity. Unfortunately, it is too easy to demoralize strangers. One need not belittle strangers to make those unlike us feel foreign. One need only ignore the stranger to make another human being feel invisible. The English word "stranger" only amplifies the problem. It implies that someone who is unlike us is strange, deepening our natural suspicion of "the other." It also describes the complex and confusing feelings of being in a new place and not being familiar with the customs, language, and culture that intensifies the alienation. The estrangement can happen at many levels; a person who is new to a country may experience the full weight of this distance, but even those new to an institution – with its own customs, language, and culture – can feel out of place and insecure. What is the role of the leader in minimizing this social isolation?

To answer this question, we turn to a verse in our Torah reading, *Parashat Behar*: "But the land must not be sold beyond reclaim, for the land is Mine; you are but resident aliens with Me" (Lev. 25:23). God says to the Israelites, in effect, you will be strangers permanently because you will have an unusual status: resident aliens. As such, when you enter the Land of Israel, you will never be allowed to sell it. It is not yours. It is Mine. The ultimate sign of God's ownership is the Jubilee year, when property returns to its original owner every fifty years. Knowing that this shift of land possession will occur within a generation or two means that a family can never fully exert territoriality. Ownership creates dominance. Lack of ownership creates humility.

Rashi confirms this reading on our verse, explaining that one must not resent this law because the land was never ours to begin with. Rabbi Abraham ibn Ezra provides a profoundly religious understanding of the Jubilee by directing us to a line from Psalm 90: "Lord, You are our dwelling place" (Ps. 90:1). We live with faith in God in a state of spiritual suspension. Rashi cites from the first chapter of Ecclesiastes that "one generation passes and another comes"; we learn to live over time with our uncomfortable impermanence.

Our founding father Abraham was the first to declare this status: "*I am a resident alien* among you; sell me a burial site among you, that I may remove my dead for burial" (Gen. 23:4). This is an unusual and oppositional term, a *ger toshav,* a resident alien. Either you are a resident or you are a stranger. Abraham suggests an identity that abides in the invisible hyphen between those words. Rashi here writes, "I have come from another land, but I have settled down among you." This is descriptive. Sforno explains why Abraham declares this to the Hittites after Sarah's death: "Because I used to be a stranger here, I do not possess an ancestral burial ground." This is proscriptive. I need to buy land because I do not have any within which to bury my beloved wife.

But maybe Abraham's statement is descriptive, proscriptive, and existential. Abraham's very identity was to be different than others. He was not allowed to stay in his birthplace and was told to go to someplace new where he would have to start again. If you do not come from a place, you never fully feel at home there. You understand the experience of the stranger and will always treat future strangers with compassion and a welcoming demeanor. Your tent flaps will stay open. God would always be your ultimate dwelling place. Territories have boundaries. But if you live in spiritual statelessness, God's love knows no boundaries. Such was Abraham's fate as a resident alien. Such was the fate of the

Israelites who left Egypt and are mandated dozens of times to treat the stranger with kindness.

In our short *sedra*, we are told multiple times to observe the Jubilee and reenter a state of homelessness because we are not masters but servants to a higher order. We are not landowners but worshippers. We can conquer a land from our enemies but never be its true vanquishers. "For it is to Me that the Israelites are servants: they are My servants, whom I freed from the land of Egypt – I, your Lord God" (Lev. 25:55).

This framework for our *sedra* takes us all the way back to the first chapter in Genesis. Rabbi Jonathan Sacks, in his essay "Loving the Stranger," describes why we were always meant to be strangers: "I made you into the world's archetypal strangers so that you would fight for the rights of strangers – for your own and those of others, wherever they are, whoever they are, whatever the colour of their skin or the nature of their culture, because though they are not in your image, says God, they are nonetheless in Mine."[25] If we are truly created in God's image then we look with admiration rather than distrust at those who do not look like us, because they are the very face of God.

Business thought leader Jon Mertz pits two words that are often strangers to each other, "authority and accountability," that should live in more friendly tension in the work of leadership. "Authority and accountability are necessary companions, yet they often are strangers. An imbalance of authority and accountability creates challenges for an organization and a leader. When lopsided, frustration rises."[26]

To this end, he offers four common leadership paradigms: (1) vague authority and vague accountability; (2) vague authority, clear accountability; (3) clear authority, vague accountability; and (4) clear authority and clear accountability. If authority is vague, the leader and the leader's followers are unsure if or how much to trust a leader's direction. The leader may not trust his or her own right to guide, mentor, and own authority. When leaders are not given sufficient authority, they are not allowed to make decisions; they are given a position but cannot be change makers. This is one of the most frustrating and ambivalent states for a leader and can lead to burnout and resignation.

Vague accountability means that leaders can claim authority but do not have to show outcomes or results in their work. This can eventually produce leaders who are authoritarian and narcissistic. They answer to no one. There are no checks and balances and few expectations. Mertz warns that this is a "peril for many." He advises the clear authority, clear accountability route. This "will not always be successful, but we will know where we stand and begin to work with others to recover and move forward again." Establishing and communicating a leader's roles and responsibilities helps everyone hold a leader accountable, especially the leader. Mertz reminds us that leaders, like land, have boundaries. In order not to become strangers in their work, leaders need clarity.

Personal Leadership Reflection

In what ways do you see yourself as a stranger in your leadership circles? Who among you lives as a stranger and needs to be less invisible?

פרשת בחקתי • *Parashat Beḥukotai*

What is Life Worth?

"How did I try to balance the claim of the fireman's widow against the stockbroker's children or the parents of an undocumented worker?"[27] These were some of the complex calculations made by Kenneth R. Feinberg, the special master of the government's 9/11 compensation fund. He shared this dilemma and many other difficult challenges in his fascinating book on the painful, delicate issue of post-9/11 compensation.

Feinberg did not sugarcoat the personal attacks leveled at him for doing an unenviable job. He took no compensation for the work because he did not want to appear mercenary, namely that he was making money out of someone else's greatest tragedy.[28] In this kind of leadership, many misunderstand the delicate nature of the work and the temperament required; it demands both empathy and an iron stomach to withstand the inevitable criticisms. Feinberg understood that when people railed against the compensation package, it had less to do with the money and everything to do with the unfairness of their circumstances.

What interests us and ties the compensation fund to *Parashat Beḥukotai* is the attempt to put a valuation on individual lives. There's an inherent unfairness and detached and impersonal objectification to an exercise that is by nature highly personal. Feinberg admits that "it's never fair to put a price on any life, but we do it all the time." As Feinberg said in a television interview: "Juries every day in New York, every village and hamlet in this country, listen to the evidence and then place a value on an injury, on a death. It is the American way of compensating victims."

In Jewish law, one of the ways we measure a life financially is through compensation for injury. "One who injures another is liable to pay compensation for that injury through five types of indemnity: he must pay for damage, for pain, for medical costs, for loss of livelihood, and for humiliation" (Bava Kama 83b). It is not enough to pay someone's medical bills. If you have injured another, you are obligated to cover the cost of physical pain that may far outlive whatever medical procedure one has to endure. There is loss of revenue from not working during convalescence. There is also the cost of psychological harm. The Talmud uses the example of one person slapping another in the face in public. There may be no medical harm, enduring pain, or loss of income, but the humiliation may be substantial. These costs are far from easy to determine.

In our *parasha*, however, the valuation (*erekh*) of individuals is for a different purpose – not as compensation for the dead, harm, or injury as a tool to give *tzedaka*, charity. In Leviticus 27:1–2, we read: "God spoke to Moses, saying: Speak to the Israelite people and say to them: When any party explicitly vows to the equivalent for a human being." Rashi, citing both a midrash and the Talmud, explains that there were fixed monetary valuations for someone who wanted to give money to the Sanctuary, as if to communicate metaphorically that the life of the Temple is dependent on the lives of those who benefit from it.

Rabbi Samson Raphael Hirsch explains that these freewill offerings come down to "*erekh*," a word used in modern Hebrew for "worth" or "value." This is not only monetary in meaning but also communicates the values we hold. Rabbi Hirsch states that we place one value – our individual lives – next to another value – the estimation of our worth as a person in relationship to the holiest of places. We do not measure every single life differently, even though we believe in the singularity of each human life. Rather, "this value is given as a fixed one; it has absolutely nothing to do with physical, spiritual, intellectual, moral or social qualities."

When valuations are fixed, some people who cannot afford to give the set amount would not be able to contribute. Thus, the Torah continues: "But if one cannot afford the equivalent, that person shall be presented before the priest, and the priest shall make an assessment; the priest shall make the assessment according to what the vower can afford" (Lev. 27:8). Rashi here explains, based on the talmudic volume dedicated to this form of charity (Arakhin 23b), that the priest works with the donor so that he can also feel the sense of belonging that comes with contributing to this remarkable spiritual center while making sure that he still has "a bed, mattress, and pillow, and the tools necessary for his trade." Additionally, the Talmud discusses what happens if a person made this vow when he was poor, became wealthy, and then became poor again. Does his commitment change?

These talmudic cases of injury and charity, like those in the 9/11 victim compensation fund, occupy the complicated space between establishing objective standards that will never be fully just with the subjectivity of one's individual financial and social standing. The process will always be inherently flawed, because we can never measure human worth with accuracy. And most of the time, we don't have to. But every once in a while, we have to, and it requires clarity, strength of character, and lots of time. It takes moral leadership. As we close the book of Leviticus, we are asked to personalize the Temple and its rituals by asking what we are willing to give to God to show what we value.

Personal Leadership Reflection

How would your charitable giving change if you assessed your personal worth in relation to the worth of what you are giving to?

Leadership in the Book of Numbers

פרשת במדבר • *Parashat Bemidbar*

Navigating Uncertainty

"To be a pioneer – as Jews know from our history – you have to be prepared to spend a long time in the wilderness," wrote Rabbi Jonathan Sacks.[1] This was the way he described the early Zionists who founded the State of Israel and the sacrifices they made to do so. We think of them with gratitude as we celebrate Israel's seventy-fifth year of existence. We can also travel back in time to those who made the perilous forty-year journey from Egypt to Canaan or further still to Abraham, our first wilderness pioneer.

This embrace of uncertainty is stamped all over the book of *Bemidbar*, or Numbers, that we open this week to read the Torah portion that carries the same name. The Israelites spent a long time in a state of unknowing. They had no first-hand knowledge of where they were going. They did not believe, given the harsh conditions of the desert, that they would get there. They questioned the character and competence of their leaders, uncertain that they could trust them in this wilderness, and unsure of God's intentions. That's a lot of uncertainty to carry.

In *Desert and Shepherd in Our Biblical Heritage*,[2] Nogah Hareuveni notes that the word *midbar* refers to arid places with very little rainfall and also, and ironically, as places to graze animals on the margins of human habitation. We also recognize the root word *d-v-r* as a thing or word. Some biblical scholars point out that *d-v-r* can mean that which comes after or that which comes about as a result of something else. It can signify both being and becoming.

The wilderness is often characterized by silence, but our wilderness trek was filled with noise. We complained. We threatened. We cried. We challenged. In the wilderness, a donkey spoke while some leaders were silenced. An enemy gave us a blessing. Someone recently asked me why there is not one recorded circumcision in the book of Numbers. I responded simply that there are no births recorded in this book. There are only deaths. There is a steep price to pay when you travel in the wilderness. It's a place you cross. You cannot stay there. The *midbar* is a provisional bridge between points of stability that can untether us if we stay too long.

No doubt, the Israelites also looked around them and up above them and murmured their wonder and gratitude at their very existence. This vulnerability of uncertainty may have allowed them the space, clarity, and willingness to receive the Ten Commandments in a desert and not in our homeland; the ten *dibrot* – "utterances," sharing a root with "*midbar*" – came to us where we least expected them. By receiving them at Sinai rather than in Jerusalem, we could carry them wherever we went. Their wisdom has no geographic boundaries.

The *midbar* is a perfect metaphor for leadership. Good leaders escort us through uncertainty. They provide the direction forward and offer their reassurances to keep going when we get stuck. In their *Harvard Business Review* article, Rebecca Zucker and Darin Rowell invite leaders to embrace the discomfort of not knowing and relinquish the need to be right or certain.[3]

They distinguish between leadership problems that are complicated and those that are complex. A complicated problem may be a technical one, where something must be broken down, often by experts, into its constituent parts in order to solve. A complex problem, however, is different. It may "contain many interdependent elements, some of which may be unknown and may change over time in unpredictable ways." This may precipitate lots of confusion and opinions without obvious solutions. "As a result, solutions to complex challenges typically emerge through trial and error and require the willingness, humility, and ability to act, learn, and adapt."

Zucker and Rowell ask leaders to let go of perfectionism, resist oversimplification, and avoid drawing quick conclusions to remove themselves from uncertainty. They encourage leaders to find partners in the work of uncertainty and zoom out, because being too close to a problem can vitiate the capacity to see it for what it is. Creating distance "provides you with a broader perspective and a systemic view of the issues and can shine a light on unexamined assumptions that would otherwise not be visible." Take an aerial view, and the issues looks different. So can possible solutions.

God helped us navigate the wilderness by commanding Moses to place the *Mishkan*, our portable sanctuary, at the heart of every encampment, as if to say: Know that in a place of uncertainty, what you stand for – your values – is stable and centered. It is, on some level, that which can never be truly in transition. In our *parasha*, we are given a protocol for moving the *Mishkan*: "When the Tabernacle is to set out, the Levites shall take it down, and when the Tabernacle is to be pitched, the Levites shall set it up" (Num. 1:51). Rashi explains: "Whenever they were about to set out on a journey in the wilderness from one station to another, they took the structure apart and carried it to the place where the clouds of glory rested, and there they encamped and erected it." The terrain may be different, but the core of the nation is always the same.

Personal Leadership Reflection

What core values provide you with stability during times of uncertainty?

פרשת נשא • *Parashat Naso*

To Be a Blessing

I was recently in a small store and overheard the clerk speaking Hebrew to a man at the register. The customer bought nothing but then gave the clerk a lengthy blessing for long life, good health, happiness with his family, and financial success. I asked in Hebrew if this came with every purchase and how I could get this special blessing for myself. When the customer left, the clerk turned to me and said, "This man has lost everything and came to ask me for work. I try my best to help him." When I asked about the blessing, he responded softly, "He is a *kohen* [a priest]. The only thing I could give him today was the opportunity to bless me so that he can help me."

I felt tears welling up. This clerk understood how to equalize a relationship of charitable giver and receiver by giving this man a sense of dignity through the instrument of a blessing. It was a magnificently tender moment of grace, one that made me think about the power of giving a blessing. How wonderful it would be if every time we felt blessed, we blessed others. And here, this unfortunate man who did not feel blessed was, nevertheless, willing to bless someone else.

The exchange made me think of the scene in Genesis when Jacob encountered Pharaoh and gave him a blessing on the way in and the way out of Pharaoh's chambers (Gen. 47:7–10). Jacob was a man broken. His homeland Canaan was in a crippling famine, but Jacob maintained his self-respect and self-worth by giving Pharaoh what he did still have: the capacity to bless. Rabbi Jonathan Sacks explains what this important impulse can do: "Making a blessing over life is the best way of turning life into a blessing."[4]

In fact, it is this that God commanded Abraham to do in the first act of revelation Abraham received: "I will make of you a great nation, and I will bless you; I will make your name great, and you shall be a blessing. I will bless those who bless you and curse the one who curses you. And all the families of the earth shall bless themselves by you" (Gen. 12:2–3). God blessed Abraham with the expectation that Abraham would become a blessing, give his blessings to others, and establish a nation that would be a blessing to the world. God articulated an endgame; founding a nation is insufficient. Abraham and those who followed him would only succeed if he and they were regarded as a blessing by others. This was essential to his leadership. For Rabbi Sacks, giving a blessing and being a blessing was an important theme in his work, as he once wrote, "In life, ask not 'What can I gain?' but 'What can I give?' Be a blessing to others and you will find that life has been a blessing to you."[5]

When we turn to our *parasha, Naso,* we find the blessing that the priests gave to Israel:

> "God spoke to Moses: Speak to Aaron and his sons:
> Thus, shall you bless the people of Israel. Say to them:
> God bless you and protect you!
> God deal kindly and graciously with you!
> God bestow [divine] favor upon you and grant you peace!
> Thus they shall link My name with the people of Israel, and I will bless them." (Num. 6:22–27)

R. Yishmael, one of the great Sages of the Talmud, commented on one of the verses in this passage, "You shall bless the children of Israel." He asked if the priests bless the people, who blesses the priests? To answer, he cited the later verse: "And they shall put My name upon the children of Israel, and I will bless them" (6:27). He concludes from this verse that just as the priests bless Israel, so does "the Holy One, Blessed be He, bless the priests" (Ḥullin 49a). Everyone deserves and needs to give and receive blessings.

Many parents give their children this very same blessing every Friday night. Blessing our children and grandchildren is one of the highlights of my week, almost a culmination of what all of the work of the week and the blessing of Shabbat is leading me to: blessing our children and helping them see the blessing they should be to others. Wherever we or our children are in the world, we try not to miss this special ritual that brings us together and also links us all the way back to this *parasha*. Sometimes guests in our home for Shabbat who do not have this custom or do not know Hebrew say, "I wish we had this family custom." My response is always the same: "Now's a great time to start." In person. On the phone. It may be awkward at first, but as with any practice, it gets easier over time. And it only takes a few minutes. Hebrew, English, Spanish, French – it doesn't matter. It's a Jewish language of love.

Priests are spiritual leaders. Parents are leaders in their families. There are leaders in corporate and nonprofit life, in intellectual life, in politics, and in houses of worship. All need to be a blessing, to be blessed, and to give blessings. The Irish poet John O'Donohue (1956–2008) wrote of the blessings leaders need in his poem "For a Leader." I want to share a few stanzas:

> May you have the grace and wisdom
> To act kindly, learning
> To distinguish between what is
> Personal and what is not
> May you be hospitable to criticism.
> May you never put yourself at the centre of things.
> May you act not from arrogance but out of service.
> May you work on yourself....
> May you learn to cultivate the art of presence
> In order to engage with those who meet you.

When someone fails or disappoints you,
May the graciousness with which you engage
Be their stairway to renewal and refinement....
May you have good friends
To mirror your blind spots.
May leadership be for you
A true adventure of growth.[6]

Personal Leadership Reflection

What's the best blessing you have received? What's the best blessing you've ever given?

פרשת בהעלתך • *Parashat Behaalotekha*

Leadership Through Separation

In Judaism, holiness is achieved through separation. We ritualize separations between holy and profane time, holy and profane foods and objects, and holy and profane behaviors. Separation, in this sense, requires conscious and deliberative choices to move away from or to move toward, to divide or to segment experiences through constant awareness and vigilance.

In our Torah reading for this week, *Parashat Behaalotekha*, Moses is told to separate the Levites for special service: "You shall place the Levites in attendance upon Aaron and his sons and designate them as an elevation offering to God" (Num. 8:13). In their service to the priests who offer sacrifices, the Levites themselves become a sacrifice. Through this service, they elevate themselves as offerings. Sacrifices come in a lot of forms. Gifts on the altar are one form of service. But people also sacrifice time, money, thought, and attention.

As the chapter continues, we see the special regard in which God holds the Levites:

> Thus, you shall set the Levites apart from the Israelites, and the Levites shall be Mine. Thereafter the Levites shall be qualified for the service of the Tent of Meeting, once you have purified them and designated them as an elevation offering. For they are formally assigned to Me from among the Israelites: I have taken them for Myself in place of all the first issue of the womb. (8:14–16)

In his commentary *Haamek Davar*, Rabbi Naftali Zvi Yehuda Berlin (1816–1893) explains that Moses was to command the Levites "to distinguish and separate themselves in their conduct for God's sake." Moses could articulate the rules and even set them apart to fulfill their duties, but it was up to the Levites themselves to make an internal decision to see themselves as different and separate themselves from the ways of the world to sanctify themselves.

Rabbi Berlin continues this theme in his explication of these verses. The Levites were to direct all of their actions and thoughts to God, to be carriers, literally and figuratively, of the *Mishkan* and its holy objects. This physical role was established in the very first chapter of *Bemidbar*: "You shall put the Levites in charge of the Tabernacle of the Pact, all its furnishings, and everything that pertains to it: they shall carry the Tabernacle and all its furnishings, and they shall tend it; and they shall camp around the Tabernacle" (1:50). In this capacity, *Haamek Davar* stresses that the Levites behave with the utmost piety so that they are genuinely worthy of carrying the Divine Presence as they lifted and transported the portable Sanctuary. God elevated the Levites so that they could elevate the boards, curtains, table, Menora, and all the constituent parts of the *Mishkan*. This was not only a job that required great strength. It required immensity of spirit and righteousness. Let no Israelite feel that those who carried the representation of God in the world be anything less than outstanding ambassadors of holiness.

It is at this point, on Numbers 8:15, that Rabbi Berlin explains the challenge. The Levites had to be fastidious about keeping themselves pure of thought, because those who are designated or designate themselves for special service run the risk of stumbling due to pride. "Anyone who sees himself as greater than another has an enlarged inclination" and in "getting close to holiness may bring impurity." In explaining how this played out in the prophetic book Malachi, Rabbi Berlin concludes that the greatness of the Levites and priests was the cause of their faltering. The Levites had the difficult job of separating themselves for God's service while making sure that their service was always an expression of humility, especially toward others who did not enjoy their status.

Earlier, in Exodus, God spoke through Moses with words designed to help all the Israelites, a few months out of slavery, see their own leadership and capacity to serve a higher order through the commandments they were about to receive at Sinai: "You shall be to Me a kingdom of priests and a holy nation" (Ex. 19:6). In Rabbi Jonathan Sacks's essay "Servant Leadership,"[7] he writes that "in Judaism to lead is to serve. Those who serve do not lift themselves high. They lift other people high." As the *parasha* reminds us, all great leadership requires intentionality, humility, and impulse control, as if we, too, are carrying the holiest vessels of the Sanctuary and moving them. That means elevating our speech, refraining from the gossip that is so often the currency of people in positions of power, and giving people the benefit of the doubt.

In his book *Serve to Lead*, James Strock writes that leaders should ask four fundamental questions: "Who am I serving? How can I best serve? Am I making my unique contribution? What am I learning?"[8] These questions lead to the foundation of service.

But serving is not all about obligation and responsibility, as evidenced by this beautiful saying attributed to the Bangladeshi poet, writer, and Nobel Prize winner Rabindranath Tagore: "I slept and I dreamed that life is all joy. I woke and I saw that life is all service. I served and I saw that service is joy." There is true delight and pleasure in service.

Personal Leadership Reflection

When, in a leadership role, did you have to work hard at being righteous?

פרשת שלח • *Parashat Shelaḥ*

Leadership and Diversity

Diversity in groups creates a higher chance of seeing positive change. Because society is diverse, diverse leadership means "greater depth and breadth of experience and perspective."[9] Diversity increases awareness of different pockets of society, sensitivity to other ways of looking at the same scenario or set of facts, and "pressure-tests assumptions and judgments." This almost always maximizes learning, innovation, and honesty. Diverse groups help create more inclusive decisions and outcomes.

"Every team must be made up of people with different roles, strengths, temperaments, and perspectives," writes Rabbi Jonathan Sacks.[10] "They must always be open to criticism and they must always be on the alert against groupthink. The glory of Judaism is its insistence that only in heaven is there one commanding Voice. Down here on earth no individual may ever hold a monopoly of leadership." Diversity in teams has many positive dimensions, but it's not always easy to create or navigate. Leadership experts Jon Katzenbach and Douglas Smith write in *The Wisdom of Teams* that good teams must balance individualism with the good of the group. Too much individualism can compromise teams: "Individual concerns and differences become a source of collective strength.[11] If there is too much consensus, diversity fails in its value.

This is apparent when reading *Parashat Shelaḥ*. "Send agents to scout the land of Canaan, which I am giving to the Israelite people" (Num. 13:2), we read as we open the *parasha*. Whereas God generally told Moses what to do, here He imbued Moses with the authority to select leaders for this reconnaissance mission from each of the twelve tribes: "… send one participant (*ish eḥad, ish eḥad*) from each of their ancestral tribes, each one a chief (*nasi*) among them." The verse stresses both the singularity of each leader within his tribe and the group as a whole, which must work together as one.

Rashi explains that "each one was a leader among them." Sforno adds that the individual selected had to be the best leader from his tribe, one who could recognize the significance of the land. For Rashi, it's a leader. For Sforno, it's *the* leader. Moses needed to think very carefully about the qualities of each person and the composition of the group. Select the wrong people, or the right individuals but not a productive combination of them, and the mission would fail. And the mission did fail.

The Torah names each person selected according to his tribe. These men had a historic role. People far into the future would need to know their names. Each of these leaders carried the important task of evaluating the land according to Moses's specific objectives: "See what kind of country it is" (Num. 13:18), he told them.

> Are the people who dwell in it strong or weak, few or many?
> Is the country in which they dwell good or bad?
> Are the towns they live in open or fortified?
> Is the soil rich or poor?
> Is it wooded or not? (13:18–20)

Moses concluded with one request: "And take pains to bring back some of the fruit of the land." It was the grape harvest season. Seeing is believing. When the people saw the sweet and large fruit, they would be impressed and feel motivated to complete the journey with enthusiasm. The tribal leaders were to figure this out together and present one report.

Nahmanides wonders why Moses sent out the mission in the first place. It was a risk. If the report was negative, was Moses going to take the people back to Egypt? Certainly not. Nahmanides explains that the Israelites wanted a group to reconnoiter the land as a standard procedure of military incursions in other foreign armies so that they could prepare themselves properly for war. Joshua did the same.

These leaders answered the questions and started on a high note: "We came to the land you sent us to; it does indeed flow with milk and honey, and this is its fruit" (13:27). But immediately afterward, they injected their own pessimism into the report, sharing how many enemies lived in the land and how well-fortified they were: "The country that we traversed and scouted is one that devours its settlers. All the people that we saw in it are of great size; we saw the Nephilim there – the Anakites are part of the Nephilim – and we looked like grasshoppers to ourselves, and so we must have looked to them" (13:32–33). Now, closer than ever to the Promised Land, the people lost all hope: "The whole community broke into loud cries, and the people wept that night" (14:1).

Here is where diversity does its hardest work. Caleb, one of the scouts from the tribe of Judah – the tribe most associated with leadership – protested. He was not prepared to speak with one voice, the voice of fear. Instead, he spoke with the voice of courage and destiny: "Caleb hushed the people before Moses and said, 'Let us by all means go up, and we shall gain possession of it, for we shall surely overcome it'" (13:30). Caleb met fear with mettle and valor. He spoke these words before Moses to assure the people that Moses's intentions were good and his judgment was sound. It must not have been easy to contradict the group, who compared themselves to grasshoppers.

Caleb was no grasshopper. He discouraged insect-like smallness and reminded the people of their own power to change their destiny and rise to the occasion. And he left us with a greater understanding of diversity's importance. Sometimes it's not consensus that creates greatness, but listening to the still, small minority voice of hope.

Personal Leadership Reflection

What leadership group do you belong to that would benefit from more diversity?

פרשת קרח • *Parashat Koraḥ*

When What You Have Is Not Enough

"You're not the boss of me!"

This was a regular part of our sibling banter as kids, and now, I have the great fortune of hearing my grandchildren say it to each other. It's a way that children indicate independence and control, especially in their absence, as if to say: I don't need to listen to you. I can determine my own direction. Thank you very much. Leave me alone.

In Tanakh, we also have a "you're-not-the-boss-of-me" moment. It occurs at the beginning of *Parashat Koraḥ*. Korah, a Levite, gathered together a number of elders and 250 leaders to challenge the leadership of Moses and Aaron. It was a dramatic, high-stakes rebellion with a very painful and shocking denouement. They accused the brothers of aggregating too much power and not sufficiently democratizing the governance of the Israelites: "They combined against Moses and Aaron and said to them, 'You have gone too far (*rav lakhem*)! For all the community are holy, all of them, and God is in their midst. Why then do you raise yourselves above God's congregation?'" (Num. 16:3).

There are many serious charges in this one verse. The rebels suggested that Moses and Aaron appointed themselves, abused their authority, and regarded themselves as superior to everyone else when the entire the community was holy. This is the way that Rashi on 16:3 interprets the events: "Much more than is proper have you taken for yourselves in the way of high office." They also hinted, with their generalized complaint, at some greater sedition that was left unnamed.

Their claim – summed up in the two words "*rav lakhem*," you have gone too far or have taken too much – was matched when Moses used the same criticism of them. He threw their words back at them: "You have gone too far, sons of Levi!" (16:7). We do not have access to the murmurings that precipitated this confrontation, but it is clear that this ground-swelling mutiny was the result of accumulated tension. They were not happy with the authority vested in their office; they wanted power. In *The Great Partnership*, Rabbi Jonathan Sacks offers us a warning about such desire: "Power is a fundamental assault on human dignity. When I exercise power over you, I deny your freedom, and that is dangerous for both of us."[12]

Moses made his charge first and then his case: "Hear me, sons of Levi. Is it not enough for you that the God of Israel has set you apart from the community of Israel and given you direct access to perform the duties of God's Tabernacle and to minister to the community and serve them? Now that [God] has advanced you and all your fellow Levites with you, do you seek the priesthood too?" (16:8–10). All those who approached Moses and Aaron already had titles and status. But it was not enough. Ironically, for Moses it was too much. He never wanted the position in the first place and protested his appointment several times. A few chapters earlier, Moses wanted to quit. He did not want more. He wanted less.

But, nearing the end of his leadership, the same word *rav* was used in reference to Moses' own leadership. Moses was told he overstepped the mark was in his last plea to cross the Jordan River into Canaan. In his review or revision of the journey, Moses told the people that it was their fault he could not cross over. "But God was wrathful with me on your account and would not listen to me. God said to me, 'Enough! (*rav lakh*). Never speak to Me of this matter again!'" (Deut. 3:26). A decree is a decree. A punishment is a punishment. Enough protest, God said to Moses. It was time for

Moses to accept his fate fully and acknowledge that a leadership transition was soon to take place. Any further argument would be fruitless.

A. D. Amar, Carsten Hentrich, and Vlatka Hlupic claim that leaders, especially in times of crisis, "strive for greater efficiency by tightening control."[13] This inevitably fails in the long term because without independence, people lose their intrinsic motivation. "... [The] truth is that relinquishing authority and giving employees considerable autonomy can boost innovation and success at knowledge firms, even during crises."[14] They call this type of shared governance "mutualism." Employees are evaluated not by revenue or other numbers but "against qualitative values such as trust, responsibility, and innovation. And it implies that leaders don't dictate vision or strategy; instead, they enable employees to create a common vision."[15]

But for this to work, these experts claim, individuals must be self-driven and committed to a common vision of shared success: "If abdication of authority is to yield value for the corporation, however, individuals must be self-motivated."[16] Such a theory would never have worked for Korah and his followers, because they wanted to grab power, not share it. Moses tried to show them the authority they already had; it was a holy authority rooted in service to God and to their followers. Yet it was not enough for them.

Every Passover, we sing the song *Dayeinu* – "It is enough." With each successive stanza, we confirm that had only this event or development happened, it would have been enough, even though we needed all of it to happen in the process of redemption. Leaders need the perspective to sometimes say, "I have enough. I am enough."

Personal Leadership Reflection

What do you have enough of in your leadership and what would you like more of?

פרשת חקת • *Parashat Ḥukat*

Have a Little Faith

One of the most debilitating and consequential moments in Moses's leadership occurs in *Parashat Ḥukat*. The *parasha* begins with the death of Moses's sister, Miriam, and ends with the death of his brother, Aaron. In between these tragic losses, Moses struck a rock with his staff instead of speaking to it and strangely lost the right to enter the Land of Israel. The loss of family and role in such a condensed time period could have shattered Moses's will to bring the people to the edge of the Jordan River. Nevertheless, he persisted. What gave him strength?

Let's turn to the first few verses of our *parasha*: "The Israelites arrived in a body at the wilderness of Zin on the first new moon, and the people stayed at Kadesh. Miriam died there and was buried there. The community was without water, and they joined against Moses and Aaron" (Num. 20:1–2). We are given no reason for Miriam's death. It is almost recorded as a passing fact of wilderness life. The people moved. A leader died. The people complained about water.

One midrash strings these events together. If water disappeared when Miriam died, it must have been in her merit that water was given to the Israelites in the form of a miraculous well throughout their travels.

This midrash is so familiar that it can distract readers from realizing the actual ignominy of her death. The people, so tired and faithless by this point, said nothing to Moses and Aaron about their loss. They allowed their leaders no personal time to mourn. They thought only of their own needs and pounced on Moses and Aaron with complaints: "Why did you make us leave Egypt to bring us to this wretched place, a place with no grain or figs or vines or pomegranates? There is not even water to drink!" (20:5).

As a result, Miriam's death was ignored by those she served. It was she who protected their savior, standing by the reeds when Moses was placed in the Nile. It was she who fetched her mother as a nursemaid for Moses, keeping him connected to his family. It was she who celebrated with joy and timbrels when her brother split the sea for the Israelites to cross to safety. But all of these memories were suddenly erased.

Instead of mourning, the brothers fell on their faces before God and awaited instruction: "You and your brother Aaron take the rod and assemble the community, and before their very eyes order the rock to yield its water. Thus, you shall produce water for them from the rock and provide drink for the congregation and their beasts" (20:8). The Israelites weren't censured. They would get what they wanted. In fact, copious amounts of water poured from the stone, making this one of the most dramatic miracles of desert life.

The Israelites got the water they were desperate for, but not exactly the way they wanted it: "Moses and Aaron assembled the congregation in front of the rock; and he said to them, 'Listen, *you rebels*, shall we get water for you out of this rock?'" (20:10). Moses, perhaps stabbed with a grief unacknowledged and lacking patience for more grumbling, did not merely speak to the rock. He did not only hit the rock with his rod. He called the people – his people – rebels (*hamorim*).

Rashi explains the word as "foolish people." Rabbi Abraham ibn Ezra similarly writes that their request was far-fetched, prompting Moses and Aaron to reply: "Do we have the power to bring forth water out of this rock for you?" Nahmanides elaborates on Ibn Ezra's position: "He [Moses] thus stressed their rebellion, telling them they were wanting in faith, and that the reason for their quarreling with him was because they thought that God would not act wondrously for them." It is as if, after all of the signs and wonders that the Israelites received, they still doubted God's salvific powers. This, Moses could not tolerate.

But Moses did not get the last word in the chapter. God was angry with Moses and Aaron and forbade them from entering the land: "Because you did not trust Me enough to affirm My sanctity in the sight of the Israelite people, therefore you shall not lead this congregation into the land that I have given them" (20:12). Rashi here is unequivocal: "For had you spoken to the rock, and it had brought forth water, I would have been sanctified before the whole congregation, for they would have said: This rock, which cannot speak and cannot hear and needs no maintenance, fulfills the bidding of the Omnipresent God. How much more should we do so?" If a rock can bring forth water, then we, too, have the capacity to follow the will of our Maker.

Moses, out of anger, hit the rock, but perhaps God ultimately punished him because he lost faith in the people he was leading. Once you stop believing in your people, you lose the privilege of leading them. "If you want to be a leader," writes Bruce Kasanoff in "Leadership in One Word: Faith," "your focus needs to be on earning the faith of people around you."[17] Faith in a leader generates faith in the mission and faith in all those engaged in the mission. The more faith you have, the more belief people will have that they can stretch themselves to do what they never thought possible. "People," Kasanoff states, "want great leaders to succeed. They want to have faith that if the leader succeeds, they, too, will succeed."[18] This was not only true for our faith in God, Moses, or Aaron. Rabbi Jonathan Sacks explains that "the deepest mystery of all is not our faith in God but God's faith in us. May that faith sustain us as we heed the call to responsibility and take the risk of healing some of the needless wounds of an injured but still wondrous world."[19]

Why did Moses continue, alone and bereft as he was? Because, through the rock incident, God held up a mirror to Moses's faith to show him the still "wondrous world" after he thought he lost everything. Water can gush out of stone just as slaves can be set free. Just as a people can return home after centuries of exile. Have faith in Me, said God with this water. Have faith in the mission. Have faith in yourself. And, above all, have faith in your people, even when they cannot see your pain or honor your loss. They are still your people. They need you to have faith in them.

Personal Leadership Reflection

Describe a time when you had enough faith to carry out a mission even though it felt impossibly hard.

פרשת בלק • *Parashat Balak*

What the Eye Can't See

As we open our Torah reading for the week, we are introduced to an unusual agreement. King Balak of Moab paid Balaam, an accomplished soothsayer, to curse the Israelites, who would be passing through on their way to the Promised Land. This, Balak believed, would diminish their military might. Balaam saddled his donkey and set out on the journey, but was then obstructed on the way by an angel he could not see. Eventually, Balaam was forced into blessing the Israelites in an ironic turn of events.

It's an intriguing story. Balaam's donkey, it turns out, is far more interesting than its rider. The donkey, in contrast to Balaam, *could* see the angel blocking the narrow path forward and refused to move. Balaam, with increasing impatience, jabbed at the donkey's side, prodding him forward: "When the donkey now saw the angel of the Lord, it lay down under Balaam, and Balaam was furious and beat the donkey with a stick" (Num. 22:27). This scene of an ill-tempered man beating an animal for non-compliance is painful but not, sadly, unusual, until the story takes another surprising turn. The donkey talked back to its owner: "What have I done to you that you have beaten me these three times?" (22:28). The donkey did not deserve this treatment and therefore advocated for himself.

As readers, we might be surprised that Balaam actually talked back to his magical donkey and explained his actions: "You have made a mockery of me! If I had a sword with me, I'd kill you" (22:29). Balaam was humiliated that while he was out on a royal mission, his insignificant donkey did not obey him. But the donkey, whose wisdom no longer astonishes us, pushed back: "'Look, I am the donkey that you have been riding all along until this day! Have I been in the habit of doing thus to you?' And he answered, 'No.'" The angel then posed the same question to Balaam. "Why did you hit your donkey three times?"

To understand this *parasha* and its compelling message about leadership, we need to answer three questions:

- How is it that this supposed visionary, who is even called a prophet in the Talmud (Bava Batra 15b), could not see what was right in front of him?
- How can it be that a man tasked with controlling the future could not even control his own simple beast?
- What is the function of this small, strange conversation when so much else of political and spiritual consequence was happening?

The answers to all three questions may be found in Rashi's comment on what the donkey saw: "*And the donkey saw*: But he [Balaam] did not, since the Holy One, Blessed be He, gave the animal the gift of sight beyond man. Since he possessed this knowledge, he became easily frightened when he witnessed danger." In this story, we find that it is precisely the lack of sophistication of the animal that allowed it to experience reality more acutely and obey the more powerful vision. The donkey served as a foil to Balaam, because of both its vision and its loyalty. The donkey protested its beatings on the grounds that it had never before behaved like this and should be trusted.

Balaam was told directly by God not to undertake this journey: "But God said to Balaam, 'Do not go with them. You must not curse that people, for they are blessed'" (22:12). Despite this clear warning,

Balaam undertook Balak's mission. Balaam had the conflicting messages of a king and the King of Kings before him and made a poor choice of what command to prioritize. Not so his donkey. When the words of his master were contradicted by an appearance of the Divine Presence, he yielded to it, even at the cost of the violence to his body.

As a result of selective hearing, Balaam suffered selective vision. He saw what he wanted to see and did not see what was actually there. The donkey, free of all human machinations, saw reality as it was. The donkey protested its beatings; it had done nothing more than face the truth of a situation that escaped the cognition of its master. Balaam, when finally confronted by the angel, confessed as much: "I erred because I did not know that you were standing in my way" (22:34).

The story line changed again when Balaam's eyes were literally unveiled, and, as Rashi intimated earlier, Balaam, like his donkey, was gifted with clear vision. Balaam's failing eyesight had been repaired, and he gained a wholly different perspective: "How goodly are your tents, O Jacob, your dwellings, O Israel! Like palm-groves that stretch out, like gardens beside a river, like aloes planted by God, like cedars beside the water" (24:5–6). Balaam described what he saw with the same set of eyes, but with a different set of mind. And what he suddenly saw was a nation worthy of blessing.

Rabbi Jonathan Sacks writes of the delicate balance between seeing the world as it is and as it should be: "A leader must have vision, but also realism. He or she must think the impossible but know the possible."[20] Senior partner of the consulting group Leader's Strategic Advantage, Inc. Debbie Zmorenski defines leadership as "a picture in the leader's imagination that motivates people to action when communicated compellingly, passionately, and clearly."[21] The problem lies in how that vision is communicated when followers cannot not see it or it not clearly communicated. Balaam could not see what was obvious to his clear-sighted donkey.

Zmorenski recommends four practical steps that a leader can take to translate vision into a reality for others:

- Isolate one challenge within an organization upon which to focus.

- Imagine what success will look like and describe it in detail so it can look real to others.
- Consider the language you will use and the context you need to make the message compelling. How, where, and how often must this vision be shared?
- Practice communicating what you have written and make sure it's sincere because "if you don't believe it, no one else will believe it either."

Vision is the capacity to describe a reality others cannot see so that you can bring others there.

Personal Leadership Reflection

As a leader, are you better at seeing reality as it is or as you think it should be?

פרשת פנחס • *Parashat Pinḥas*

The Zealous Leader

We admire zeal – a sense of fervor, ardor, and eagerness pursued with intensity – and we are also afraid of it. Leadership consultant Ken Byler writes about "zeal appeal." We need people to be zealous champions for causes, but we don't want them to be fanatical, inflexible, or intolerant. Byler observes that we rarely see good examples of zealous behavior today in leaders: "In today's workplace zeal seems strangely absent. It is rare to find a leader or employee whose passion shines bright as they flawlessly execute their appointed duties. When zeal does emerge, it is a breath of fresh air in an otherwise stale and listless environment."[22] He finds zeal most in people who love what they do. To find or rekindle that enthusiasm, we need to tap into our calling again and again.

Zeal is both a problem and a solution in the *parasha*. As the book of Numbers inches to a close, a significant number of Israelites began to unravel morally. Men fornicated with Moabite women and worshipped foreign gods. The stresses of desert life and wilderness leadership were taxing. The encampment was on the brink of losing its spiritual core. God was angry and told Moses to rid the camp of the wrongdoers. Then, in mid-conversation to resolve the problem, Moses was stunned by an act that rang of complete zealotry and anarchy: "Just then a certain Israelite man came and brought a Midianite woman over to his companions, in the sight of Moses and of the whole Israelite community who were weeping at the entrance of the Tent of Meeting" (Num. 25:6).

The rebellion was no longer on the margins but right in front of Moses's eyes and exactly where Moses received divine revelation. Nothing was sacred. There was no shame. Every boundary was pushed. The people wept over who they had become. Moses was silenced.

Jonathan Haidt argues in *The Righteous Mind: Why Good People Are Divided by Politics and Religion* that "when a group of people make something sacred, the members of the cult lose the ability to think clearly about it. Morality binds and blinds."[23] Here, a member of the leadership elite broke every rule in a very public way. The group was blinded. They began to see their illicit behaviors as normative. This may explain R. Yosei bar Yehuda's reasoning in a statement recorded in the Talmud: "When a person commits a transgression the first time, he is forgiven; a second time, he is forgiven; a third time, he is forgiven; but the fourth time, he is not forgiven" (Yoma 86b). Sin enough times, and it becomes acceptable in your mind. Do the same sins as those around you, and you feel validated. Aristotle and R. Yosei agree. Habituated bad behavior can become part of one's character.

Suddenly, in the thick of the crowd, an unexpected leader took control of the chaotic situation: "When Pinhas, son of Eleazar son of Aaron the priest, saw this, he left the assembly and, taking a spear in his hand, he followed the Israelite man into the chamber and stabbed both of them, the Israelite man and the woman, through the belly" (Num. 25:7–8). Pinhas stopped adultery and idolatry with one act of astonishing violence. Passionate sin was met with passionate rectitude. For this, God rewarded Pinhas with a covenant of peace.

We are left puzzled and upset. We are disturbed that the Israelites reached this low point and also distressed that it was stopped in this way. We are uncomfortable that violence was rewarded, even if there were positive outcomes. The means do not always justify the ends.

Rabbi Jonathan Sacks alerts us to what happens when there is an imbalance of power that leads to this degree of passion: "Violence is what happens when you try to resolve a religious dispute by means of power. It cannot be done. Trying to resolve ultimate issues of faith, truth, and interpretation by the use of force is a conceptual error of the most fundamental kind.... You cannot impose truth by force. That is why religion and power are two separate enterprises that must never be confused."[24]

When reflecting on this story from a distance, however, we can see more clearly the heat of the moment that produced the heat of the response. The dangerous cocktail of eros, profanity, public duplicity, and groupthink right in front of Moses meant that someone besides Moses had to defend the integrity of the Torah unambiguously. That individual met shock with shock to stop what was happening and provide the space for change. Someone needed to lead with commitment. "Commitment requires hard work in the heat of the day," writes John Gardner in his book *On Leadership*. "It requires faithful exertion on behalf of chosen purposes and the enhancement of chosen values."[25]

There is one detail that is often ignored when studying this story that may hold a key to understanding it. Pinhas was a *kohen*, a priest. He was committed, like his father and grandfather before him, to a life of service and to the continuity of a mission. He was not allowed any contact with death except in the rarest of circumstances. His role was not to put his hand out to others holding a spear but to hold his hands out in blessing. It was out of his character and against his job description to act this way.

But crisis situations can call for extreme stopgap measures. Situations like this, therefore, cannot be judged by the moment but by what happens *after* the moment. By awarding Pinhas with a covenant of peace, God was saying to him, to Moses, and to the encampment that his act of courage saved the day in the short term but would never work in the long term. God was, in effect, telling Pinhas that his ultimate task was to return to the work of peace – of blessing and service. The Netziv, Rabbi Naftali Tzvi Yehuda Berlin, contends that for Pinhas, the *brit shalom* was a way of removing such impulsive and violent tendencies that become an ever-present danger to one who has committed murder.

The demands of leadership can take us temporarily out of our lane, but an enduring commitment to our values puts us back in it.

Personal Leadership Reflection

What are you zealous about? When has that passion fueled your drive and when has it been a source of trouble? How can you channel it in constructive ways?

פרשת מטות • *Parashat Matot*

Adjusting Sights

In *Parashat Matot,* we have one of the most significant quiet and understudied rebellions in the Torah, and one that has always troubled me. In chapter 31, the Israelites waged war against the Midianites, collected the spoils, and divided them. Suddenly, two tribes found themselves in possession of an impressive stock of cows: "The Reubenites and the Gadites owned cattle in very great numbers. Noting that the lands of Jazer and Gilead were a region suitable for cattle" (Num. 32:1). It was challenging to progress in their journey in the wilderness with a now unmanageable herd. The lands just outside Israel, on the other side of the Jordan, were also, by implication, more fertile and better for grazing.

In 1915, geographer G. A. Smith published *The Atlas of the Holy Land,* which was reviewed and recommended with "unqualified admiration." Smith wrote wistfully about Gilead as a place where cattle grazed in the heat of the day, and at night, in his tent, he "would hear the shepherd's pipe far away, and the sheep and the goats, and cows with heavy bells, would break over the edge of the hill, and come down the slope to wait their turn at the troughs. Over Jordan we were never long out of the sound of the lowing of cattle or of the shepherd's pipe."[26]

Smith paints an enticing picture, so enticing that these tribes requested they stay there permanently and not enter the land. They approached Moses with their question: "It would be a favor to us,' they continued, 'if this land were given to your servants as a holding; do not move us across the Jordan'" (32:5). They seem to ask Moses casually if he wouldn't mind compromising on the dream and the vision that all of Israel cross the Jordan and finally return to the Land of Israel. This could only smack of betrayal. How could theses tribes prioritize cows over the Holy Land? This was, in its own way, a material revolution. *Leadership in the Wilderness* contains this observation about this historic moment: "If it took them a little longer, and they had to graze the cattle on land not quite as fertile, it was a small price to pay for the gift of a land to call their very own."[27]

Like the Reubenites and the Gadites, we nervously await Moses's response: "Moses replied to the Gadites and the Reubenites, 'Are your brothers to go to war while you stay here? Why will you turn the minds of the Israelites from crossing into the land that God has given them?'" (32:6–7). Wounded by the recent betrayal of the spies or scouts, Moses reads into their request nothing but self-serving cowardice. They were not prepared to go to war again. Others would do so while they grazed their cattle.

While Moses was concerned that these tribes privileged their safety over the larger collective vision of a united Israel in the Land of Israel, one midrash in Numbers Rabba 22:9 steps in with its censure that they valued their animals over their families:

> The tribes of Reuben and Gad cherished their own property more than human life, saying to Moses: "We will build here sheepfolds for our flocks and towns for our children." Moses said to them, "That is not right! Rather do the important things first. 'Build towns for your children' and afterward 'sheepfolds for your flocks.'" ...The Holy One, Blessed be He, said to them: "Seeing that you have shown greater love for your cattle than for human souls, by your life, there will be no blessing in it."

The author of this midrash regarded the tribes' request as deeply unsettling. These tribes promised to settle their cattle before settling their families. Not only were they undermining the promise to become a covenantal community together in Israel, they put what they owned before whom they loved.

Moses interrogated their intentions; they said they would settle their holdings and families and then fight as vanguards for Israel and even wait until the tribes were allocated their land: "We will not return to our homes until the Israelites – every one of them – are in possession of their portion" (Num. 32:18). After this exchange, Moses reluctantly agrees to let them stay on the "wrong" side of the Jordan, as long as they did so under God's stewardship and they maintained close ties to the rest of the Israelites. They could not lose their distinctive national commitment even if they lived elsewhere.

This decision had to be difficult for Moses on a personal level, a detail not shared in the Torah. Moses begged and pleaded to enter the Land of Israel and was consistently told, "No." What else could he say to those who elected volitionally not to go? As leaders must on occasion, Moses did not share his own emotional stake in this change of plan. No longer was he marching the tribes up to the border. He was leaving two tribes behind.

Was this a leadership failure? No. It was an act of genius. Moses understood that had he forbidden these tribes to live in Gilead, they likely would have done it anyway, and he would have been responsible for the ten, rather than the twelve, tribes. Given the difficult, painful choice of one people or one land, Moses opted for one people. As the chapter concludes, those on the other side of the Jordan ended up expanding the geographic reach of Israel and staying collectively intact.

Moses was open to change. This was not the first time his "No" turned into a "Yes." But these course corrections were not performed impulsively. He interrogated intentions, determined what was of real consequence, and agreed with conditions. By doing so, he maintained a fragile community and, counterintuitively, made it stronger. Rabbi Jonathan Sacks sums up in very few words the impact of change: "If we change the way we think, we can change the way we feel, which changes the way we act, which changes the person we become."[28]

Moses had what the American psychologist and professor at Stanford University Carol Dweck calls "a growth mindset" instead of "a fixed mindset," a now famous distinction from her book. [29] "In the fixed mindset, everything is about the outcome. If you fail – or if you're not the best – it's all been wasted. The growth mindset allows people to value what they're doing regardless of the outcome. They're tackling problems, charting new courses, working on important issues." This is deep and hard work and requires a high degree of flexibility and adaptation. "Mindset change is not about picking up a few pointers here and there," Dweck concludes. "It's about seeing things in a new way. When people... change to a growth mindset, they change from a judge-and-be-judged framework to a learn-and-help-learn framework. Their commitment is to growth, and growth takes plenty of time, effort, and mutual support."[30]

Personal Leadership Reflection

What is your Moses's moment: a radical mindset change you made that enabled you to grow and to flourish through a challenge?

פרשת מסעי

Parashat Masei

Leadership of the Land

Parashat Masei contains one of the strangest laws of the entire Torah: a detailed description of the city of refuge as a place where an accidental killer can live to escape capital punishment. The accidental killer is consigned to an interstitial space – a place not of his own choosing that signifies his removal from society for murder while, simultaneously, acknowledging his innocence. It is a difficult place to be, a place of guilt and limbo, but a place of life, nonetheless. Someone has died. Someone is responsible for that death even if it was unintended.

The playwright David Mamet wrote a book of his own Torah interpretations, *Five Cities of Refuge*. There, he invites us to visualize life in a city of refuge: "What must it have been like to live in a city of refuge, this place of neither acquittal nor punishment? Every single person you'd meet, every single day, had accidentally murdered another human being.... They were all united by shame; they all had innocent blood on their hands. And there was no escape either."[31] He concludes: "Perhaps it was no different from life in any city, anywhere, anytime."[32] Cities of refuge had other residents who were not guilty of manslaughter, but it's not clear if you could tell them apart. Casual encounters with shopkeepers and neighbors must have had a small charge of danger and mystery.

The chapter that discusses these laws concludes with a general warning: "You shall not pollute the land in which you live; for blood pollutes the land, and the land can have no expiation for blood that is shed on it, except by the blood of the one who shed it. You shall not defile the land in which you live, in which I Myself abide, for I God abide among the Israelite people" (Num. 35:33–34). Keep the land pure by keeping yourselves pure. Devote yourselves wholly to God by remaining spiritually clean through good moral choices.

Understand that the land is a reflection of its inhabitants. It cannot withstand hypocrisy. This exhortation reaches a crescendo in the book of Leviticus: "Thus the land became defiled; and I called it to account for its iniquity, and the land spewed out its inhabitants" (Lev. 18:25). Land that cannot withstand human destruction will spit out its residents. What happens to the spilled blood of those who are murdered? It seeps into the ground, as God told Cain after the very first murder: "What have you done? Hark, your brother's blood cries out to Me from the ground!" (Gen. 4:10).

This outcry is more than an environmentalist's creed. In the Hebrew Bible, the land and those who reside in it do so in equipoise, a counterbalance of forces that are delicately aligned and dependent on human behavior and an aspiration of purity or freedom from moral contamination.

Purity, like sacrifice, submission, and sin itself, is central to all major faiths but alien to modern sensibilities.

In her book *Purity and Danger: An Analysis of Concepts of Pollution and Taboo*, Mary Douglas introduces her subject by stating that "rituals of purity and impurity create unity in experience. So far from being aberrations from the central project of religion, they are positive contributions to atonement."[33] The impurity of sin distances us from God, from others, and from ourselves. Douglas believed that "ideas about separating, purifying, demarcating and punishing transgressions have as their main function to impose a system on an inherently untidy experience."[34] Nothing is morally messier than murder. Rabbi Joseph

Soloveitchik contends that the sinner needs to withdraw, acknowledge that the sin has distanced him from God, confess, and repent so that he can bridge that lonely abyss.[35]

Rabbi Jonathan Sacks writes that "there are aspects of Judaism that never change, wherever and whenever we are. The laws of purity and impurity, permitted and forbidden, sacred and secular – [these] have barely changed through the centuries."[36] We no longer observe many of these laws, because we do not have a Temple. But these laws are still studied because they teach us about how we demarcate experiences in the attempt to achieve holiness as individuals and as a society.

There is no greater breach for sacred societies than murder. The Talmud is explicit about this:

> Due to the sin of bloodshed, the Holy Temple is destroyed and the Divine Presence leaves Israel, as it says: "So you shall not pollute the land wherein you are; for blood, it pollutes the land; and no expiation can be made for the land for the blood that is shed therein, but by the blood of him that shed it. And you shall not defile the land which you inhabit, in the midst of which I dwell; for I the Lord dwell in the midst of the children of Israel" (Num. 35:33–34). However, if you defile the land, you will not inhabit it, and I will not dwell in it. (Shabbat 33a)

One midrashic reading of these verses helps us understand why the city of refuge was critical to the creation of a holy community. When it states in Numbers 35:34 that "I the Lord dwell in the midst of the children of Israel," the midrash suggests that even when the Israelites are impure, the Divine Presence remains among them (*Sifrei Bemidbar* 160:15; see also Yoma 56b–57a). When you are marked by a sin so great it disturbs the universe, you can feel that you are your sin. There is no escaping from the terror of self-loathing. You do not feel that God is with you. You are wracked by shame and guilt for a murder you never intended. But in a city of refuge, you are with others who share this burden. Your vulnerability is acknowledged. You can express other parts of your being. You know that the Divine Presence is with you.

We have no modern-day equivalent of the city of refuge. The most we can do is create environments that feel both safe and accepting and also inspire personal and communal growth. In her *HBR* article, Janice Omadeke asks, "How do you create a culture where your team feels empowered to be honest, share without fear of retribution, and ask for what they need?"[37] She observes that "the perception of what it means to be vulnerable has shifted from the grand gesture to the small act of bravery." Leaders have to model that bravery to "open the door for people with less formalized power to safely emulate your behavior."[38]

Omadeke suggests two ways to open that small, important door of vulnerability. (1) Be honest about your own struggles. You cannot expect others to share their obstacles and frustrations if you cannot do so. This means asking for help when you need it or mentioning the difficulty of a task. It may mean sharing a hardship in your life that may be getting in the way of your best performance. (2) Do the difficult thing – even when others are hesitant. What Omadeke means by this is "standing up for your values and beliefs, publicly and privately." This means speaking up and challenging groupthink. It means being a voice for others who may be mistreated in the workplace or society. And it means respectfully addressing uncomfortable issues that are papered over in leadership.

No one can live free of sin and without regrets. The city of refuge was a place where those guilty of manslaughter could continue to live despite sin and regret and be accepted and productive. One role of leaders today is to create similar environments of shelter and psychological refuge so that others may live.

Personal Leadership Reflection

What step can you take as a leader in creating a spiritual city of refuge for yourself and others?

Leadership in the Book of Deuteronomy

פרשת דברים • *Parashat Devarim*

Leadership Stars

Many years ago, I was invited to teach a leadership class in a large tech firm on the topic of intrinsic and extrinsic motivation. At some point, one department head commented, "I don't have to praise people who work for me. I pay them." The others in the room looked uncomfortable. It wasn't hard to understand why his department was shrinking.

In *Parashat Devarim*, Moses praised his people, even as he criticized them. He began his farewell speech to the nation about to enter the Land of Israel. He had to prepare them to live without him. Succession is one of the hardest leadership transitions, both for the leaders who are coming and going and for those who have to adapt to new models of governance. Moses was the people's faithful guide, who freed them from slavery, brought their laws down from Sinai, and escorted them through the desert. All of these formative national experiences were associated with one person.

In his remarks, Moses sandwiched praise of the Israelites with criticism of them. It's hard to know what we as readers should feel when we read this contradictory summation:

> Thereupon I said to you, "I cannot bear the burden of you by myself. Your God has multiplied you until you are today as numerous as the stars in the sky. May God, the God of your ancestors, increase your numbers a thousandfold, and bless you as promised. How can I bear unaided the trouble of you, and the burden, and the bickering!" (Deut. 1:9–12)

First Moses complained that he could not handle the people. Then he commented that the people were numerous as stars and should be blessed, which was then followed by how difficult the people were; they were argumentative and burdensome. It's a confusing, inconsistent message. If we take a longer, retrospective view, however, it's easier to understand the order of these baffling words.

"You are today as numerous as the stars in the sky" in the first chapter of Deuteronomy is a majestic culmination of a vision from the first chapter of Genesis. God blessed Adam and Eve: "Be fertile and increase, fill the earth and master it" (Gen. 1:28). But the blessing was a struggle. Everything having to do with children was difficult. Eve was cursed with pain in childbirth. Her first son killed her second, and she disappeared after the first verse in Genesis 4.

Abraham and Sarah, too, were given national aspirations, but, as a couple, they struggled with infertility and how to make sense of God's mandate. They tried a variety of options, including adopting Lot as an heir and suggesting Eliezer as a successor. When the first two options did not work out, God took Abraham outside each time to count that which could not be counted, first the dust of the earth and then the stars in the sky: "Look toward heaven and count the stars, if you are able to count them, so shall your offspring be" (Gen. 15:5). Eventually, Sarah and Abraham had Isaac. Only one grain of earth. Only one star in the sky.

When stuck in a difficult place, with no options before you, look above, God advised Abraham. Look far off into a future unseen. Look up rather than ahead. That is what vision is: seeing the impossible, even the improbable, and making it so. God used the image of the twinkling stars set in a dark night to ask Abraham for a little more faith.

The book of Genesis is filled with painful stories of infertility, making it difficult, story after story, to see a nation emerging. But by the time we begin the book of Exodus, the blessing first given to Adam and Eve and to all of humanity to propagate and fill the earth had borne fruit: "The Israelites were fertile and prolific; they multiplied and increased very greatly, so that the land was filled with them" (Ex. 1:7). The aerial view of the stars that sustained our ancestors for generations carried them across the chasm of barrenness. But when they finally experienced a population growth, they were in someone else's land. Their numbers were a threat and a cause for punishment and oppression.

Only when we arrive in Deuteronomy, on the cusp of a homeland, did Moses note the historic realization of the dream in Genesis 1, the mystery of Genesis 15, and the anguish of Exodus 1. Finally, we became a nation beyond count with autonomy beyond measure. Numerous and free, we shined like Abraham's stars. We were made of the earth and imbued with the sky, as Rabbi Jonathan Sacks writes: "We may be dust of the earth, the debris of exploded stars, a concatenation of blindly self-replicating genes, but within us is the breath of God."[1]

Moses did what leaders must always do. He told the people they had actualized and fulfilled a long-term dream of their ancestors. They achieved a great objective in their history. He named it and celebrated it. He also acknowledged that this growth had consequences for leadership. He was proudly outnumbered. But with growth came other challenges that would need to be addressed by future leaders, such as the unwieldly quarrels and demands of the masses. Moses tried to remind them of the larger, grander picture, but they could only see the mess right in front of them.

Sometimes leaders, when they reach an impasse, need to name the special moments, revel in the milestones, and remind people how far they've come and what new challenges they must tackle.

A *Forbes* panel discussion opens with the observation that many leaders find it easy to make requests but hard to give praise. Instead, the members of the panel recommend praising often, sincerely, and specifically. As worshippers, we are asked to relate to God first and primarily through praise – not because God needs praise, but because we are changed when we name and acknowledge the good in the world that God has created.

A corporate leader interviewed in the article commented that "giving praise, when deserved, can help balance out one-sided developmental feedback."[2] Employees and volunteers need a balance of positive and productive feedback to grow. If giving praise liberally is difficult, one leader suggests that it may be time to do some deep and reflective work about "their own relationship with praise and authenticity and articulate better what the fear is about." Sometimes, when leaders don't need praise themselves, they forget that others thrive on it.

But Moses did more than praise. He began his farewell by offering the Israelites a lesson in perspective. When what you see on the ground looks problematic and you cannot see a way forward, don't get stuck. Look up.

Personal Leadership Reflection

When in your leadership did a long-term vision get you through a short-term problem?

פרשת ואתחנן • *Parashat Va'etḥanan*

Words on Fire

"Take utmost care and watch yourselves scrupulously," Moses advised in *Parashat Va'etḥanan*, "so that you do not forget the things that you saw with your own eyes and so that they do not fade from your mind as long as you live. And make them known to your children and to your children's children" (Deut. 4:11–12). The foundational experiences of becoming a nation may fade over time, so Moses asks that his people – our people – bear witness to what they have gone through and share it with the power of story.

One of those indelible experiences was the giving of the Torah at Sinai. Moses has specific details burnished in his mind about that nascent time in Israelite history: "You came forward and stood at the foot of the mountain. The mountain was ablaze with flames to the very skies, dark with densest clouds. God spoke to you out of the fire; you heard the sound of words but perceived no shape – nothing but a voice" (Deut. 4:11–12). Moses's description is rich and sensory, as if to say: These are "the things you saw with your own eyes." Never forget them.

The Jerusalem Talmud offers an incredible commentary on how this specific scene and verse was passed from father to son. Elisha, the

Talmud's famous heretic, was extolling his father Abuya with the story about the day of Elisha's *brit*, his entrance into the covenant (Y. Ḥagiga 2:1). Abuya was a wealthy man who invited all the important people of Jerusalem to this event. They were in one room feasting, dancing, and clapping. In the next room, the sages R. Eliezer and R. Yehoshua were studying Torah.

The rabbis said to each other, "While they are occupied in theirs, let us be occupied with ours." They studied an array of subjects with such intensity that "fire descended from Heaven and surrounded them." Abuya ran next door and chastised the pair: "Why do you come to burn down my house?" The sages were unapologetic. They exclaimed, "The words were joyful as at their giving on Sinai." Since the words of Torah were given with fire, they told Abuya, they received them with fire as well. They then cite our *sedra*'s verse: "The mountain was ablaze with flames." Abuya was so impressed with the power of Torah that he said he would dedicate his new son to the Torah.

The message of the story is clear. Words given in fire are received in fire. The passion of study and learning attracts, magnetizes, and burns brightly.

Rabbi Jonathan Sacks teaches that the power of the Torah's words is singular to our faith: "For Judaism God is to be found not in a person or a place but in words, the words of the Mosaic books, Torah in its narrow sense. Neither Moses, the greatest of the prophets, nor Sinai, the place of revelation, have intrinsic sanctity. They were the vehicles of revelation, not its embodiment. That description belongs to Torah alone."[3]

The metaphor of a burning mountain as a symbol of intellectual charisma reminds us that if the words we use are on fire, they will be received with fire. When we are passionate about a cause or an idea, we can generate passion in others. When we are unmoved by our own words, so too will those hearing them be unmoved. Leaders understand this. Followers want charisma in their leaders. They want to feel inspired, stimulated, and motivated.

Hannah L. Miller describes charismatic leaders as "charming, caring, motivational, supportive, infectious, and warm."[4] She believes they have unusually good emotional intelligence, confidence, and potent energy. Their charm and likeability resonate with others and help drive results. This is especially important, Miller contends, in companies with a strong social cause: "The leader drives people to stay positive, upbeat, and keep fighting the good fight."[5]

There are dangers, though. Fire burns. Jim Collins, in *Good to Great,* discusses the liability of charisma.[6] The passion of a leader for an idea or a strategy can blind him or her to other opinions. Egos and tempers can be high when followers do not achieve the desired results. Followers may not buy into the prevailing zeitgeist with the same level of commitment. This can lead to burnout. Sometimes, passion can falsely compete with content or real work. Words on fire become meaningless if they are not backed up with outcomes. Some researchers have concluded that charisma is unessential for leadership and may contribute negatively to the environment and to conflicts withing organizational structures."[7]

In our *sedra,* Moses challenged the Israelites to hold fast to the visual image of a burning mountain so that the words of Torah would continue to simmer within them. He was also telling them how to transmit God's law to the next generation. Words given in fire are received in fire. So was it then. So is it now.

Personal Leadership Reflection

What words, advice, or events are burnished in fire within you that you have passed down?

פרשת עקב • *Parashat Ekev*

Leadership and the Destination Postcard

In *Parashat Ekev*, we are given a beautiful set of images to describe the Land of Israel: "Your God is bringing you into a good land, a land with streams and springs and fountains issuing from plain and hill; a land of wheat and barley, of vines, figs, and pomegranates, a land of olive trees and honey; a land where you may eat food without stint, where you will lack nothing; a land whose rocks are iron and from whose hills you can mine copper" (Deut. 8:7–9). It's a compelling picture of the future and one that might have helped the Israelites complete the journey ahead with greater enthusiasm and inspiration. It's also a sharp contrast to the negative images of danger communicated by the leaders who reconnoitered the land as told in Numbers 13.

There, they brought back some of the fruit mentioned again in our verse here: "They reached Wadi Eshcol, and there they cut down a branch with a single cluster of grapes – it had to be borne on a carrying frame by two of them – and some pomegranates and figs" (Num. 13:23). The fruit was not only sweet but of enormous size. When Moses offered his description of the land many chapters later, he clearly spoke the truth as affirmed by those who had already been there. Yet the leaders who came back did not speak exclusively of the fruit. They spoke of being literally eaten by enemies instead of being the ones doing the eating: "The country that we traversed and scouted is one that devours its settlers" (13:32).

Moses amplified his visualization of the land beyond its produce to counter these attacks and to prepare the group for the miracle of normal, domestic life they were soon to experience. He mentioned that the scarcity the Israelites endured in the desert would be reversed when they arrived in Israel. Instead of an arid wilderness that contained no resources, Israel would find iron beneath the surface of the land. On the land would be magnificent trees and vines. And above the land's surface, the hills would yield copper. Water would flow freely in this good country. It is a place "where you will lack nothing," instead of the persistent complaint that the Israelites lacked everything.

Sforno on Deuteronomy 8:9 believes that Moses's descriptive choices were intentionally chosen to augment the good by bringing together many desirable assets in Israel that are generally not found in any one place. Nahmanides adds that Moses's words were used to raise expectations: "In the place where you expect stones, you will find iron, for it will be mined from the dust thereof. He thus brought them the joyful message that in the Land of Israel there is a quarry of copper and iron, which are a great necessity for the inhabitants of the land."

The people listening knew they had traveled a long way through different places symbolized by food. They reminisced about the foods of Egypt, but the taste of this food was, by and large, bitter. They were parched: "The riffraff in their midst felt a gluttonous craving; and then the Israelites wept and said, 'If only we had meat to eat! We remember the fish that we used to eat free in Egypt, the cucumbers, the melons, the leeks, the onions, and the garlic. Now our gullets are shriveled. There is nothing at all! Nothing but this manna to look to!'" (Num. 11:4–6). They may have looked back in longing and craved the pungency of garlic, onions, and leeks in their current monochromatic lifestyle, but these left an unpleasant residue, much the way that their suffering as slaves would stay with them as a bad taste they could never remove.

In their wilderness years, in contrast, they had a different food. God was their grocer, supplying them with a special food unknown to them called manna to see if they could stay true to the sacrifices of those years. God was the one "who fed you in the wilderness with manna, which your ancestors had never known, in order to test you by hardships only to benefit you in the end" (Deut. 8:16). This transitional, mysterious food and its daily delivery stopped when they arrived in the land. It was as transitional as the people who ate it. It represented God's sustenance through difficult times and Israel's commitment to reaching the Promised Land.

Now, so close to the finish line of this trek, Moses gave them a new set of foods and a new set of hopes. The Land of Israel is a place of sweetness, not bitterness. It is a place where bountiful trees have deep roots, unlike the transitional manna that came and went from day to day. Farming was to be a partnership between God's grace and human industry. The Israelites would not be dependent only on God for their food. Finally, their mouths would be full with the tastes of freedom, sweetness, rootedness, and independence.

Moses offered the Israelites what leadership experts Dan and Chip Heath call a "destination postcard" in their book *Switch: How to Change Things When Change Is Hard.*[8] When people want or need to change something, they have to have a lot of self-control. This can be exhausting, and the mental fatigue of discipline and impulse control can become an obstruction to thinking creatively and expansively, diminishing the exact qualities needed to make big changes. We rarely acknowledge just how difficult this shift of mindset and behavior really is: "When you hear people say that change is hard because people are lazy or resistant, that's just flat wrong. In fact, the opposite is true: Change is hard because people wear themselves out…. What looks like laziness is often exhaustion."[9]

What provides respite and stimulates people to keep going is what the Heath brothers term a "destination postcard" – "a vivid picture from the near-term future that shows what could be possible." Leaders need to understand that words alone are insufficient to stimulate change. People need to visualize what success looks like. Good leaders understand the difficulties; their portraits of the future address the issues and reverse these problems. They paint a granular picture of optimism. But more than any of these motivators, high-impact leaders create the conditions necessary for success. "A good change leader never thinks, 'Why are these people acting so badly? They must be bad people.' A change-leader thinks, 'How can I set up a situation that brings out the good in these people?'"[10]

We conclude with a challenge then and now. Once the Israelites were settled, safe, and productive in their own land, would they remember the tastes of slavery enough to see and address poverty and pain in others still suffering? Rabbi Jonathan Sacks reminds us that "we cannot enjoy the food of affluence while others eat the bread of affliction. We are not fully free if others are oppressed." As we read this *parasha*, it's a good time to think about those who struggle to put food on their tables and consider volunteering at a shelter or donating to a local food pantry. When we have more than enough, it's time to help those still embittered by the taste of hunger.

Personal Leadership Reflection

What destination postcard do you need right now to inspire change in yourself or others?

פרשת ראה • *Parashat Re'eh*

The False Prophet

"I ain't no false prophet – I just know what I know. I go where only the lonely can go," sings Bob Dylan in his song "False Prophet." A false prophet makes claims to have secret knowledge that others cannot access. The false prophet uses this information to persuade followers to a particular agenda. Dylan warns against making him into this kind of person: "What are you lookin' at – there's nothing to see. Just a cool breeze encircling me." A false prophet can only exert the authority others give him. Look elsewhere, Dylan asks.

It is for this reason that our Torah reading, *Parashat Re'eh*, does not caution people *not* to become false prophets but instead tells potential followers not to listen to such inauthentic leaders. The false prophet is nothing without followers. Do not give him – or her – that power. The way you know if the prophet is false is clear according to our verses; if a prophet tells you to go against the Torah, you know that he is misleading you: "If there appears among you a prophet or a dream-diviner, who gives you a sign or a portent, saying, 'Let us follow and worship another god' – whom you have not experienced – even if the sign or portent named to you comes true, do not heed the words of that prophet or that dream-diviner" (Deut. 13:2–4).

Maimonides, in his encyclopedic legal work, alerts his readers to the dangers of false prophets. A false prophet does not have to prove himself through signs and wonders, Maimonides writes, like Moses or Elijah. The true test of a prophet is "the fulfillment of his prediction of future events" (*Mishneh Torah, Hilkhot Yesodei HaTorah* 10:1). We should not taunt the prophet by saying, "'Split the sea for us, revive the dead, or the like, and then we will believe in you.' Instead, we tell him, 'If you are a prophet, tell us what will happen in the future.' He makes his statements, and we wait to see whether [his 'prophecy'] comes to fruition or not."

This process of testing must happen, according to Maimonides, many times. The self-appointed prophet may have been lucky with his early prediction. To assume such a lofty place in Jewish life means proving oneself again and again. There are simply too many charlatans out there to believe in any human being with complete faith unless this leader's predictions hold true, endure over time, and uphold the laws and principles of the Torah. A veneer of authenticity is not the same as being loyal to the cause.

Rabbi Jonathan Sacks writes that "those who are disloyal are eventually distrusted and lose whatever authority they might once have had. Leadership without loyalty is not leadership. Skills alone cannot substitute for the moral qualities that make people follow those who demonstrate them. We follow those we trust, because they have acted so as to earn our trust.... Always be loyal to the people you lead."[11] Our *parasha* asks leaders to be loyal to the people, loyal to the Torah, and loyal to God. Anything else can become the bluster of the narcissistic leader anxious to be worshipped.

Maimonides differentiates the work of diviners and sorcerers from prophets precisely because it can be hard to tell them apart. A true prophet "will arise for the sole purpose of telling us the future events which will transpire in the world, whether there will be plenty or famine, war or peace, and the like. He even will inform a particular individual regarding his needs.... These are the types of things that a prophet will say. He will not come to found a new faith or add or diminish a mitzva" (*Mishneh Torah, Hilkhot Yesodei HaTorah* 10:3).

Rather than leave us with a didactic teaching, the Torah, in this instance, uses the lyrical language of the soul to explain why the appointment of a false prophet is so problematic: "For your God is testing you to see whether you really love your God with all your heart and soul. It is your God alone whom you should follow, whom you should revere, whose commandments you should observe, whose orders you should heed, whom you should worship, and to whom you should hold fast" (Deut. 13:4–5). These are the words that undergird any covenantal commitment that demands loyalty. It should be total and uncompromising. It requires trust, faith, and humility. It demands both the heart and the mind.

If false prophets are so problematic, why are we drawn to them? In a universe of uncertainty, moral opacity, and political confusion, we want someone to tell us that all will be fine, that we are wonderful, and that there is one right answer. We want clarity and certainty in our leaders. But truly great leaders will never offer that. "Leadership is an improvisational art," write Ronald Hefeitz and Marty Linsky. "You may be guided by an overarching vision, clear values, and a strategic plan, but what you actually do from moment to moment cannot be scripted. You must respond as events unfold."[12] No one can or should script the future. Do not become a false prophet. Do not believe in false prophets.

Too many leaders have the messiah complex. They think they know it all and can fix it all. And with this false advertising, they rob us of our agency to fix our own problems. That is why the obligation is upon us not to create false idols, rather than on individuals not to set themselves up as prophets. There are false leaders everywhere. Will we believe in them and give them power or not?

Throughout Jewish history, we have had examples of charismatic figures who tried to lead others astray, from Bar Kokhba to Shabbetai Tzvi to Jacob Frank. They may have started life as innocent and insightful Jews with a gift for persuading others. But at some point in their complicated lives, they used their talents to undermine the convictions and traditional practices of their followers and often flamed out.

Today we have modern-day prognosticators who make their own predictions about the future fate of the Jewish people. They are often doomsayers. The twentieth-century thinker Simon Rawidowicz, in his famous essay "Israel: The Ever-Dying People," writes that in our view of ourselves and in what others have said of us, we are "constantly on the verge of ceasing to be, of disappearing."[13] Salo Baron famously called this perspective the "lachrymose conception of Jewish history." And yet, here we are still, alive and flourishing. Rawidowicz leaves us with an ironic blessing of continuity: "Let us be the last as our fathers and forefathers were. Let us prepare the ground for the last Jews who will come after us, and for the last Jews who will rise after them, and so on until the end of days." In other words, don't believe the false prophets who predict our demise. Look around. We are still here.

Personal Leadership Reflection

When have you believed you could fix someone else's problems and deprived that individual of his or her own agency?

פרשת שפטים • *Parashat Shofetim*

Leadership and Bias: Blinding Wise Eyes

"What do you do?"

"I'm in compliance."

"That's a very important job."

"You're the first person who's said that to me. Most people see me and walk in the opposite direction."

This was my conversation with a lovely young woman I met after giving a class recently. She laughed and then shrugged as she admitted that she's not the most popular person in her office. Instead of viewing compliance as a critical mechanism to keep an organization ethical, the people she works with may regard her as an uncomfortable, judgmental presence.

Some researchers have concluded that ethical leaders need to play a role as models, use reward and punishment to decrease unethical behavior, and hire those prone to ethical behavior in order to avoid corruption within their organizations.[14] You cannot merely hope that people will behave ethically in the workplace. You have to model it and build it into systems. As human beings, we've been given a mandate not just to live in a just world but to shape it. As Rabbi Jonathan Sacks notes in *To Heal a Fractured World*, "God in making humanity conferred on us the right and duty to see things from a human point of view.... Making us human, not Divine, God calls on us to judge and act within the terms of our humanity."[15]

In *Parashat Shofetim*, we find an unambiguous statement about judging others with the highest moral standards and expecting compliance: "You shall not judge unfairly: you shall show no partiality; you shall not take bribes, for bribes blind the eyes of the wise and upset the plea of the just" (Deut. 16:19). Whereas sometimes the Torah is authoritative and didactic in its presentation of commandments, here it is explanatory. The verse tells us what taking bribes can do both to the judge and to those being judged.

Rashi here writes poignantly that at no time during the presentation of a case should a judge "be lenient to one and harsh to the other," and he gives a simple illustration. A judge asks one party to stand and the other to sit as he listens to a case. This visible display of difference may falsely and even unwittingly communicate a preference. Judges must review every one of their small actions and gestures and what they may inadvertently communicate.

Rashi, citing Shevuot 30a, then moves from the judge to those being judged. Should there be even the slightest hint of favoritism, the litigant who feels disrespected may be hampered in his plea. Once he thinks there is any bribery or preference in a case, he may feel defeated and lose all confidence. What's the point of making a case if the judge has already predetermined the outcome?

Someone told me that during meetings of his senior team, the CEO regularly looked at the second most senior person in the room for approval or rolled her eyes at that employee to show disagreement with something that was said. This gesture was slight. No speaking was involved, but pretty soon other members of the team self-censored and did not speak up about important issues. The room was not safe. They felt they would be judged unfavorably, so they kept quiet. When this behavior was brought to the CEO's attention, she instantly denied it. "I don't know what you're talking about." Nobel Prize winner Daniel

Kahneman, in his book *Thinking, Fast and Slow,* writes that "we can be blind to the obvious, and we are also blind to our blindness."[16]

Rashi, on our same verse, also states that when a judge takes a bribe, no matter how much he thinks he can be impartial, he cannot: "As soon as he has accepted a bribe, it is impossible for him not to incline his heart to that one and try to find something in his favor." Rashi bases himself on a passage in the Talmud (Ketubot 105b) that explicates our verse. There, the Sages discussed what this verse adds to our understanding of Jewish justice, since all the way back in Exodus 23:8 we learned: "You shall take no bribe." The Talmud concludes that even in a case in which these is no concern that justice will be perverted, a judge should, nevertheless, not take anything from any litigant. In the United States, for example, there are strict and intricate gift-giving restrictions in place for government employees, lest accepting a gift – even one of nominal monetary value – influence judgment, even subconsciously. This is where compliance work does its heavy lifting.

The Talmud continues in its interpretation of our verse: "For bribes blind the eyes of the wise." If bribes can blind the eyes of the wise, the Sages concur, then they can certainly blind the eyes of a fool. Is a fool likely to be appointed as a judge? We assume that only those who are intelligent, discerning, and knowledgeable would be selected to such positions. But this is not always the case. When a wise person takes a bribe, the Talmud states, "He will not leave this world without suffering blindness of the heart." He will become a fool.

Compliance regulations in all fields help us check our conscious and unconscious biases and prevent us from making small errors of judgment that may become larger over time if not monitored and supervised. This is true for judges and in all arenas of leadership. We carry our beliefs and our biases with us wherever we go and in whatever we do. And at times, when we find ourselves faltering, our values carry us.

Personal Leadership Reflection

When did partiality – in work or within your family – hurt you?
When did you hurt others with your unfair display of preference?

פרשת כי תצא • *Parashat Ki Tetzeh*

Leadership and Favoritism

Many sensitive relationships are mentioned in the opening chapter of *Parashat Ki Tetzeh*. The first is the status of the captive woman who was taken in battle and captured the fancy of a soldier in that war. She was completely vulnerable and, in principle, unprotected. The Torah understood that the situation was one of natural exploitation and thus placed parameters around her care. The captive woman's hair and nails were to be trimmed, and she was to exchange her old clothes for new ones, presumably resembling those worn by other Israelite women. The exoticism associated with foreign women was to be tempered to measure whether or not the soldier had true feelings for *this* woman.

This concern was not only about externalities; it was also about the emotional weather in the relationship: "She shall spend a month's time in your household lamenting her father and mother; after that you may come to her and thus become her husband, and she shall be your wife. Then, should you no longer want her, you must release her outright" (Deut. 21:13–14). This poor woman, ripped from the bosom of her family, no doubt suffered greatly. She was to be given time to grieve, after which the soldier must decide if he had the patience and tenderness to commit to this woman in earnest.

If not, he was forbidden to sell her into slavery, as if she were owned by him. The way she was to be treated is discussed in the first person, as if the reader is the one in this unenviable position. It's as if the Torah wanted us to be in the heart of this casualty of war, understand its complexities, and feel the captive woman's shame and loss. The case provokes us to ask if there are limits to love.

The second situation in chapter 21 of Deuteronomy brings sensitivity to bear to another human tangle not commonly experienced today. A man had two wives. He loved one, but the other was unloved. Both women had sons, but the first child born was the son of the unloved one. Here, too, love is the commodity, and here, too, love, is overshadowed by fairness: "He may not treat as first-born the son of the loved one in disregard of the son of the unloved one who is older" (21:16).

Ordinarily, the first son would inherit a double portion. Some believe that this is because the oldest child either had more household responsibilities within the family or would one day assume more responsibility than any of the other siblings in managing the estate. One interpretation I came across suggests that the first-born receives twice what other children inherit because parents make the most mistakes with their first-borns! In our situation, justice trumps partiality in Jewish law, even though, in the case of our first Jewish families in Genesis, this was usually not true. Maybe the law in the last of our five books of the Torah is there as a future corrective. Favoritism can do permanent damage within a family dynamic.

This unfortunate reality does not stop our children and, I suspect, many other people's children from asking that fateful question: "Who's your favorite child?" Worse still is this assumption: "Your favorite is…" Current research in psychology suggests that even when parents show no visible preference for a child, children still assume a preference. In her radically titled article in *Psychology Today*, "Why Most Parents Really Do Have a Favorite Child,"[17] Dr. Tracy Asamoah states that we try as parents to cover up our partiality out of shame for the psychic costs to a child. She discusses many factors that lead parents not to disclose this information. The silence may be related to guilt, to the perceived damage this can do to this unfavored child/children, or to the damage that preferential treatment may do to the family dynamic or to the favored child. She also suggests that parents explore their own feelings; in their effort to deny favoritism, they may not be examining their own feelings and how these are reflected in subconscious behaviors.

Asamoah concludes that "favoritism has little to do with loving one child more. It is more about how your personality resonates with one child's personality more than the other's. Essentially, it's a question of like."[18] One person explained it to me this way: "It's not that you have favorites. It's that you have allies." Relationships, Asamoah writes, have deep roots. Some children trigger what we might call ancient feelings and associations both positive and negative that we have with our own parents or grandparents. We might respond lovingly or apprehensively to traits in our children that mirror our own biases and preferences. Asamoah also states that our feelings for our children are "seasonal." Different times and situations in our lives may bring us closer to or distance us from one child over another. Nevertheless, Asamoah concludes that while we might like our children differently, they must all "receive equal love and nurturance."

While favoritism can have tragic consequences in families, as the Torah and modern research suggest, it can contribute to positive and significant developments in leadership when kept in check. Those chosen or appointed for leadership roles are most often those who demonstrate a higher degree of responsibility, obligation, and drive to action than others. Their selection for leadership roles validates this and generates more leadership possibilities as leaders assume more responsibility. They then get selected for more authoritative roles. This leadership cycle of selection can create higher and higher aspirations. This, I believe, is why favoritism is a repeated trope in the families of Genesis. Genesis is not a family manual. It's a leadership manual. The same favoritism that is devastating in families can be generative in identifying and growing talent in organizational cultures.

But, as with all partiality, it must be tempered and leavened by fairness. In our Torah reading, we encounter two situations where love can be damaging rather than nurturing. Rabbi Jonathan Sacks writes this explicitly: "You cannot build a society on love alone. Love unites, but it also divides. It leaves the less-loved feeling abandoned, neglected, disregarded, 'hated.' It can leave in its wake strife, envy, and a vortex of violence and revenge.... We must learn to love; but we must also know the limits of love, and the importance of justice-as-fairness in families and in society."[19]

Personal Leadership Reflection

When has being selected had both beneficial and detrimental outcomes in your leadership?

פרשת כי תבוא • *Parashat Ki Tavo*

Climb Every Mountain

In *Parashat Ki Tavo*, Moses gave the Israelites an unusual command. He told the people that after they crossed the Jordan River, they were to separate into two distinct groups; each group was charged with a different recitation. On one mountain, Mount Gerizim, six tribes were to stand: Simon, Levi, Judah, Issachar, Joseph, and Benjamin. On the other mountain, Mount Ebal, the remaining tribes were positioned: Reuben, Gad, Asher, Zebulun, Dan, and Naphtali. The Levites would first call out a litany of curses and then a string of blessings "in a loud voice (*kol ram*)" (Deut. 27:14), and the people would respond "Amen" in unison, to signify that they heard these words clearly and understood their significance. The text of these blessings and curses are listed in our *sedra*. When read in synagogue, the curses are chanted in a low voice. It is as if we do not wish to hear the words, because they speak to a reality we cannot accept. Ironically, when the words are read this way, we must strain to pay attention, and their sobering message penetrates even more.

Imagine the scene. *Parashat Ki Tavo* offers the staging. The mountains provided an expressive and dramatic backdrop, amplifying the curses and affirming the blessings. The people understood that if they were at a mountain, something grand and important was to take place. Mount Moriah was where Abraham, the knight of faith, was willing to risk it all for his faith in God. His individual commitment on that mountain was mirrored by the collective covenant we undertook as a people at Mount Sinai, when, with the natural orchestra of thunder and lightning, we were given the Ten Commandments. Suddenly, not far from the Jordan River that was to liberate us from the wilderness, we were presented with not one, but two mountains. And this time, the people were standing on the mountain instead of a single leader. With each "Amen," the twelve tribes were affirming their commitment to live a covenantal life.

The Talmud makes clear that both the curses and blessings recited by the Levites were equal in the way they were articulated to suggest that in the many arenas of private and public behavior described in this declaration, there are choices to be made:

> Just as the curse is recited by the Levites, so too, the blessing is uttered by the Levites. Just as the curse is proclaimed loudly, so too, the blessing is proclaimed loudly. Just as the curse is proclaimed in the sacred tongue, so too, the blessing is proclaimed in the sacred tongue. Just as the curse is proclaimed both in general and in detail, so too, the blessing is proclaimed in general and in detail. And just as after the curse is uttered, both groups of people on each mountain respond and say "Amen," so too, after the blessing is uttered, both groups respond and say "Amen." (Sota 37b)

These stark choices will be a reflection of the entire community; thus, the entire community spoke in one voice in response.

These mountains represent the different stages in the spiritual development of a people. The first mountain, Abraham's mountain, represents faith. The second, Moses's mountain, represents law. But what does this set of mountains represent?

To answer this question, we turn to the verses that immediately precede ours. The chapter begins with the mandate to the people to inscribe all of the commandments on large boulders after crossing the Jordan River. The boulders were to be plastered, and "all the words of this Law" were to be written directly on the plaster. Commentators debate what these words were and if it was indeed possible to contain every law on these large stones. At this same location, the Israelites were to build an altar to God, also made out of stone. The stones of the law were twinned with the stones of worship to consecrate this new land immediately upon entry. If the people had any doubt about the values embedded in this new stage of their lives or the difference between where they came from, Egypt, and where they were going, the Land of Israel, these stones sent an unambiguous message of conviction.

Then, right before the tribes were to break up and climb their respective mountains, the Israelites heard a surprising announcement: "Then Moses and the Levites spoke to all Israel: 'Be still and listen, Israel. Today you have become the people of the Lord your God. Therefore, listen to the Lord your God, keeping His commandments and decrees, with which I charge you this day'" (Deut. 27:9–10). During the forty long years of desert wandering, they were, we assumed, already God's people. God freed them from slavery, gave them the tablets, protected them day and night with a cloud and a pillar of fire, and gifted them daily with manna. These are acts that indicate a strong and growing bond. Yet, until that moment, that very day, our verses imply that the people were not yet truly God's people.

Each mountain experience represented a new stage of collective identity precipitated by an immersive, transformative experience. The Israelites first crossed a body of water as an act of liberation. They were going to cross yet another body of water to become a nation. It was not enough to put words on stones or to arrange rocks into an altar. They had to understand the ramifications and consequences of their behavior: the good, the bad, and the ugly. Moses would no longer be there to guide them or beg for forgiveness when they sinned. They needed to co-create and own a collective moral spirit embodied in the curses and blessings they heard spoken out loud in the echo chamber in between each mountain. The words, both inspiring and frightening, made them accountability partners to each other. When they were not saying "Amen," they were told to be still and listen.

Leaders cannot carry the full weight of accountability alone. Leadership accountability reduces the way we often shift blame on others and, ultimately, decreases mistakes. It also encourages a culture of experimentation, because only those who are truly accountable can assess gains and risks. Accountability requires courageous followers who have learned to stand up for what they believe in and commit to action. It often requires a strenuous climb. Rabbi Jonathan Sacks writes about the essential nature of accountability to creating the kind of universe where morality thrives: "A free society is a moral achievement, and without that, we will lose it. We've forgotten that without a shared moral code to which we are all accountable, into which we are all educated and which we have internalised, we will lose the trust in public life on which our very freedom depends."[20]

With the climb up their respective mountains and their confirmation of curses and blessings, the Israelites figuratively and emotionally imitated Moses and became the masters of their own destiny. They had to be the mountain climbers. For leaders to grow, they have to be willing not only to climb mountains, but to identify the next mountain to climb.

Personal Leadership Reflection

What mountain lies before you right now that you need to scale?

פרשת נצבים • *Parashat Nitzavim*

Stand Strong

There is something magical about a crowd. We may fear groupthink, mobs, the stampede and rush of an uncontrollable group and forget the power and validation that comes when a diverse group of people come together to support a belief, to protest, to sing joyously at a concert, or to cheer a favorite team in a competition. There are so few occasions when we experience the vastness and reach of a shared moment in unison, what Emile Durkheim called a "collective effervescence." Think for a moment of the largest, most powerful memory you've ever experienced as part of a large group. Why was it so much fun or so meaningful?

In *Parashat Nitzavim*, Moses asked all the Israelites to gather in a standing position: "All of you are standing today before the Lord your God – the leaders among you, the tribes, the elders and officials, all the men of Israel, the children, the women, the strangers in your camp, from woodworker to water-drawer – to enter the covenant of the Lord your God" (Deut. 29:9–11). Rashi explains that Moses asked all the Israelites to join as one group, unified by a covenant on the last day of his life. Rabbi Abraham ibn Ezra adds that they were to congregate around the ark, signifying that they were making the Torah the focal point of their current and future lives. Stand up for what you believe in this moment, and you will know what to stand up for with conviction for the rest of your lives.

Nahmanides ties these two points together. Moses assembled the people as a group, every one of them, to affirm a covenant around the ark: "He made them bring the little ones, in order to include them in the covenant, for he made the covenant even with the future generations." With this call across the generations, Moses asked the Israelites to confirm their belief in the Torah, in Jewish unity, and in Jewish continuity. What good is a covenantal commitment that only lasts a generation? This was a potent question then and no less an urgent question now. If we were all asked to gather together to affirm our belief in the Torah and in the future, would our children and grandchildren be in the room with us of their *own* volition? If not, we have our work cut out for us.

Nahmanides also obliquely suggests that this may have been a new covenant, without explaining the contents of that new covenant. If this was to be the last day of his life, Moses may have been asking the Israelites to sustain their beliefs and practices in his absence. The Jewish way of life cannot only center around the insistence of a particular leader. Its greatest validation lies in its sustainability after that leader is no longer there.

Perhaps there is another way of looking at this request to gather. In Deuteronomy 34, only five chapters later, Moses was told to climb Mount Nebo, where he was given a magnificent aerial view of the Land of Israel: "Gilead as far as Dan; all Naphtali; the land of Ephraim and Manasseh; the whole land of Judah as far as the Western Sea; the Negeb; and the Plain – the Valley of Jericho, the city of palm trees – as far as Zoar" (Deut. 34:1–3). There, right before he died, he was given the privilege of seeing the fruit of a lifetime of leadership. It was a majestic sweep of beauty and the last image his eyes took in before Moses departed this world. But it was not the only view Moses was given. If our *sedra* did indeed take place on the last day of Moses's life, then he was to see not only the Land of Israel as his chief accomplishment but also all the Israelites together as the nation he formed, nurtured, and carried. This twin vision of the people and the land was God's parting gift to Moses.

There is one more detail that is essential in this remarkable imprint of Moses's last hours. The very people who complained, who fought him, and who rebelled were told to adopt a new mindset gently and tenderly: "The Lord your God will circumcise your heart and the hearts of your descendants, so that you may love the Lord your God with all your soul, with all your might, *that you may live*" (30:6). Rabbi Jonathan Sacks, in his commentary on the Koren *Tanakh* writes, "... He will soften their hearts, allowing them to devote themselves to Him."[21]

Circumcising one's heart is an unexpected, unsettling image. It is, in contrast to the crowd, a very individualized request. One person's heart is not another's. The reward for making a hole in their hearts, according to this verse, enabled them to live. Physically, a hole in the heart may be dangerous. Emotionally, it is the only way to live. The hard-heartedness that enveloped Pharaoh and obstructed his compassion for the exploited masses became the source of his eventual demise and the death of all of Egypt's firstborn. If you want to live truly and freely, the verse suggests, you must be vulnerable. The hard-heartedness that characterized the Israelites' behavior in the wilderness needed to give way to a more open, more loving, and less judgmental attitude, lest they inherit the land but forget how to live.

Ron Heifetz and Marty Linsky, in their classic *Leadership on the Line: Staying Alive through the Dangers of Leading*, call this the "sacred heart" of leadership: "The most difficult work of leadership involves learning to experience distress without numbing yourself. The virtue of a sacred heart lies in the courage to maintain your innocence and wonder, your doubt and curiosity, and your compassion and love even through your darkest, most difficult moments."[22] When leaders experience crisis or personal attacks, they are often given the worst advice: Develop a thick skin. That callousness can, over time, create insensitivity to the suffering of others and undermine the very inspiration to lead in the first place: "A sacred heart allows you to feel, hear, and diagnose, even in the midst of your mission, so that you can accurately gauge different situations and respond appropriately."

Heifetz and Linksy remind us that "leading with an open heart means you could be at your lowest point, abandoned by your people and entirely powerless, yet remain receptive to the full range of human emotions without going numb, striking back, or engaging in some other defense. In one moment you may experience total despair, but in the next, compassion and forgiveness."

We are with Moses in these last hours. God has brought the Israelites together for him and for them. In these painful chapters of Moses's farewell, he leaves them with a potent message. It is time to let go of a recalcitrant heart. Be compassionate partners to each other. Stand side by side. In the future, speak of this moment when you stood strong and together across the generations, and you committed to a future of the wholeheartedness that can only come through cutting through a layer of stubbornness and revealing the grace beneath.

Personal Leadership Reflection

Describe a moment you felt affirmed by the power of a crowd.

פרשת וילך • *Parashat Vayelekh*

After Leadership

The word "*vayelekh*", literally means "and he went," but the *sedra* ironically opens with Moses's confession to the Israelites that he could no longer go on: "He said to them: I am now one hundred and twenty years old, I can no longer be active" (Deut. 31:2). Moses, for the past four books of the Torah, was always on the move. But at 120, he told his followers that he was unable to continue. Rashi explains that this was his announcement that the end of their journey and the end of his days would coincide: "Today my days and my years become full." Moses was to die on the seventh of Adar, the same day that he was born (Sota 13b).

Rabbi Abraham ibn Ezra explains that Moses was telling the people he could no longer go out to war. There comes a time in every leader's life when the glories and triumphs of old are no longer possible. But this was not, Rashi reminds us, because Moses did not have the physical strength, as one might assume to be true of someone of his advanced years. In the last chapter of Deuteronomy, we are told outright that Moses had his physical capability intact: "His eye were undimmed, and his strength was undiminished" (Deut. 34:7).

This is a touching portrait of aging, captured by an observation Rabbi Jonathan Sacks made when visiting seniors as the chief rabbi. He met a woman who was 103 and retained her liveliness. He asked her for the secret of her youth and the delight she had in being alive. "With a smile she said, 'Never be afraid to learn something new.'" Rabbi Sacks, in *Lessons in Leadership,* concluded that "if you are prepared to learn something new, you can be 103 and still young. If you are not prepared to learn something new, you can be twenty-three and already old."[23]

If Moses was still sprightly, then why couldn't he continue leading? According to Rashi, he was not *permitted* to continue. His leadership position was being taken from him and given to Joshua. God had determined that the time had finally come. The same passage of Talmud that identified his birth and death date offers another distressing reading of Moses's vulnerability at this moment. Moses could no longer teach the people because he no longer had the wisdom he once had.

Nahmanides challenges this reading. He explains that the wisdom that was taken from Moses at this time was a miracle and a kindness to prevent him from being unsettled and upset about the transference of power to Joshua. No matter how much he believed he found a fit successor for leadership, Moses had to be devastated to lose his authority. His identity was wholly wrapped in his leadership. Who was Moses without his role?

I've spoken to many people who completed terms as presidents, CEOS, or executive directors of organizations, and to lay leaders who served as chairs, to find out what leadership is like in the days, weeks, and months after they step down. Some have described it as relief tinged with sadness. They are relieved to get their normal lives back after the many hours a day they spent managing people and managing crises. The day-to-day wear and tear of leadership can be exhausting. They appreciated the time to recover and being able to spend more time with family.

But they also missed the excitement. They missed the decision making and the people. They missed being needed or valued for their experience and expertise. Many shared with me the hurt that although they often knew more about the inner workings than almost any other person in an organization, they were rarely consulted for their knowledge and experience. This left them feeling undervalued by the very institutions they sacrificed years of their lives to sustain and improve.

They tried to give space to the next leader to establish a distinct platform and offered an open door to help with problems, but more than one person shared that the phone never rings. Once gone, leaders can feel that they never existed. A woman told me she even wrote a poem about it! What they fail to teach you when you take the most senior role in leadership is what it's going to feel like one day after leadership. It's clear we need to create a different, more ennobling exit ramp for professional and volunteer leaders.

Bill George, a professor at Harvard School of Business, writes that it's important to know when to leave and how to plan for what's next.[24] He understands the dilemma. A leader's "self-worth is often connected to their work, and the questions they face go to the heart of their self-image: How can I remain vital and relevant? Will people still respect me without my title? Where should I live now that I'm not tied to headquarters? How will I fill my days? Without an organization to lead, how can I continue to make a difference in the world?"

He advises leaders to finish strong and leave before they are asked to leave. He recommends meeting with a career coach or therapist a year before retiring to discuss fears, expectations, and directions. It's important to discuss transitions with family and to think about adventures, hobbies, and activities that were not possible because of work. Say meaningful goodbyes, make a clean break, and only come back when you're invited. He suggests a hiatus of six to twelve months to explore options before making new commitments. For those looking to stay engaged, find ways to mentor, to serve on other boards, to teach, and to write.

This stepped approach to leaving is not only about a change of role but, as we mentioned earlier, it's about a change of identity. Sensitivity to this is evident in the Torah in a verse from an earlier book. In Numbers, we read that Levites begin their work at the age of twenty-five and "at the age of fifty they shall retire from the work force and shall serve no more" (Num. 8:24–25). Fifty is a bit young to retire. The very next verse, however, softens the change: "They may assist their brother Levites at the Tent of Meeting by standing guard, but they shall perform no labor. Thus you shall deal with the Levites in regard to their duties" (8:26).

Rashi explains that at fifty, the Levites no longer had to carry the parts of the *Mishkan,* the portable sanctuary, when the Israelites changed encampments. But they were still allowed to sing and to help load the sacred vessels onto wagons. No doubt, they "assisted their brother Levites" by helping novices understand the roles and responsibilities of the office, thus mentoring a new generation of Israel's spiritual leaders.

Personal Leadership Reflection

What have you done to show gratitude to a leader who has retired or finished a role? How can you learn from his or her wisdom?

פרשת האזינו • *Parashat Haazinu*

Healing Leadership

We usually think of leaders as ambitious drivers, people who stand in the front of the room, take charge, and direct others toward a particular goal. If they are kind and respectful, they engage followers with that kindness and respect. If not, their service can be fueled by the need for dominance and authority. Thoughtless ambition can result in callousness, ruthlessness, narcissism, and exploitation. In this *parasha,* we find a remarkable description of God that challenges this dominant paradigm: "See, then, that I, I am the One. There is no god beside Me. I deal death and give life; *I wounded, and I will heal.* None can deliver from My hand" (Deut. 32:39).

God's singularity, tied into life and healing, models a different leadership modality – that of Healer. In this verse, when God hurts people, God also brings solace and comfort. If God acknowledges that God hurts people, how much more so can we do the same. Now we, too, must heal the wounds we create.

Our *sedra* is not the first or only place to refer to God in the "first person" as a healer. "You shall serve the Lord your God, and He will bless your bread and your water, and *I* will take sickness away from among you" (Ex. 23:25). God says to the Israelites that He will have a sustaining and therapeutic presence throughout their wilderness years.

In the book of Isaiah, God is also described as binding up the wounded: "And the light of the moon shall become like the light of the sun, and the light of the sun shall become sevenfold, like the light of the seven days, when God binds up the wounds of this people and heals the injuries it has suffered" (Is. 30:26). Malbim explains that when someone breaks a bone, the bone must first be set properly, and only then can the injury be healed. The broken bone is on the inside; thus the recovery must begin on the inside first. Healing, he suggests, is both physical and emotional.

We read a similar sentiment twice in Jeremiah. The first is a simple yet powerful request that God heal: "Heal me, O Lord, and I shall be healed; save me, and I shall be saved, for You are my praise" (Jer. 17:14). Later, God promises future healing: "Behold, I will bring to it health and healing, and I will heal them and reveal to them abundance of prosperity and security" (33:6). In Psalms, we also find a verse that expresses human pain in need of repair: "Be gracious to me, O Lord, for I am languishing; heal me, O Lord, for my bones are troubled" (Ps. 6:2). God is also described as the One to heal that pain: "He heals the brokenhearted and binds up their wounds" (147:3). Moses, in Numbers 12, begs for Miriam's healing.

Nicholas Janni devotes his entire book, *Leader as Healer*, to restoring the imbalance that leaders today experience between their inner and outer lives We need leaders who are strategic *and* sensitive, hard-working *and* thoughtful, efficient *and* empathic.[25] But today, especially post-pandemic, he contends that leaders cannot be effective if they are overly transactional. People need and are demanding a more humanizing path forward. Healers need to make sure that their emotional and physical selves are intact and aligned with their intellectual, professional selves.

Leaders should not only heal the wounds of others, but they should also find ways to name and integrate their own wounds into their leadership. The theologian Henri Nouwen acknowledges as much in his book *The Wounded Healer*: "Our service will not be perceived as authentic unless it comes from a heart wounded by the suffering about which we speak."[26] We are, all of us, the walking wounded. We are bruised by difficult life circumstances, losses, transitions, family challenges, insults, and the injustices of the world. We cannot pretend these do not exist. Recognizing our own wounds opens pathways of empathy for the wounds of others. Rabbi Jonathan Sacks gives us this very charge: "If I were to sum up what faith asks us to be, I would say: a healing presence."[27]

The Talmud relays a remarkable and unexpected dialogue between the sage R. Yehoshua b. Levi and Elijah about healing leadership.

> "When will the Messiah come?" R. Yehoshua b. Levi asked the prophet.
> Elijah replied: "Go ask him yourself."
> R. Yehoshua asked: "Where can he be found?"
> He replied: "At the entrance of Rome."
> R. Yehoshua asked: "By what sign will I be able to recognize him?"
> He replied: "He sits among the poor who suffer from various ailments; untying and tying their bandages." (Sanhedrin 98a)

If you want to know where the Messiah is right now, look to the poor and the one who bandages them. If we want the Messiah to come, we should do the same. The grand, dramatic gestures of leadership will be surpassed by the gentle and tender touch to the wounds of those who require healing.

Personal Leadership Reflection

Name a leader who healed you in some physical or emotional way. What could you do to pay the kindness forward today and help heal someone else?

פרשת וזאת הברכה • *Parashat Vezot Haberakha*

The Greatest Leadership Legacy

What endures when a leader leaves us?

A lyrical passage in the Jerusalem Talmud informs us that when certain scholars died, their expertise and uniqueness died with them. When Ben Azzai died, for example, diligent students ceased to exist. When Ben Zoma died, Torah interpreters ceased. When R. Yehoshua died, goodness ceased from the world (Y. Sota 9:16). The list of scholars and the gaps they left are lengthy. This does not imply that there would never again be diligent students, expounders of Torah, goodness in the world, or the many other virtues and skills discussed. It suggests that these traits and behaviors were associated with particular rabbis, and the world was significantly diminished without them. This is what is lost, but the Talmud here does not tell us what endures after a leader dies.

For that, we turn to our Torah reading, *Parashat Vezot Haberakha*. After an entire book of farewell speeches, Moses no longer spoke. He was spoken to. The last chapter of Moses's life is one of the shortest in the Hebrew Bible, almost mirroring the pace at which a single human life is gone. One day there is a pulse. There is vibrancy; there is life. The next moment, there is not. The twelve verses in Deuteronomy 34 are all focused on this immense change in the Israelite universe. No one could ever replace Moses. God spoke to Moses face-to-face and performed signs and wonders through him. No one ever did what Moses did "in the sight of all Israel" (Deut. 34:12). And then, just like that, his many decades of service were over.

Here, Moses is identified as God's servant, an appellation of simplicity and profound honor. "And Moses the *servant of the Lord* died there in Moab, as the Lord said. He buried him in Moab, in the valley opposite Beit Peor. To this day no one knows where his grave is" (34:5–6). Moses was buried in enemy territory, opposite the place of one of his lowest points as a leader, as if the stain of this incident would forever remain close to him. Unlike the vast pyramids of Egyptian royalty and aristocracy, Moses's grave is unknown. It would neither become a place of cult worship nor signal to those who survived Moses that they should return to Moab. His death, like his life, was shrouded in mystery.

There is a well-known argument in the Talmud (Bava Batra 15a) as to who wrote the last eight verses in the Torah. Was it Moses writing about his own death , or was it Joshua, Moses's successor? R. Shimon, using a prooftext from Deuteronomy 31:26, argues that Moses wrote every single letter in the Torah. God dictated each word; thus, Moses also wrote the last eight verses.

R. Yehuda claims it was Joshua. Moses laid his hands on Joshua, imbuing him with God's spirit, which would allow him to write the final words of the Torah after Moses died: "Now Joshua son of Nun was filled with the spirit of wisdom because Moses laid his hands on him. So the Israelites listened to him and did what the Lord had commanded Moses" (Deut. 34:9). It is hard to imagine that Moses, with his characteristic humility, would have written lines like the closing verses of this chapter: "Since then no prophet has risen in Israel like Moses" (34:10).

The Talmud adds one small detail to this scene. Moses, if he wrote these last eight verses, did so in tears. How could he not cry over his own death, over leaving the Israelites whose joys and burdens he carried these past forty years, over not being allowed into the Promised Land? "We now sense the full force of the drama of these last days of Moses's life," writes Rabbi Jonathan Sacks. "Moses knew he was about to die, knew he would not cross the Jordan and enter the land he had spent his entire life leading the people towards. Moses's confronting his own mortality, asks us in every generation to confront ours."[28]

Contemporary research suggests that when leaders have thoughts about death, they tend to want more power rather than less, are more generous with their charity, and have an increased sense of purpose. Social scientists call this reality check "mortality salience." Manfred Kets de Vries, a professor of leadership development and organizational change, writes in "Death: The Ultimate Motivator" that "death anxiety underlies much executive behaviour and action and as this anxiety intensifies, there are three common maladaptive responses."[29]

The first he calls "the manic defence." Leaders, he claims, protect themselves from death through workaholism, what he calls an executive's "immorality system." Overwork is both valorized and compensated in many work environments, which blinds leaders from seeing the underlying cause of the tension they are really running from. This self-generated overload can be unhealthy for them and for those they work with. It can lead, according to de Vries, to low morale, enhanced turnover, substance abuse, and other collateral damage.

The second problem this denial amplifies is a refusal to deal with succession issues. The leader tells herself, "If I keep going, I will not die." This can create situations in which leaders hold onto positions long past their prime and lessen their impact and efficiency. The third issue de Vries identifies is what he calls the "edifice complex." Leaders afraid of death want to create tangible legacies. I cannot die, but if I do, I will live on in bricks and mortar or I will create unrealistic or unfair expectation that the next generation continue my legacy. In this way, I will still live.

Returning to our *sedra*, we might examine Moses's death in light of these three defenses. Moses certainly worked around the clock, but his position was never something he personally desired. He refused several times, and even threatened to stop leading when he felt himself unable to do the work. Moses had a healthy desire for succession, even telling God explicitly that there cannot be a flock without a shepherd. By lovingly placing his hands on Joshua, he demonstrated that he was not trying to hold on to leadership by obstructing Joshua's success. And lastly, Moses neither built nor commanded others to build something tangible as a physical testimony of his leadership. His only building project was the *Mishkan* , which enabled God to abide with His people.

"Unresolved death anxiety," de Vries writes, "can result in heightened stress and psychological burnout."[30] Instead of resorting to the three behaviors he warns leaders against, he advises people to confront their mortality by building meaningful relationships with family and friends, giving charitable gifts, and processing the anguish of death with emotional maturity.

Writing one's own death in tears is the way, according to one opinion in the Talmud, Moses faced his demise. He stopped pleading with God to let him into the land and instead turned his attention to a future without him. He gave us the ultimate and enduring gift of meaning to pass on to the next generation: the Torah.

But Moses gave us two other enduring gifts. We are told that "Moses was a hundred and twenty years old when he died, yet his eyes were not weak nor his strength gone" (Deut. 34:7). Moses, whose young eyes saw social injustice and a burning bush, was taken from this world full-sighted. His strength was intact. And in departing with these bodily functions undiminished, he left us the inheritance most necessary for developing Israel then and now: vision and strength.

Personal Leadership Reflection

In what way have you confronted your own mortality, and what legacy do you want to leave for those who come after you?

Hadran: Finishing and Beginning Again

Congratulations. We've concluded studying the fifty-four weekly Torah portions together. With Moses's death and the Israelites at the cusp of the Promised Land, we complete the last chapter of the Torah. Like all good endings, we finish with mixed emotions about how far we've come and how much we have ahead of us. Endings fill us with sadness, loss, hope, excitement, and immense possibility. They also prepare us for new beginnings. Historically, as a nation, we said goodbye to one era and stage marked by freedom, growth, transition, and uncertainty and then turned our attention to leadership succession and a return to our homeland, embracing a new national adventure with all of its advantages and challenges.

As a community of Torah readers, we pause at such moments for reflection. Every time we finish reading one of the first five biblical books in synagogue, we invite the congregation to rise and recite three Hebrew words, "*Ḥazak ḥazak venitḥazek*," which are loosely translated as, "Be strong, be strong, and we will strengthen each other." We recite this blessing of completion and continuity in the plural, acknowledging that the Torah is a source of pride and vitality that shapes us as human beings and as a spiritual society. The scroll represents our religious, narrative, legal, national, and historical roots and has given us wings to reach heavenward. When we complete the fifth book, this brief recitation gets audibly louder. I've always cherished this moment and close my eyes when I hear the person reading the Torah say it and then we repeat it in unison.

It's easy to understand the desire to sanctify this completion. We've read the Torah's 187 chapters together, from the creation of the world to the release from Egyptian slavery, from Sinai to the building of the *Mishkan* – our portable sanctuary – from the hot sands of the desert until the edge of the Jordan River. We're about to enter the Land of Israel. We've accomplished all that, and before we read it all again, we take a few seconds to celebrate. But why this call for strength? We the listeners didn't physically cross any finish line. It's all been a journey of the imagination.

Long ago, there was a custom to recite "*Ḥazak ḥazak venitḥazek*" after every *aliya* to the Torah (see the Rema, *Oraḥ Ḥayim* 139:11). The person called up to bless the Torah before the reading of each of its seven segments was sent off with a message of fortitude. In Sephardic congregations, the Torah's parchment is wrapped in an elaborate, self-standing container, but in Ashkenazi synagogues, the Torah scroll used to be physically held up straight by each person who came up to the altar to read it. The weight of the Torah signaled the seriousness of our commitment and the sacrifices required to observe the words inside it. By the time we reach chapter 34 of Deuteronomy, when the Torah scroll is totally unwound, it is very heavily weighted to one side and unwieldy. The reader was blessed with the strength to uphold the Torah quite literally. And even when the Ashkenazi custom evolved to reading the Torah on a table, this vestigial saying remained because it speaks to a profundity we experience that is worthy of articulation as a sacred community. The Torah holds us up, and we hold it up.

As a result, those who physically hold up the Torah today must do so slowly and securely. If a Torah drops to the ground, it is a sign of grave offense and disrespect both toward the materiality of the Torah and toward what it represents. The great Jewish legalist Rabbi Eliezer Waldenburg (1915–2006) wrote extensively on the custom to fast if a person who lifts the Torah drops it by accident, God forbid. In some cases, the entire congregation fasts if they witness a Torah falling (*Tzitz*

Eliezer 5:1). Rabbi Waldenberg even discusses whether or not a person who is blind must fast if he or she is in the sanctuary when a Torah is dropped but didn't actually see it fall. Some rabbinic authorities discuss the practice of fasting for forty days if the person holding the Torah up unintentionally released it and it fell as a parallel to the forty days Moses was on Sinai receiving the tablets. He stayed up on the mountain for weeks not eating and drinking; he negated his physical needs to prepare himself for this spiritual gift. If someone drops a Torah, it may signal a failure to prepare properly to carry its weight and receive this gift anew as Moses did in the days of old.

Of course, there are other resonances to this Exodus story that emerge when a Torah is dropped. It reminds us of the moment when Moses saw the Israelites worshipping a golden calf and then dropped the tablets. At this moment in text, film, and paintings, Moses is depicted as an angry leader who hurled the Ten Commandments in utter defiance. Those who were unworthy of them would never be able to receive them in this shattered state. One midrash contends, however, that when Moses was delivering these heavy stones, his love and excitement gave him the physical strength to carry them. But all of that vigor dissipated when he witnessed who the Israelites had become in his short absence. The tablets simply slipped from his grip. He could hold them no longer. Rembrandt was one of the few artists who did not paint an angry Moses, but depicted the leader as worn down and heartbroken, his face riddled with pain.

Today, after someone explains an idea in the Torah or finishes teaching a Torah study class, we often wish them a hearty "*Yasher koaḥ*" – "May your strength be firm." In so doing, we revisit that dark moment in time when the tablets were broken and ask that the person speaking have the personal strength to continue holding the Torah up today as recompense. Every time we teach and learn, we are making up for a loss, as the sage Reish Lakish observed in the Talmud and Rashi explained: "May your strength increase [*Yishar koḥakha*] in response to the fact that you broke the tablets" (Shabbat 87a).

The blessing of strength given from one to another also appears four times in the first chapter of Joshua (Josh. 1:6, 7, 9, 18), when Joshua desperately needed the courage to lead after Moses's death and was preparing himself and the nation for conquest. The people bolstered him with their words. Later, in Scriptures, an angel confronted Daniel at a time when he felt weak and vulnerable and gave him strength: "'Have no fear, precious man, all will be well with you; be strong, be strong!' As he spoke with me, I was strengthened, and said, 'Speak on, my lord, for you have strengthened me!'" (Dan. 10:19). When we require strength, we are strengthened by the belief others have in us. When we complete the Torah and chant "*Ḥazak ḥazak venitḥazek*," we honor the Torah as the source of our spiritual strength.

When we complete a work of Jewish text, a *sefer* (book), we also recite the *Hadran*, which means "return" and also signifies beauty or splendor (Lev. 23:40; Mishna Sukka 4:5). We return and recommit to the beginning and to the study that has filled our lives with additional meaning. The text of *Hadran* that is printed at end of every volume of Talmud is a pastiche of sayings from different scholars who completed their study of a book with a religious recitation. The person completing the book usually offers a discourse on the book's very last teaching, often tied into the beginning of the book, or summarizes central ideas in the book to show some degree of mastery. The following is an excerpt from one *Hadran* that communicates our desire to focus and retain our learning, that our study be sweet, that we are grateful to be able to study and to observe mitzvot, and that with this study we are also engaged in an act of Jewish continuity:

> We will return to you, _____ [fill in the name of the book or tractate], and you will return to us; our mind is on you, _____, and your mind is on us; we will not forget you, _____, and you will not forget us – not in this world and not in the next world.
>
> May it be Your will, our God, and God of our ancestors, that we should be loyal to Your Torah in this world, and it should be with us in the next world.
> Please make sweet, Lord, our God, the words of Your Torah.
> We give thanks before You, Lord, our God, and God of our fathers, for You gave us a share among those who sit in the study hall,

> May it be Your will, Lord, my God, just as You have helped me to complete ______, so too may You help me to start other tractates and books, and to complete them, to learn and to teach, to observe and to enact and to fulfill all the words of the teaching of Your Torah with love.
> And may the merit of all of the *Tanna'im* and *Amora'im* and Torah scholars be present for me and for my descendants, to ensure that the Torah does not depart from my mouth and from the mouths of my descendants for all eternity.

This is generally recited in the presence of a group of people and then *Kaddish DeRabbanan* is recited to sanctify the gathering and complete the ritual. Then it's time to return our strength quite literally with a celebratory meal, a custom as old as the Talmud (Shabbat 118b–119a). This meal to fete the completion of a book is so significant that it may take religious precedence over certain fast days (*Shulḥan Arukh, Yoreh De'ah* 246:26). With this prayer and with this meal, we rejoice in the intellectual, psychological, and spiritual accomplishment of completing the study of one book or a set of books and feel refreshed and inspired to return to the act of study.

For thousands of years, this virtue cycle of study has been foundational to Judaism. And now, with the completion of the fifty-four Torah readings for this year, it is time to finish and to begin again. Be strong, be strong, and we will strengthen each other.

Acknowledgments

One of the few and great gifts of Covid's isolation was teaching a weekly online class on the weekly Torah portion for the Wexner Foundation called "The Torah of Leadership." Preparing and teaching that weekly half-hour session was a joy, especially seeing the beautiful faces of new and old students across the country who came together to study ancient texts and their contemporary application. I am grateful to the president of the Foundation, Elka Abrahamson, and Angie Atkins, Becca Thomas, and Tali Zelkowicz for creating this online community and for providing terrific feedback. I want to also thank my Jewish Sistas – Elka Abrahamson, Deborah Lipstadt, Arna Poupko Fisher, and Cindy Chazen – for their friendship and professional guidance, especially during those long days. Special thanks to my other soul sisters and brothers – you know who you are – who have a special place in my heart and from whom I have learned so much about leadership.

It is my hope that Audrey Wagner, extraordinary leader, teacher, and mother, and whose husband and children lovingly dedicated this book in her honor, will be blessed to enjoy the fruits of all of her labors and the abundant love and respect of her children for many years to come.

Many individuals helped me produce these essays on the Torah reading of the week that form the core of this book. I'd like to thank Aliza

Abrams Konig, Dr. Shira Weiss, Rabbi Rob Shur, and our intern David Rubin. Uri Westrich was our very patient, very professional videographer for a year of filming. Rabbi Dr. Marc Eichenbaum was thorough and thoughtful in reviewing the manuscript. Thank you all. My gratitude extends to my other wonderful colleagues at Yeshiva University for their insights and friendship; special thanks to President Ari Berman for his encouragement and support of my work. I'm grateful to Rabbi Dr. Stu Halpern for suggesting that I take these essays and put them into a book. None of this would have been possible without Terri and Andrew Herenstein. Hats off to you and to all you've made possible. I'd also like to acknowledge Lady Elaine Sacks and my friends at the The Rabbi Sacks Legacy who partner with us in honoring the memory of Rabbi Lord Jonathan Sacks.

I'm grateful to my friends at Koren who were enthusiastic about this book and helped me structure and edit it: Matthew Miller, Rabbi Reuven Ziegler, Caryn Meltz, Nechama Unterman, Meira Mintz, and the whole crew at Maggid.

I extend blessings to my parents and extended family. May you enjoy good health and happiness, laughter and love. As always, my husband and my rock, Jeremy, has been by my side and together we continue to parent and grandparent and share the blessings God has given us: four children and four wonderful new children who married our children. Ori has joined Erez, Amir, Adi, and Lev as our shining lights of Jewish continuity. May you grow up to lead our cherished people and help perfect this remarkable world we've been given.

Notes

PREFACE

1. Erica Brown, *Inspired Jewish Leadership: Practical Approaches to Building Strong Communities* (Jewish Lights, 2008).
2. Jonathan Sacks, *Lessons in Leadership* (Maggid Books, 2015).
3. Adam Grant, "Your Email Does Not Constitute My Emergency," *The New York Times* Opinion , April 13, 2023, https://www.nytimes.com/2023/04/13/opinion/email-time-work-stress.html.
4. Jonathan Sacks, "Naso: The Politics of Envy," *Covenant & Conversation*, https://www.rabbisacks.org/covenant-conversation/naso/the-politics-of-envy.
5. Robert Jay Lifton, *The Protean Self: Human Resilience in an Age of Fragmentation* (Basic Books, 1995), 1.
6. Daniel Kahneman, *Thinking Fast and Slow* (Farrar, Straus and Giroux, 2013), 218.
7. Ibid., 12.
8. Ibid., 14.
9. Ibid., 416.
10. https://www.youtube.com/watch?v=qHMHK4i_oLg. Davis expanded the talk into a book called *Dedicated: The Case for Commitment in an Age of Infinite Browsing* (Simon and Schuster, 2021).

LEADERSHIP IN THE BOOK OF GENESIS

1. Richard Powers, *The Overstory* (W. W. Norton & Company, 2019), 424.
2. Ibid., 132.

3. Peter Wohlleben, *The Hidden Life of Trees: What They Feel, How They Communicate* (Greystone Books, 2016).
4. *The Overstory*, 499.
5. Jonathan Sacks, *Studies in Spirituality* (Maggid Books, 2021), 7.
6. John Gardner, *On Leadership* (Free Press, 1993), 169.
7. *Lessons in Leadership*, 11.
8. Simon Sinkek, *Start with Why: How Great Leaders Inspire Everyone to Take Action* (Portfolio Publishing, 2011), 136.
9. Jonathan Sacks, *Essays on Ethics* (Maggid Books, 2016), 198.
10. "Leaders, Stop Avoiding Hard Decisions," *Harvard Business Review*, April 13, 2018, https://hbr.org/2018/04/leaders-stop-avoiding-hard-decisions.
11. Jonathan Sacks, *Morality: Restoring the Common Good in Divided Times* (Maggid Books, 2020), 167.
12. Jonathan Sacks, "Nitzavim: The World Is Waiting for You," *Covenant & Conversation*, https://www.rabbisacks.org/covenant-conversation/nitzavim/world-waiting-for-you.
13. Aviva Gottlieb Zornberg, *The Murmuring Deep: Reflections on the Biblical Unconscious* (Schocken, 2011), 210.
14. Robin J. Ely and Anne Morris, "Managing Yourself: Stop Holding Yourself Back," *Harvard Business Review*, January–February 2011, https://hbr.org/2011/01/managing-yourself-stop-holding-yourself-back.
15. *Morality: Restoring the Common Good in Divided Times*, 173.
16. Dan Ariely, *The Honest Truth About Dishonesty: How We Lie to Everyone – Especially Ourselves* (Harper Perennial, 2013), 23.
17. Jonathan Sacks, *Morality: Restoring the Common Good in Divided Times*, 167.
18. Meir Shalev, *Beginnings: Reflections on the Bible's Intriguing Firsts* (Harmony, 2011), 34–39.
19. Ibid., 34.
20. Ibid.
21. Jonathan Sacks, *The Home We Build Together: Recreating Society* (Bloombury Continuum, 2009), 142.
22. Susanne Biro, Leaders: Dreaming Matters," *Forbes*, December 3, 2020, https://www.forbes.com/sites/forbescoachescouncil/2020/12/03/leaders-dreaming-matters/?sh=5b98306a7599.
23. Sigmund Freud, *The Interpretation of Dreams* (Basic Books, 2010), 92.
24. Marcel Mauss, *The Gift: Forms and Functions of Exchange in Archaic Societies* (Hau Books, 2016).
25. Lewis Hyde, *The Gift* (Vintage, 2019), xxxii.
26. Jonathan Sacks, "Toldot: Why Did Isaac Love Esau," *Covenant & Conversation*, https://www.rabbisacks.org/covenant-conversation/toldot/isaac-love-esau.
27. Dan and Chip Heath, *Decisive: How to Make Better Choices in Life and Work* (Crown Currency, 2013), 226.

28. *Lessons in Leadership*, 5.
29. Doris Kearns Goodwin, *Leadership in Turbulent Times* (Simon and Schuster, 2018), 164.
30. Richard Breitman and Allan J. Lichtman, *FDR and the Jews* (Belknap Press, 2014).
31. Raphael Medoff, *The Jews Should Keep Quiet: Franklin D. Roosevelt, Rabbi Stephen S. Wise, and the Holocaust* (Jewish Publication Society, 2021).
32. Deborah Ancona and Hal Gregersen, "The Power of Leaders Who Focus on Solving Problems," *Harvard Business Review*, April 16, 2018, https://hbr.org/2018/04/the-power-of-leaders-who-focus-on-solving-problems.
33. Jonathan Sacks, *Not in God's Name* (Maggid Books, 2015), 219.
34. Ibid., 26.
35. Susan Scott, *Fierce Conversations: Achieving Success at Work and in Life One Conversation at a Time* (Berkley, 2004), 33.
36. Ibid., 31.
37. Ibid., 32.
38. Ibid.
39. J.W. Shenk, "Lincoln's Great Depression," *The Atlantic*, October 2005, https://www.theatlantic.com/magazine/archive/2005/10/lincolns-great-depression/304247.
40. Jonathan Sacks, "Vezot HaBracha Staying Young," *Covenant & Conversation*, https://www.rabbisacks.org/covenant-conversation/vezot-habracha/staying-young.

LEADERSHIP IN THE BOOK OF EXODUS

1. A. O. Scott, *Better Living Through Criticism: How to Think About Art, Pleasure, Beauty, and Truth* (Penguin Books, 2017), 42.
2. Jonathan Sacks, "Bereshit: The Three Stages of Creation," *Covenant & Conversation*, https://www.rabbisacks.org/covenant-conversation/bereishit/the-three-stages-of-creation.
3. Joyce E. A. Russell, "Positive Leadership: It Makes a Difference," *Forbes*, May 29, 2021, https://www.forbes.com/sites/joyceearussell/2021/05/29/positive-leadership-it-makes-a-difference/?sh=31ed7e7e7d7a.
4. Emma Seppälä and Kim Cameron, "The Best Leaders Have a Contagious Positive Energy," *Harvard Business Review*, April 18, 2022, https://hbr.org/2022/04/the-best-leaders-have-a-contagious-positive-energy.
5. Jonathan Sacks, *Radical Then, Radical Now* (Continuum, 2004), 69.
6. Gregory Burns, *Iconoclast: A Neuroscientist Reveals How to Think Differently* (Harvard Business Review Press, 2008), 7.
7. Jonathan Sacks, "Naso: The Priestly Blessings," *Covenant & Conversation*, https://www.rabbisacks.org/covenant-conversation/naso/the-priestly-blessings.

8. Liz Wiseman, *Multipliers: How the Best Leaders Make Everyone Smarter* (Harper Business, 2017).
9. Jonathan Sacks, *The Dignity of Difference: How to Avoid the Clash of Civilizations* (Bloomsbury Continuum, 2003), 36.
10. Kory Kogon, Adam Merrill, and Leena Rinne, *The Five Choices* (Franklin Covey, 2016), 11.
11. David Villa, "How Celebrating Success Can Lead to More of It," *Forbes,* May 12, 2022, https://www.forbes.com/sites/forbesagencycouncil/2022/05/12/how-celebrating-success-can-lead-to-more-of-it/?sh=5893e8902eca.
12. Jonathan Sacks, "Vayakhel-Pekudei, Celebrate," *Covenant & Conversation,* https://www.rabbisacks.org/covenant-conversation/pekudei/celebrate.
13. Abraham Joshua Heschel, *Who is Man?* (Stanford University Press, 1965), 117.
14. Ron Carucci, "How Leaders Should Handle Public Criticism," *Harvard Business Review,* December 12, 2022, https://hbr.org/2022/12/how-leaders-should-handle-public-criticism.
15. Jonathan Sacks, *Judaism's Life-Changing Ideas* (Maggid Books, 2020), 290–291.
16. *Lessons in Leadership*, 97.
17. Thomas Maran, Simon Liegl, Sebastian Moder, Sascha Kraus, and Marco Furtner, "Clothes Make the Leader! How Leaders Can Use Attire to Impact Followers' Perceptions of Charisma and Approval," *Journal of Business Research,* January 2021, https://www.sciencedirect.com/science/article/pii/S0148296320307797.
18. Matthew Hutson and Tori Rodriguez, "Dress for Success: How Clothes Influence Our Performance," *Scientific American,* January 1, 2016, https://www.scientificamerican.com/article/dress-for-success-how-clothes-influence-our-performance.
19. Silvia Bellezza, Francesca Gino, and Anat Keinan, "The Red Sneakers Effect: Inferring Status and Competence from Signals of Nonconformity," *Journal of Consumer Research* 41, no. 1 (2014), 35–54.
20. Hajo Adam and Adam D. Galinsky, "Enclothed Cognition," *Journal of Experimental Social Psychology,* 48.4 (2012), 918–925.
21. Jonathan Sacks, "Nitzavim: Defeating Death," *Covenant & Conversation,* https://www.rabbisacks.org/covenant-conversation/nitzavim/defeating-death.
22. Muriel Maignan Wilkins, "Signs That You're Being Too Stubborn," *Harvard Business Review,* May 21, 2015, https://hbr.org/2015/05/signs-that-youre-being-too-stubborn.
23. Jonathan Sacks, "Beshallach: The Turning Point," *Covenant & Conversation,* https://www.rabbisacks.org/covenant-conversation/beshallach/the-turning-point.
24. Sarah Jaffe, *Work Won't Love You Back: How Devotion to Our Jobs Keeps Us Exploited, Exhausted, and Alone* (Bold Type Books, 2021), 321.
25. Ibid., 15.
26. Ibid.
27. Ibid., 3.

28. Abraham Joshua Heschel, *The Sabbath* (Farrar Straus Giroux, 2005), 3.
29. Jonathan Sacks, *A Letter in the Scroll: Understanding Our Jewish Identity and Exploring the Legacy of the World's Oldest Religion* (Free Press, 2004), 136.
30. Jim Loehr and Tony Schwartz, *Power of Full Engagement: Managing Energy, Not Time, Is the Key to High Performance and Personal Renewal* (Free Press, 2003), 37.
31. Daniel Shapiro, *Negotiating the Nonnegotiable: How to Resolve Your Most Emotionally Charged Conflicts* (Penguin Books, 2017), xvii.
32. Jonathan Sacks, *Community of Faith* (Peter Halban Publishers Ltd, 1995), 111.
33. Dave Logan, John King, and Halee Fischer-Wright, *Tribal Leadership: Leveraging Natural Groups to Build a Thriving Organization* (Harper Business, 2011), 28.

LEADERSHIP IN THE BOOK OF LEVITICUS

1. Larry Bossidy and Ram Charan, *Execution: The Discipline of Getting Things Done* (Crown Currency, 2002), 40.
2. Ibid., 17.
3. Jonathan Sacks, *The Great Partnership* (Maggid Books, 2011), 69.
4. Jonathan Sacks, "The Flame of Faith That Has Survived All Tyranny," *The Times*, December 19, 2008.
5. Moshe Halbertal, *On Sacrifice* (Princeton University Press, 2012), 18.
6. Ibid., 15.
7. *Lessons in Leadership*, 53–54.
8. Gifford Thomas, "Leaders Take All the Blame and Give Away All the Credit," *Leadership First*, May 8, 2020, https://www.leadershipfirst.net/post/leaders-take-all-the-blame-and-give-away-all-the-credit.
9. Jonathan Sacks, *Ceremony & Celebration* (Maggid Books, 2017), 49.
10. Tracy Bower, "How To Lead Through Hard Times: The 5 Most Important Things To Know," *Forbes*, August 16, 2020.
11. Matthew Desmond, *Evicted: Poverty and Profit in the American City* (Crown, 2017), 300.
12. Ibid., 293.
13. Jonathan Sacks, *Faith in the Future* (Darton, Longman & Todd Ltd., 1995), 133.
14. *Judaism's Life-Changing Ideas*, 226.
15. Suket Gandhi, "Beware the Rise of Scapegoat Leaders," *LinkedIn*, April 17, 2016, https://www.linkedin.com/pulse/beware-rise-scapegoat-leaders-suket-gandhi.
16. Roberto Motta, "Are You a Leader or a Scapegoat," *Medium*, September 19, 2015, https://robertomottaoficial.medium.com/are-you-a-leader-or-a-scapegoat-6e32d8d4609f.
17. Jonathan Sacks, "Mishpatim: Loving the Stranger," *Covenant & Conversation*, https://www.rabbisacks.org/covenant-conversation/mishpatim/loving-the-stranger.

18. Douglas Stone, *Thanks for the Feedback: The Science and Art of Receiving Feedback Well* (Penguin Books, 2015), 8.
19. Ibid., 1.
20. David Burkus, "How to Get Better at Receiving Feedback," September 15, 2021, https://ideas.ted.com/how-to-get-better-at-receiving-feedback.
21. Anne Lamott, *Traveling Mercies: Some Thoughts on Faith* (Anchor, 2000), 134.
22. Dan McCarthy, "Leadership Scruples: What Would You Do? 20 Ethical Dilemmas for Leaders," *Great Leadership*(Jan. 28, 2009). https://greatleadershipbydan.com/2009/01/leadership-scruples-what-would-you-do.html.
23. Ibid.
24. *Morality: Restoring the Common Good in Divided Times*, 311.
25. Jonathan Sacks, "Mishpatim: Loving the Stranger," *Covenant & Conversation,* https://www.rabbisacks.org/covenant-conversation/mishpatim/loving-the-stranger.
26. Jon Mertz, "Leadership Strangers: Authority and Accountability," June 11, 2016, https://www.thindifference.com/2016/06/leadership-strangers-authority-accountability.
27. Kenneth Feinberg, *What Is Life Worth?: The Inside Story of the 9/11 Fund and Its Effort to Compensate the Victims of September 11th* (Public Affairs, 2006), x–xi.
28. Ibid., 26.

LEADERSHIP IN THE BOOK OF NUMBERS

1. Jonathan Sacks, "Noach: The Courage to Live with Uncertainty," *Covenant & Conversation,* https://www.rabbisacks.org/covenant-conversation/noach/the-courage-to-live-with-uncertainty.
2. Nogah Hareuveni, *Desert and Shepherd in Our Biblical Heritage* (The Biblical Landscape Reserve in Israel, 1991), 26.
3. Rebecca Zucker and Darin Rowell, "6 Strategies for Leading Through Uncertainty," April 26, 2021,https://hbr.org/2021/04/6-strategies-for-leading-through-uncertainty.
4. Jonathan Sacks, *Celebrating Life: Finding Happiness in Unexpected Places* (Bloomsbury, 2019), 16.
5. Jonathan Sacks, "Behar: We Are What We Do Not Own," *Covenant & Conversation,* https://www.rabbisacks.org/covenant-conversation/behar/we-are-what-we-dont-own.
6. John O'Donohue, *To Bless the Space Between Us: A Book of Blessings* (Doubleday, 2008), 152.
7. Jonathan Sacks, "Korach: Servant Leadership," *Covenant & Conversation,* https://www.rabbisacks.org/covenant-conversation/korach/servant-leadership.
8. James Strock, *Serve to Lead: 21st Century Leaders Manual* (Serve to Lead Group, 2019), 10.

9. Forbes Council Panel, "14 Important Benefits of a More Diverse Leadership Team," *Forbes,* June 24, 2021, https://www.forbes.com/sites/forbescoachescouncil/2021/06/24/14-important-benefits-of-a-more-diverse-leadership-team/?sh=7d20e4861f9b.
10. Jonathan Sacks, "Tetzaveh, The Counterpoint of Leadership," *Covenant & Conversation,* https://www.rabbisacks.org/covenant-conversation/tetzaveh/the-counterpoint-of-leadership.
11. Jon Katzenbach and Douglas K. Smith, *The Wisdom of Teams: Creating the High Performance Organization* (Harvard Business Review Press, 2015), 8.
12. *The Great Partnership,* 139.
13. A. D. Amar, Carsten Hentrich, and Vlatka Hlupic, "To Be a Better Leader, Give Up Authority," *Harvard Business Review,* December 2009, https://hbr.org/2009/12/to-be-a-better-leader-give-up-authority.
14. Ibid.
15. Ibid.
16. Ibid.
17. Bruce Kasanoff, "Leadership in One Word: Faith," *Forbes,* July 23, 2015, https://www.forbes.com/sites/brucekasanoff/2015/07/23/leadership-in-one-word-faith/?sh=5962ddee2074.
18. Ibid.
19. Jonathan Sacks, "Ha'azinu: The Leader's Call to Responsibility," *Covenant & Conversation,* https://www.rabbisacks.org/covenant-conversation/haazinu/leaders-call-responsibility.
20. Jonathan Sacks, "Pinchas: The Pace of Change," *Covenant & Conversation,* https://www.rabbisacks.org/covenant-conversation/pinchas/the-pace-of-change.
21. Debbie Zmorenski, "Why Leaders Must Have Vision," *Reliable Plant,* https://www.reliableplant.com/Read/29109/leaders-have-vision.
22. Ken Byler, "Zealous Leaders," *LinkedIn,* April 29, 2019, https://www.linkedin.com/pulse/zealous-leadership-ken-byler.
23. Jonathan Haidt, *The Righteous Mind: Why Good People are Divided by Politics and Religion* (Vintage, 2013), 34.
24. *Not in God's Name,* 238.
25. *On Leadership,* 190.
26. G. A. Smith, *The Atlas of the Holy Land* (Hodder & Stoughton, 1915), as cited in Jacob Milgrom, *The JPS Commentary: Numbers* (Jewish Publication Society, 1990), 267.
27. Erica Brown, *Leadership in the Wilderness* (Maggid Books, 2013), 208.
28. *Judaism's Life-Changing Ideas,* xxii.
29. Carol Dweck, *Mindset: The New Psychology of Success* (Random House, 2007), 48.
30. Ibid., 254.
31. David Mamet and Lawrence Kushner, *Five Cities of Refuge* (Schocken, 2003), 129.

32. Ibid., 130.
33. Mary Douglas, *Purity and Danger: An Analysis of Concepts of Pollution and Taboo* (Ark Paperbacks, 1984), 3.
34. Ibid., 5.
35. Joseph D. Soloveitchik, "Catharsis," *Tradition* 17, no. 2 (Spring 1978), https://traditiononline.org/catharsis.
36. Jonathan Sacks, *Covenant & Conversation: Numbers – The Wilderness Years* (Maggid Books, 2017), 113.
37. Janice Omadeke, "The Best Leaders Aren't Afraid to Be Vulnerable," *Harvard Business Review*, July 22, 2022, https://hbr.org/2022/07/the-best-leaders-arent-afraid-of-being-vulnerable.
38. Ibid.

LEADERSHIP IN THE BOOK OF DEUTERONOMY

1. *The Great Partnership*, 160.
2. Forbes Panel, "How Leaders Can Get More Comfortable Praising Employees," *Forbes*, Oct. 6, 2022, https://www.forbes.com/sites/forbescoachescouncil/2022/10/06/how-leaders-can-get-more-comfortable-praising-employees/?sh=1ae992e9268f.
3. Jonathan Sacks, *Crisis and Covenant: Jewish Thought After the Holocaust* (Manchester University Press, 1993), 177.
4. Hannah L. Miller, "4 Ways You Can Practice Charismatic Leadership," *Leaders*, August 24, 2023, https://leaders.com/articles/leadership/charismatic-leadership.
5. Ibid.
6. Jim Collins, *Good to Great: Why Some Companies Make the Leap and Others Don't* (Harper Business, 2001), 80.
7. Igor Kotlyar and Len Karakowsky, "Falling over Ourselves to Follow the Leader," *Journal of Leadership & Organizational Studies* 14:1 (2007), 46.
8. Dan and Chip Heath, *Switch: How to Change Things When Change Is Hard* (Crown Business, 2010), 78–93.
9. Ibid., 220.
10. Ibid.
11. Jonathan Sacks, "Balak: Leadership and Loyalty," *Covenant & Conversation*, https://www.rabbisacks.org/covenant-conversation/balak/leadership-and-loyalty.
12. Ronald Heifetz and Marty Linsky, "A Survival Guide for Leaders," *Harvard Business Review*, June 2002, https://hbr.org/2002/06/a-survival-guide-for-leaders.
13. Simon Rawidowicz, *Judaism* 16:4 (Fall 1967), 423.
14. Muhammad U. Manara, Suzanne van Gils, Annika Nübold, Fred R. H. Zijlstra,

"Corruption, Fast or Slow? Ethical Leadership Interacts With Machiavellianism to Influence Intuitive Thinking and Corruption," *Frontiers in Psychology,* November 2020, 1–17.

15. Jonathan Sacks, *To Heal a Fractured World: The Ethics of Responsibility* (Schocken, 2007), 26.
16. Daniel Kahneman, *Thinking Fast and Slow* (Farrar, Straus, and Giroux, 2013), 24.
17. Tracy Asamoah, "Most Parents Really Do Have a Favorite Child," *Psychology Today,* September 14, 2018, https://www.psychologytoday.com/us/blog/lets-reconnect/201809/why-most-parents-really-do-have-favorite-child.
18. Ibid.
19. *Studies in Spirituality,* 271.
20. Jonathan Sacks, "Post-Truth and the Erosion of Trust," https://rabbisacks.org/videos/post-truth-erosion-trust.
21. *The Koren Tanakh: Magerman Edition* (Koren Publishers, 2021) 488.
22. Ron Heifetz and Marty Linsky, *Leadership on the Line: Staying Alive through the Dangers of Leading* (Harvard Business Review Press, 2002), 227.
23. *Lessons in Leadership,* 301–302.
24. Bill George, "The CEO's Guide to Retirement," *Harvard Business Review,* November-December 2019,https://hbr.org/2018/09/the-ceos-guide-to-retirement?utm_medium=paidsearch&utm_source=google&utm_campaign=domcontent&utm_term=Non-Brand&tpcc=paidsearch.google.dsacontent&gad_source=1&gclid=Cj0KCQiA6vaqBhCbARIsACF9M6nd4yiZmUiglCSDbVsaQNvPea7j6HcqNT0AhLw-PjiTurSHSI4feQIaApE7EALw_wcB.
25. Nicholas Janni, *Leader as Healer: A New Paradigm for 21st-Century Leadership* (LID Publishing, 2022).
26. Henri J.M. Nouwen, *The Wounded Healer: Ministry in Contemporary Society* (Doubleday, 1972), 4.
27. *To Heal a Fractured World,* 264.
28. Jonathan Sacks, "Defeating Death," *Nitzavim, Covenant & Conversation,* https://www.rabbisacks.org/covenant-conversation/nitzavim/defeating-death.
29. Manfred Kets de Vries, "Death: The Ultimate Motivator," *Insead,* March 4, 2014, https://knowledge.insead.edu/leadership-organisations/death-ultimate-motivator.
30. Ibid.

The fonts used in this book are from the Arno family

Maggid Books
The best of contemporary Jewish thought from
Koren Publishers Jerusalem Ltd.